Preface

This book makes a tripartite argument. Its first claim, at once philosophical and historical, is that life is held together by contradictions. Life is fractured, lacking, death-driven. Although these contradictions are a permanent fixture—or deficit—of being, the contemporary climate catastrophe has aggravated them, or made them harder to disavow. The second claim, critical and disciplinary, is that the thinkers tending to ecological existence have too often smoothed over life's contradictions. They have equated life with the Good and insisted on its availability for new and improved relational configurations.

Let us consider Donna J. Haraway's influential periodizing notion of the "Chthulucene," which is "made up of ongoing multispecies stories and practices of being-with in times that remain at stake, in precarious times, in which the world is not finished and the sky has not fallen—yet."[1] We agree with Haraway that these are troubling times, wherein life is hazardous, a mere em-dash away from annihilation. Our fidelity to this fact constitutes our response to her call to "stay with the trouble." We diverge from Haraway, however, on what it means to do so. Haraway urges us to "make kin" with both human and nonhuman beings—a practice that, she maintains, the more-than-human world itself can teach us. She advocates "*learning* to be truly present," "mak[ing] kin in lines of inventive connection as a practice of *learning* to live and die well with each other in a thick present," "*learning* to stay with the trouble of living and dying in response-ability on a damaged earth," and displaying "intense commitment and collaborative work and play with other terrans."[2] Life and death may exist in uncomfortable proximity in these excerpts, but Haraway stands firmly on the side of the "flourishing [of] rich multispecies assemblages that include people."[3] While this flourishing is not guaranteed, she has a plan for achieving it: to give all "refugees, human and not," the "refuge" they need.[4] We press upon a pair of assumptions that appear in Haraway's scholarship but are in no way exclusive to it: that ecological losses past and future can be remedied through better modes of presence and co-presence within an inclusive multispecies federation; and that we can and should expect the natural world to dispense a pedagogy legible to us as kinship.

Thus we move, belatedly, to our third claim, this one aesthetic: that form, particularly cinematic form, exposes what structures life's contradictions. Form enables an encounter with life's negative value, its resistance to a sanitized or, as we put it, pastoralized ethics of relation. The "negative life" concept, which we elaborate in conjunction with psychoanalytic and queer accounts of disturbance and disorganization, refers to that which is both of and against life, that which filibusters the conversion of staying with the trouble into making kin.

Negative Life: The Cinema of Extinction is, in essence, a theoretical inquiry. It asks broad questions and makes broad claims about subjectivity, sexuality, and environmentality. It touches on aesthetics in a general sense and builds a case for a formalism that would intervene in the geopolitics of climate catastrophe. The following pages, however, concern themselves mainly with one medium: the cinema. They focus on a limited number of contemporary narrative feature films, the majority of which were released in the decade prior to this book's publication. Our choice of medium and archive is not arbitrary. This isn't to say that a study that applied similar premises to, say, ecopoetics would fail to reach valid conclusions. We certainly could trace a genealogy of damaged life through the queer, settler ecopoetics that problematizes how we desire in environments that do not and should not desire us in return. Take Brian Teare's *Doomstead Days*, which opens with a poem that, in one portion, turns "life against itself":

> the toxins piggybacking
> on reproduction to turn
> life against itself ::
> I can't forget how we've made
> a poison nature's
> second nature, how the real
> seems dependent on this fact ::[5]

In this excerpt and beyond, "Clear Water Ranga" describes life from the vantage point of disaster. Teare began to write the sprawling poem after the 2007 *Cosco Busan* oil spill in San Francisco Bay, and he was still working on it when, in 2010, the *Deepwater Horizon* oil spill took place in the

NEGATIVE LIFE

SUPER
IMPOSITIONS

PHILOSOPHY AND THE MOVING IMAGE

Series editor Brian Price

Superimpositions: Philosophy and the Moving Image takes philosophy and visual media as related practices. Books in this series do not simply apply philosophy as a method for reading art or redundantly representing its extant ideas. Following the visual logic of superimposed imagery, we see what philosophy and art share and what remains distinct, and distinctly generative. Superimposition, moreover, resembles thinking itself: an encounter with an object summons the idea of something like it and yet not the same. Twentieth-century philosophers turned increasingly to literature to replace generalized axioms with thick descriptions of the world and our psyches. *Superimpositions* takes the moving image, in all its limitations and possibilities, as central to the task of twenty-first-century philosophy and its refusal to foreclose either thought or difference.

Negative Life

THE CINEMA OF EXTINCTION

Steven Swarbrick and
Jean-Thomas Tremblay

NORTHWESTERN UNIVERSITY PRESS
EVANSTON, ILLINOIS

Northwestern University Press
www.nupress.northwestern.edu

Printed in the United States of America

10 9 8 7 6 5 4 3 2 1

Library of Congress Cataloging-in-Publication Data

Names: Swarbrick, Steven, 1984– author. | Tremblay, Jean-Thomas, author.
Title: Negative life : the cinema of extinction / Steven Swarbrick and Jean-Thomas Tremblay.
Description: Evanston : Northwestern University Press, 2024. | Series: Superimpositions | Includes bibliographical references and index.
Identifiers: LCCN 2024006371 | ISBN 9780810147195 (paperback) | ISBN 9780810147201 (cloth) | ISBN 9780810147225 (ebook)
Subjects: LCSH: Motion pictures—History—Philosophy. | Motion pictures—Philosophy. | Motion pictures—History. | Extinction (Biology)—Philosophy.
Classification: LCC PN1995 .S925 2024 | DDC 791.4301—dc23/eng/20240329
LC record available at https://lccn.loc.gov/2024006371

Contents

Gulf of Mexico.[6] The poet predicates "the real" on a toxic hybridization of life that "we've made": we both produce and embody "a poison nature's // second nature." The lines regularly end with a double colon notation that invites analogies never completed; life lacks something to compare itself to, something that would confirm its self-identicality. Death "piggyback[s]" on reproduction: note the idiomatic animality. There is an undeniable affinity between the worldview relayed by the poet in "Clear Water Ranga" and that relayed by the filmmakers who appear in this book—filmmakers who, too, it will become clear, detach reproduction from vitality and futurity. Still, rather than adopting a comparative approach that would survey how each medium or form makes and remakes negative life, we have chosen to posit a privileged intimacy between the cinema and our titular concept.

In the cinema, as one of us has summarized elsewhere, life and death, absence and presence are not antithetical.[7] Louis-Georges Schwartz lists three ways that moving images have historically been "entwined in the thinking of life": (1) proto-cinematic technologies that took photographs at different intervals decomposed the movement of living beings; (2) early brand names related to film projection, including Biograph, Vitascope, and Animascope, sold "the cinema as a machine for seeing or writing life"; and (3) theorists and philosophers have seized the occasion of the cinema's invention and development to reconceive life.[8] We may identify, as an example of the third point, André Bazin's statement that "the screen is not a frame like that of a picture, but a mask which allows only a part of the action to be seen. When a character moves off screen, we accept the fact that he is out of sight, but he continues to exist in his own capacity at some other place in the decor which is hidden from us."[9] More recently, Kara Keeling has posited that "the cinematic," a term borrowed from Gilles Deleuze, produces and reproduces social reality, including the "common sense" of life amid anti-Blackness and homophobia.[10] Films, as theorists and philosophers have noted, immortalize the movement, or vitality, of the dead, the dying, and the precarious. This immortalization isn't itself immortal, for film, the material, decays. Moreover, most films today aren't printed on film; the art and the artwork are named after an absent medium.

Scaling these observations up and down reveals the cinema as an art of extinctions large and small. The cinema incepts, occupies, and destroys worlds. We make worlds, notes Jennifer Fay, in part to come to terms with the inhospitability and unlivability of our own. Bazin turns to decors to generate a cinematic ontology of life out of sight, and Fay turns to the human-made environments that are sets to consider how we estrange ourselves from life on Earth. "The Anthropocene," Fay specifies, "is to natural science what cinema, especially early cinema, has been to human culture. It makes the familiar world strange to us by transcribing the dimensionalities of experience into celluloid, transforming and temporally transporting humans and the natural world into an unhomely image."[11] In a loop of "formal recursivity," Derek Woods would add, we then "[terraform] earth," expecting the planet to match the criteria of "earthlikeness" that we derived from the realm of representation.[12]

The label "cinema of extinction," used throughout this book, may be pleonastic: all cinema concerns itself with life absented or extinguished. The titles in our corpus—specimens of transcendental, melodramatic, and disaster cinema by Julian Pölsler, Kelly Reichardt, Lee Isaac Chung, Mahesh Mathai, and Paul Schrader, as well as specimens of ecohorror by Alex Garland, Ben Wheatley, Lars von Trier, Valdimar Jóhannsson, and Ti West—merit the pleonasm because they thematize and formalize film's inversion, diversion, and eradication of life. We take the mission of the *Superimpositions: Philosophy and the Moving Image* series as an opportunity to investigate the cinema as its own mode of thinking, or failing to think, about extinction.[13] To inhabit this mode we must take our time, so we do. We invite readers to follow us through often-extensive accounts of shots, scenes, and narratives—accounts that, if our gambit pays off, should show how life turns against itself as the world recedes.

Those who have come into contact with this text, including our extraordinary editors and astute anonymous readers, have noted its polemical status. The text identifies a set of interpretive and analytical habits that, in our estimation, have jammed up ecocriticism, or the formations of environmental humanities and environmental studies wherein the aesthetic constitutes one evidentiary register. We make no secret of our conviction that ecocriticism has gotten itself stuck as it has intoned the hymns that nature is our teacher, and that its lesson pertains to better ways of living together in the multispecies commons. "Ecocriticism," of course, is an imperfect synecdoche for the trends we critique: we consider ourselves internal to the field and favorably cite many scholars who also are. We nevertheless believe that the ideas we present as dominant within ecocriticism are so, and we strive to make good-faith assessments.

We have sometimes joked that cowriting this book has been "enabling"—that it has granted us the permission to indulge pleasures, and vices. Collaborating has authorized us to protect the integrity of certain claims that, on our own, we might have preferred to deflate. The humor in having relied on each other in order to divest from relation and belonging isn't lost on us. Readers will be better judges of whether we managed to combine our voices into one. Steeped as we are in psychoanalysis, deconstruction, and other languages of self-difference, we would contend that our solo-authored monographs are no less polyvocal.

A psychoanalytic language informs key aspects of our argument. This has led us to wonder whether our attempts to get ecocriticism unstuck have immobilized it in a different position, one conveniently isometric with psychoanalysis. A version of this debate plays out at a pivotal moment in *Sex, or the Unbearable*, another collaborative text, this one dialogic. Although both authors of that book have been richly inspired by psychoanalysis, it is Lee Edelman who, as Lauren Berlant sees it, funnels arguments into a rigid, structural Lacanianism. Berlant addresses Edelman: "One of your styles of response, Lee, is to pose some version of the question 'Is *x* necessarily so?' Then, if you can show that *x* is not necessarily so, you return to your structuring view, for to you, a structure is necessarily so."[14] Edelman replies a few pages later: "If I claim that I don't 'return' to such a view, it's because I don't think I ever left it (which, given my position, should hardly come as much of a surprise). I do believe that what I call structures are 'necessarily so'; it's precisely that belief that leads me to define them as structures in the first place."[15] We rehearse this antagonism not because it neatly reflects our individual proclivities but because we've occupied both positions, often together and at once. In fact, these positions have not appeared so disjointed to us. Recognizing structures as structures—which, we wager, ecocriticism has yet to do—allows us to wrestle with and within them, even if they "are necessarily so." What we wish for, in the end, is, rather than the migration of ecocritical inquiry toward psychoanalysis, an ecocriticism that would engage objects and ideas that do not parrot the field's pedagogical and moral scripts.

This book is not hospice care. We do not purport to know, and so will not teach, how to die in the Anthropocene or the Chthulucene. *Negative Life* stands on the side of unknowing and non-belonging, on the side of an emancipation that, we hazard, is every side, for emancipation, the exception from the status quo, belongs to no *one*.[16] We wrote this book to struggle against our catastrophic present, and to achieve the minimal separation[17] that might make available to us that situation's contours.[18]

NEGATIVE LIFE

[INTRODUCTION]

Ecocriticism against *The Wall*

"The domain of the pastoral is never absent from civilization; it never fails to offer itself as a solution to the latter's discontent," rules Jacques Lacan.[1]

"It," "the pastoral," "never fails," "is never absent." We have by now memorized the pastoral lesson: nature—no, ecology—is always available, always present, to dispense insights into living better, feeling better, and knowing better.

What if ecocriticism absented from that lesson?[2] What if, by risking the absurd, ecocriticism did not take for its master-signifier the moral handed down by civilization—the palliative to our "discontent"—and instead adopted the negativity of Lacan's above "never[s]"? Might there be, beyond the pastoral regime, a pedagogy (or lack thereof) of ab-sense, one that gave up being, feeling, and meaning as grounds for a recuperative ethics?

One could argue that ecocriticism's main task has been to unlearn the anthropocentric schoolbook. Yet this process has only reasserted the importance of education. We are now called from all corners of the ecological sphere to learn from allospecies companions, wonder at comradely critters, and study epistemologies from below.[3]

Amid the concurrent climate crisis and crisis of the humanities, ecocriticism has put a premium on coherence. Deriving from their objects—climate fiction, ecopoetics, and, of particular interest to us here, ecocinema—a portable and communicable program for sharing an imperiled planet has empowered ecocritics to justify their place in both the austere university and public life more broadly.[4] Ecology, by this scheme, has something to tell us, and receiving its message—a message relayed once by art, then by scholarship—makes life in precarious times meaningful. However, the formulas that to experience art is to know better, and that to know better is to do better, leave little room for contradictory desires, attachments, and commitments. And existential contradictions, we contend, are exacerbated in a contemporary moment that, as Patrick Whitmarsh puts it, is "characterized by an intensifying awareness of destructive feedback loops that tie together cultural institutions and geophysical systems, and usher humankind toward mass extinction."[5] When a paradox imposes itself between individual longevity (which entails a growing pollution footprint) and species viability (which necessitates an inhabitable milieu), human subjectivity fractures under the weight of differing pressures. *Negative Life: The Cinema of Extinction* registers those pressures, modeling an ecocriticism of contradictions wherein nature appears not as a benevolent pedagogue but as a resistance to intelligibility.

We will not listen to the pastoral lesson. We will not remain at ecocriticism's educative impasse. There will be no charismatic animals or enlightening vegetals to light the way. We shall instead, throughout this introduction, follow a film with nothing to teach.

NO PASTORAL

Set in the Austrian Alps, *Die Wand* (*The Wall*, 2012), Julian Pölsler's adaptation of Marlen Haushofer's 1963 novel of the same name, begins with the familiar pastoral tropes.[6] An unnamed woman (Martina Gedeck) and her friends, Hugo, Luise, and their dog Lynx, travel to a lodge to find rural respite from the world of postmodern capitalism, whose defining pastiche the film soberly rejects. They no sooner arrive at the lodge when Hugo and Luise decide to fetch supplies in the nearby village, leaving Lynx and the woman behind. Day and night pass without their return. Discomfited by their absence, the woman sets out on foot to learn of their whereabouts. She is traveling along a winding dirt road through a picturesque landscape when she hits an invisible wall.

Nature, her escape, gives her no egress—no exit. The wall is impassable.[7] For a while, she resembles a zoo animal, pressed against the glass enclosure (figure 1). Her hands feel searchingly across the transparent wall, mimicking Ingmar Bergman's overture to *Persona* (1966), where a flash of light bursts from a celluloid void, connecting the life of images to thought, and thought to the negativity of the film medium.[8] Among *Persona*'s flashing images—numbers, an erect penis, cartoon figures, a skeleton, a devil, a spider, the killing of a lamb, viscera, and corpses—hands play a significant role. They appear in rapid succession, signing in one moment, splayed and crucified in another, and limp and cadaverous in yet another. The overture ends with a boy who wakes in a morgue and extends a single hand at the camera lens, or the spectator, feeling, searching, and thinking through the prehensile organ. The hands of *Persona* and *The Wall* function as *monstrations* (showing, demonstrating a will to connect) and *monstrosities*, as in Jacques Derrida's "Heidegger's Hand (*Geschlecht* II)," where the hand of thought grasps at nothing and shows the nothing that cleaves thought from itself.[9] The hand of *Persona* reaches toward Woman (figure 2), and the woman's hands in *The Wall* reach toward Nature. Yet the organs of thought, the hands, arrive at nothing. *The Wall*'s terrarium does not give. Confused and fearful, the woman returns to the hunting lodge with Lynx and goes to sleep. As she dreams, her face fills the screen in close-up before fading in mineral dissolve (figure 3). Her image trades flesh for stone, petrifying around a limit that she will try, and fail, to circumvent, fleeing the lodge only to slam against the cold, hard transparency's walled obstruction. Flattened, she appears in photo-negative, silhouetted by the moon's terrible radiance (figures 4 and 5). She appears, not for the last time, as negative life.

I

2

3

4

5

"Negative life," the concept to which this book owes its title, names the materialization and formalization by film of life's intensified contradictions in a climate emergency. Encounters with negative life are precipitated by the hyper-contemporary form to which we refer as the "cinema of extinction," one manifest in Mahesh Mathai's *Bhopal Express* (1999), Paul Schrader's *First Reformed* (2017), Kelly Reichardt's *First Cow* (2019), and Lee Isaac Chung's *Minari* (2020), as well as a number of titles—Lars von Trier's *Antichrist* (2009), Alex Garland's *Annihilation* (2018), Ben Wheatley's *In the Earth* (2021), Valdimar Jóhannsson's *Dýrið* (*Lamb*, 2021), and Ti West's *X* (2022)—that also qualify as ecohorror.[10] We don't call the cinema of extinction a genre. It wouldn't be ill-informed to do so; readers will quickly notice the thematic, ideological, and audiovisual conventions that unite our examples. Our purpose, however, isn't to tender a novel classification that would, in a positivist sense, fill a proverbial gap in the scholarship. In prioritizing form, we follow Eugenie Brinkema's example and track how the cinema of extinction configures reality, its geometry.[11] This cinema punctures ecocriticism's pastoralism by obstructing characters' and spectators' access to the realm of multispecies entanglement or enmeshment—a realm often made by ecocritics to accommodate an ethics of harmonious co-living that scales up and down, from the planetary to the subatomic.[12]

The term "negative life" invokes the psychoanalytic theories of negativity developed by queer scholars with varying degrees of fidelity to the "antisocial thesis" label.[13] Negativity, for Lee Edelman and Lauren Berlant, designates "the psychic and social incoherences, conscious and unconscious alike, that trouble any totality or fixity of identity. It denotes, that is, the relentless force that unsettles the fantasy of sovereignty."[14] This account of incoherence assumes increased pertinence in the context of the climate crisis, albeit under an altered configuration. Whereas previous iterations of queer negativity figured the death drive through an ethics of individual refusal, we observe, from an environmental vantage point, a more generalized negativity, one that frustrates the distinction between intentionality and unintentionality undergirding imaginaries and practices of refusal. Gone is the sovereign subject who only by experiencing ego-shattering can access a subverted social order.[15] Subjects are instead caught a priori in what Mari Ruti describes as "circumstantial and context-specific forms of negativity, wounding, decentering, and suffering."[16] Negativity may inform and deform the cinema of extinction, but few of the filmmakers who populate this book would rebel against the status quo at all costs. Just as our corpus registers an exhaustion around ecocritical positivity, it occasionally registers one around oppositional, or properly queer, negativity; this is entropic cinema.

The term "negative life" also refers to the film negative, the hidden condition of the cinema and its will to animate. This hidden condition becomes one of absence in an era when, with few exceptions, films are no longer printed on film. Nadia Bozak, James Leo Cahill, and Jennifer Fay have documented the cinema's development as an ecological medium with regard to its participation in "hydrocarbon culture," its relation to turn-of-the-century anatomical and zoological experiments, and the status of its sets as anthropogenic microcosms.[17] In the cinema of extinction we find the apotheosis of this development: film, the artwork, and film, the material support, are caught in a loop, each at once allegorizing and concretizing the conditions—decay, absence, extinction—expressed by the other.

Negative life incurves *The Wall*, trapping the woman; she does not belong in and around the lodge, and her existence as a historical subject and a cinematic entity is not so much presence as trace, a backlit figure impressed upon her milieu. The day after her initial encounter with the wall and the many days—how many?—that follow, she resolves to keep negative life at bay. She hunts, she gardens. She assembles a rotating cast of animals: in addition to Lynx, there is a cat and a milk cow, Bella (figure 6). She walks the perimeter of her ghostly cell, testing the boundary of what lies beyond the clear wall. Beyond it, there is stasis—death. On the other side, we see villagers frozen in repose, two still-life figures: an old man taking water from a well, an old woman staring off into the distance (figure 7). They are animacy mortified. So are we, at least part-time. The camera most often shares the woman's enclosure, but in some shots, it is located on the other side of the wall. In such moments, it is—we are—dead.

6

7

Picturing life without a future in a landscape surrounded by stasis, the woman tries at first to make kin with the animals, caring for them with great physical and emotional toil. Yet the scene before us hardly qualifies as a pastoral of entanglement or enmeshment. Companion species these animals are not, for there is no inhibiting wall to the companionate being that ecotheory palms off. In a diary entry recited as a voice-over narration, the woman writes, "I was the owner and prisoner of a cow." The tranquility of her alpine escape turns into deafening silence. "The great silence descended on me like a bell jar," she reports. The lodge that shelters her, for its part, gives way to Edenic horror. She finds herself "in a bad situation," outside the pastoral regime.[18] "I slowly changed back into the only creature that didn't belong here," she recounts; "A human being. Troubled by chaotic thoughts, cracking branches with clumsy shoes. And engaged in the bloody business of hunting." This is life on the edges of death.

The whole of *The Wall*'s narrative frame could be described in Lacan's transcendental framework as an act of elevating the ordinary object, the trash the woman engraves, to the dignity of the lost Thing: the incognizable Real that the wall, "this dreadful, invisible thing," disincarnates.[19] The wall approximates the "lamella" in Lacan's horror story of sexual existence; it is super smooth and flat, a terrible simulacrum of life.[20] Ultimately, it is this indestructible life that the woman hits, that we hit as witnesses to her anguish, nullifying the pastoral. She muses:

> I was desperately clinging to the meager remnants of the civilized life that I still had. I don't know why I am doing this. It's almost an inner compulsion driving me on. Perhaps I'm afraid that if I behaved differently, I would slowly cease to be a human being and would soon end up crawling around, filthy and stinking, making incomprehensible sounds. Not that I'm afraid of becoming an animal. That would not be so bad. But a human can never become an animal. He plunges past an animal existence into the abyss.

This statement echoes what the existentialist philosopher Alexandre Kojève, who likewise wields the axe of negativity to cut through the thicket of our ecological relations, says of the desiring animal: "Desire dis-quiets"; "For desire taken as desire—i.e., before its satisfaction—is but a revealed nothingness, an unreal emptiness."[21] *The Wall*: a human can never become an animal. Or become-with animals, for that matter.[22]

UNTANGLING ECOCRITICISM

The woman's and Kojève's statements do not sit well with the current idiom of ecological entanglement or enmeshment and its associated orthodoxy: that there is no nature out there but ecology all around. The rubrics of new materialism, speculative realism, and object-oriented ontology may have seen their popularity wane over the past ten or fifteen years, yet their legacy within the environmental humanities is undeniable. One aim of these theoretical formations has been to displace the human as the arbiter of being and meaning. To do so, they have traded "correlationism," whereby the world is apprehended through the correlation between the distinct processes of being and thinking, for a "world of panexperiential meshes" in which phenomena largely exceed and escape human cognition.[23] The mesh shows up—as "the vast mesh of interconnection" and "the interrelatedness of everything"—throughout Timothy Morton's work, where it promises an alternative to anthropocentric ontologies and phenomenologies. "The mesh isn't a background against which the strange stranger appears," Morton speculates; "It is the entanglement of all strangers."[24] Thinking from the entanglement of matter and meaning has been Karen Barad's modus operandi; Barad's "agential realism" favors "intra-action," which "recognizes that distinct agencies do not precede, but rather emerge through, their intra-action," over the usual interaction, "which assumes that there are separate individual agencies that precede their interaction."[25] The "molecular turn" personified by Barad, sums up David Hollingshead, denotes "a complex and multivalent longing to escape the realm of identity-based power relations by dissolving or decomposing into a space of anonymous material processes."[26]

While there is now far less scholarship produced under the umbrella of these once-new materialisms, the idiom of entanglement or enmeshment—whereby we are and should be one with a world of interconnection and interdependence that includes human and nonhuman life, the living and the nonliving—has been naturalized, so to speak, as ecology itself. It is gauche to name nature as one's object of study, for doing so opens a can of worms: the pastoral image of a source of potential and plenitude out there, beyond culture. Ecology, on the other hand, is here and now. The notion of ecological entanglement encounters little resistance from ecocritics, who instead strive to prove that we are entangled to a higher degree than previously imagined. Melody Jue and Rafico Ruiz even propose that entanglements are not entangled enough; these scholars offer "saturation" as a means of "addressing configurations of matter on edge, blurred agencies, gestalts, and sublimations."[27]

The wide adoption of ecological entanglement as the condition of ecocriticism may have merely displaced the pastoral. The source of potential and plenitude is no longer transcendent but immanent. Ecocriticism is bound to repeat the pastoral lesson by presuming entanglement or enmeshment an infinitely expanding, never enclosed, and inevitable terrain for ethics, specifically an ethics of harmony. Within new materialism, as one of us (Swarbrick) has argued elsewhere, such an ethics derives in part from a willfully optimistic, and partial, interpretation of the work of Gilles Deleuze and Félix Guattari as well as their predecessor, Henri Bergson.[28] If, among new materialists, Barad argues that the "infinite alterity" entailed even by self-touching opens onto ethical relations, and Jane Bennett that matter's status as "vibrant, vital, energetic, lively, quivering, vibratory, evanescent, and effluescent" makes it "the starting point of ethics," in the ecocritical camp, Thom van Dooren maintains that "paying attention to avian entanglements" enables us "to care for endangered birds," Eben Kirksey, Craig Schuetze, and Stefan Helmreich that multispecies "colli[sions]" are cause for "biocultural hope," and Karin Bolender that "the act of dividing 'human' and 'animal' . . . too often excludes interspecies wisdom."[29]

The Wall is a fright to ecocriticism because, per the woman's previously cited monologue, it "plunges [us] . . . into the abyss" of "a revealed nothingness." Consider the Daphne-esque flight she once takes into the woodenness of a tree branch, her flesh and garb echoing the tawny bark (figures 8 and 9). This arboreal resemblance does not settle her restless negativity. It does not lead to the expansiveness of mind suggested by tree-friendly and friendly-tree literature like Richard Powers's *The Overstory*, an ecocritical favorite.[30] Rather, the resemblance vitiates the pastoral scene. "I didn't go into the old raptures again," the woman states, writing her end of days on scraps of paper.

8

9

The Wall and the cinema of extinction call for revised theoretical and critical habits. This is why, in *Negative Life*, we perform the admittedly déclassé gesture of externalizing nature. We do so not out of nostalgia for a wild or wilderness that, in connoting a pure beyond that is ultimately available to human transformation, would sustain fantasies of colonial mastery.[31] Instead, the cinema of extinction urges us to rethink nature as a limit: a limit to an ethics of belonging that one ought to teach or be taught. It may seem strange for a duo whose combined bibliography includes a monograph on respiration (Tremblay's) to insist on nature's externality. After all, there may not be any more convincing proof than breathing of the enmeshment of human and nonhuman life. *Breathing Aesthetics*, however, does not deem respiratory relations endlessly productive or constructive.[32] To breathe, as the book announces in its opening line, is to encounter morbidity.[33] Breathing proffers no positive content, no positive value. Any ethics to be abstracted from respiration comes not from some good inherent to it but from synchrony (in which case the ethics is contentless; the practice of collective attunement is the point) or from opacity (in which case coalitions are authorized by our recognition of the limits to what we can learn about embodiment and experience).[34]

Negative Life radicalizes this reasoning, approaching being in relation and the contradictions therein as relentlessly horrific amid climate catastrophe. We are not the first scholars to locate our investigation in entanglement's afterlife. Eva Haifa Giraud, for instance, has observed that theorists and critics too readily accept the fact of entanglement as elaborate enough an ethics.[35] In a circular fashion, entanglement serves as both thought's origin and its destination. Giraud proposes "an ethics of exclusion" that "pays attention to the entities, practices, and ways of being that are *foreclosed* when other entangled materialities are materialized."[36] This is an ethics that "take[s] account of the constitutive exclusions that underpin any form of ethical and political intervention, as any set of relations necessarily occurs at the expense of other possibilities."[37] Giraud shows that the world of harmonious co-living dreamed up by ecocritics implies a cut: the disavowal of different worlds, including those where harmony is not achievable and those where it is so only without us. While Giraud examines the interplay between the worlds environmentalists and ecocritics recuperate and those they relinquish, between the worlds they create and those they destroy, we risk a thought experiment that film, in its ontological and formal negativity, uniquely authorizes: we cross into, and dwell on, the natures, like the one antagonizing the woman in *The Wall*, that do not care for us. The natures that cannot bear us. The natures we may never call home.

INHUMAN CALCULATION

As they turned to ecology and the sciences more broadly, humanities and post-humanities scholars have threaded relations of home and place (Ryan Hediger), composition (Bruno Latour), worlding (Donna J. Haraway), ethics and care (Anna Lowenhaupt Tsing and María Puig de la Bellacasa), intimacy (Lowell Duckert and Jeffrey Jerome Cohen), and kinship, companionship, and love (Haraway again, Deborah Bird Rose).[38] All these terms—home, place, composition, worlding, ethics, care, intimacy, kinship, companionship, love—are common enough to a humanities education, not to mention a certain normative conception of the human. Scholars have refracted these relations through the language of "sea ontologies" or the "more-than-human temporalities of the ocean" (Elizabeth DeLoughrey), food sustainability or post-human agency (Elspeth Probyn), and the "milieu-specific analysis" of "wild blue media" (Jue), to name a few, strictly aquatic, samples.[39] Humanists and post-humanists, some blue, others blue-curious, have thereby found *themselves*, to a surprising extent, beyond the wall imposed by *The Wall.*

Stacy Alaimo, for example, cites Barad's influence on her "conception of the trans-corporeal subject who is 'situated' in a more material manner, as the very substances of the world cross through her, provoking an onto-epistemology that reckons, in its most quintessential moments, with self as the very stuff of the emergent material world."[40] As an emergent property of the world—with "world" taken to mean not the brute facticity of objective reality but an openness of becoming—the "trans-corporeal subject" runs athwart the transcendent subject of post-Cartesian calculation. As Alaimo explains, "transcendent epistemologies have fueled environmental destruction and harm to wild, domesticated, and laboratory animals by reducing the latter to a calculus of consumption—mere standing reserve."[41] By contrast, the "trans-corporeal subject," as emergent, worlding practice, exposes us to the ethical, ontological, and scientific fact that, again for Alaimo (who here is quoting Barad), "humans 'are part of the world-body space in its dynamic structuration,' and the 'becoming of the world is a deeply ethical matter.'"[42]

Would it not be more accurate to say that the becoming of the world is a deeply ethical matter *for us*, and that even with the sciences in tow, the reason why we are always finding ourselves in nonhuman worlds beyond us is that we are unwilling or unable—even at this late stage of critical climate feedback—to imagine a world without us? The humanities and post-humanities left the prison house of language behind and discovered that we are woven into the fabric of ecology. If you throw a signifier into the water, it'll wash up at your feet. Or worse, in your drinking water. The sciences are enlisted to rescue the humanities from their false isolation from not only coral and mycelium but also plastics, pesticides, and fossil fuels.

At what point does our exposure to the world's substances become auto-immunizing, in the sense of immunizing us to the thought of worldlessness and our structural relation to it? The insistence on the world's becoming might belie a greater structure of panic behind the disaster scenarios imagined in blockbuster films or in the speculative accounts of scientists. It is a structure more destructive even to our way of life than oil spills or hurricanes, which, no matter how terrible, still signify within a world of human meaning. The structure in question is the abyss of nonmeaning that voids every claim to world-making. To the question, *how blue are you?* asked by the blue humanities, we would reply: not nearly blue enough, for we humanists and post-humanists still misrecognize the libidinal economy at work in the concept of world and therefore allow ourselves to believe that this blue-green planet, it turns for us.

"Pastoralism" is shorthand for the hyper-humanism at work in present-day calls to make good of tragedy by returning to an ethics of care, kin, and world—as if insisting on our place made the existential problem of compromised survival any less unbearable. It is not that these words no longer have meaning; insofar as they are the language of ethics, they are indispensable. Still, the scale of the problem now outstrips our insistence on a Holocene language that speaks to the human as a totality. All the while, underneath the worlding drive, we find the same Cartesian calculation: *how, in a world that does not guarantee my existence, should I think and live?* Instead of this necessary calculation, which arises for Descartes in the absence of a world and any semblance of interconnection, ecocriticism is asking how to remake "our" future, "our" world. For all the talk of the post-human, Freud was right all along: the "oceanic feeling" is about finding or rather refinding "ourselves" (the eternal lost object) in life-worlds that, on the surface (blue, green, whatever), act as screens for our images of human authenticity.[43]

In a symptomatic logic, the emphasis on world-making in the environmental humanities conceals a greater failure of recognition: that the problem of climate change and planetary disaster is not an invitation to re-create the world in our image, or at least as we like to see ourselves, but, as Afropessimism wagers, an urgent and impossible demand to destroy the world.[44] Consider Frank B. Wilderson III's point in *Afropessimism* that Black life *matters* because without it, there would be no world.[45] The structuring antagonism of existence, according to Wilderson, isn't Black versus White but Black versus Human. Blackness matters to humanity because humanity would not exist without it; there would be nothing, strictly speaking, against which to define the Human.

The insistence on "our" place and "our" world perpetuates an ideology of health and viability whose life drive is matched by a death drive pernicious in its ability to thrive undercover. As Alexis Shotwell has forcefully argued, the criterion of purity that often organizes attachments to health and viability interferes with the pragmatics of environmental justice by overlooking existing dynamics of complicity in favor of a utopia of achieved purification; at worst, the criterion actively disseminates racist and colonial constructions of hygiene.[46] Related discourses of sustainable development and growth posit, as a solution to climate crisis, the seemingly benign manifestations of a violent capitalist order to which the problem remains confined.

Even before climate catastrophe shifted the scales of disaster, the humanities had been about maintaining "our" health. A normative understanding of the human as open and emergent—in short, on the side of life—has long underwritten the aesthetic education of Man to the exclusion of everything outside the worlding frame: the enslaved, the colonized, the vagrant, the deviant, the nonhuman, the less-than-human. Gayatri Chakravorty Spivak defines this aesthetic education as the "*programmed* access to the concept of freedom," that is, "the humanizing of the human through culture," which Kant's "man in the raw" fails to achieve.[47] This structure of exclusion does not collapse with the arrival of the post-human; so long as we continue to privilege our worlding capacity, we ignore that the very idea of our world is bound up with exclusionary sentiment. We fail to see that conceiving of the world as ours necessitates the worldlessness of others, human and nonhuman.[48]

Ecocriticism convokes a "we" by refusing the gap between self and world, being and knowing. That this refusal inevitably creates more gaps (this, not that) must also be rejected. Refusal thus spirals *en abyme*. The fact, obvious to some minoritized subjects, that being in the world means calculating the gap between having and not having a world isn't simply a contingency that can be explained away and solved by recourse to entanglement or enmeshment. On the contrary, what we call the "inhuman calculation"—the subject's relation to lack—is the condition of possibility and impossibility for ecological ethics.

Our own use of the first-person plural—already complicated, in this very sentence, by the collaborative nature of *Negative Life*—therefore harnesses theory's power to make general claims while insisting on its own impossibility. An ecocritical "we" is impossible in a sociological sense, for there may be an existential condition proper to climate catastrophe, but there is no universal experience of said condition. This "we" is impossible from a philosophical standpoint, as well. We don't mean that it is not *yet* possible—an assertion that would relay a utopian belief in the multispecies commons to come. Rather, we mean that the first-person plural self-negates; it collects the residue of simultaneously having and not having a world. In *The Wall*, the woman more than once lays out the inhuman calculation. As "the only creature that didn't belong there," one who resorts to "the bloody business of hunting," she must renounce the fantasy of a world of multispecies entanglement that would remedy her worldlessness or that of any given creature.

ATEMPORAL, APEDAGOGICAL

Neither the woman in *The Wall* nor we as spectators ought to learn anything from the deflagrated pastoral. The scene of relation is evacuated of insights on home, place, composition, worlding, ethics, care, intimacy, kinship, companionship, and love. The film and much of the cinema of extinction are stubbornly apedagogical.

The titular wall gives no ontological justification—where it came from or why it came to be. It is. This insistence bars the pastoral romance while offering no educative out. The negative life of *The Wall* elides the temporality of education ("I had no thoughts, no memories," the woman states finally), dispatches Heideggerian being-toward-death, and rules out the authentic temporality of life in favor of a different type of horror: the horror of pure stasis.[49] If *The Wall* has a thesis, it is this: the wall does not move. We and all manner of beings move around it. Which is to say, we move nothing. This thesis ought to bother theory. There is, after all, a whole cottage industry of queer, phenomenological, and existential accounts of time and temporality. These theories have one thing in common: they maintain that time is of the essence. Time teaches, and time gives: life, becoming, and agency (Elizabeth A. Grosz), potentiality (Jed Samer), plasticity (Catherine Malabou), reorientation (Alison Kafer), materiality (Gayle Salamon), dissonance (Elizabeth Freeman), cruising (José Esteban Muñoz), and so on.[50] These theories clash with the static genesis of *The Wall*. The film is apedagogical because it is atemporal. In Haushofer's novel, the narrator once reasons: "if time exists only in my head, and I'm the last human being, it will end with my death. The thought cheers me. I may be in a position to murder time."[51] Time, *The Wall* suggests, is easy. No one runs from time. We run to time to avoid the deadlock of negativity.

We make a leap of faith if we assume that the woman in *The Wall*, or the ecocritic, or the environmentally minded subject, really wants to learn how to live, that our civilizational discontent results from a lack of education, and that, deep down, we're all nature's students. The ecocritical enterprise relies not just on nature's guiding light but also on the student's will to learn. There is, of course, a will to know, but only to the extent that knowledge doesn't shake the structure of ab-sense.[52] Like any other symptom, ecocriticism is a compromise between knowledge and ab-sense: the non-knowledge of eco-negativity. That compact is not betrayed willingly, for such a betrayal collapses our self-image as willing, knowing subjects. Meanwhile, the surplus satisfaction of knowing nothing, and solving nothing, keeps ecocriticism firmly in place, stuck—immobilized by an ab-sense it dismisses in favor of the time and direction (~~ab-~~sense) that education purports to give.

The cinema of extinction trades one stasis (the misrecognition of the educative impasse as progress) for another (an existence structured by negation: there is neither time nor meaning, nor presence). In so doing, this cinema fulfills the task of a queer theory of negativity that, according to Edelman, necessarily manifests as a "*counter*pedagogy."[53] "It follows" from the argument of *No Future: Queer Theory and the Death Drive* "that queerness, as the figure of . . . a radical unbecoming, maintains an intensely negative link to the logic of education. Queerness, wherever it shows itself (in the form of a catachresis), effects a *counter*pedagogy that refutes, by its positivization, the reality that grants it no place—or that grants it the place of what nullifies: the nonplace of the null."[54] Queerness promotes, as the antithesis to a "good education" that "serves the *social* good by negating whatever refuses that good and thereby endangers the Child," a "*bad education*" that "teaches us nothing more than the nothing of '*the Thing which is not*.'"[55] *The Wall* similarly teaches nothing but ab-sense. We call the film apedagogical, rather than outright counter- or anti-pedagogical, because it displays none of the willful defiance or deviance in Edelman's bad education. Some titles in the cinema of extinction even showcase an attachment to the usual icons of normativity: the couple, the family. What makes such titles available to queer-theoretical interpretation is the remarkable failure of this iconography to represent, let alone protect, the social good *qua* reproduction and futurity.

Embedded in our historical claim regarding negativity's intensification and propagation amid the climate crisis is a pair of disciplinary and methodological gambits. First: we propose that the pertinence of models of negativity to contemporary environmental existence is such that the transdisciplinary pairing is worth pursuing even if queerness, as it hovers further away from sexual subcultures, risks becoming more elusive than it already is. We don't have to emulate Barad or Sam See in positing a queerness inherent to nature to evaluate the impressive reach of queer theory's accounts of fractured subjectivity across the ecological realm.[56] As we situate our study within a landscape of inequalities and hierarchies, we vow to sidestep the trap of transforming negativity into a demographic datum, or sorting any given population as more or less negative than others. We wish not to ascribe negativity to this or that identity—negativity's structure is, after all, non-self-identicality—but to follow in the footsteps of James Bliss, David Marriott, and more recently Edelman by interrogating what "posited identities" are "inflect[ed] (in particular communities and at particular historical moments) as embodiments of negativity inassimilable to being."[57] The tasks, as we see them, are to investigate what identities are made to stand in, as "catachres[e]s," for nonbeing, as well as to interrogate what subjects are expected to serve an exemplary function in the theorization of negativity.[58]

And second: if it is to face the contradictions of present-day environmental existence, ecocriticism ought to give up a tendency in its engagement with queer theory to sweep negativity away on the basis of its perceived irresponsibility. Angela Hume and Samia Rahimtoola's introduction to a special issue of *ISLE: Interdisciplinary Studies in Literature and Environment* on "Queering Ecopoetics," for instance, aligns Edelmanian negativity with industrial capitalism's displacement and destruction drives:

> From an environmental standpoint, . . . [Edelman's] message comes all too close to the extractivist logic of today's resource industries, which might happily join Edelman in saying, "Fuck the social order and the Child in whose name we're collectively terrorized . . . fuck Laws both with capital ls and with small; fuck the whole network of Symbolic relations and the future that serves as its prop." . . . Like those coal companies that move from one West Virginia mountaintop to the next without concern for the exhausted landscapes they leave behind, the rejection of futurity risks reaffirming the live-for-today attitude that defines our social and environmental relations.[59]

Hume and Rahimtoola discard negativity in favor of "new ways of imagining stewardship and care" owed to Muñoz, projecting onto a planetary canvas the debate that has long opposed the antisocial and utopian branches of queer theory.[60] We would note that a radical shift in scale is necessary to argue that theorists are "like those coal companies." More to the point, the equation between a queer distrust of futurity and an acquiescence to the orchestration of environmental collapse ignores that the social order refuted by Edelman doesn't exceed extractive, industrial, and racial capitalisms; it corresponds to these very systems. Negativity is allergic to the status quo—to things as they are, to self-identicality, to the logic of the *one*. An ecocritical encounter with negativity, as Rahimtoola herself has shown elsewhere, can inhibit the compulsive narratives of economic overcoming and environmental repair that redeem and excuse Black suffering.[61]

The psychoanalytic nomenclature of negativity makes available to us, as proper objects of inquiry, the attachments that inform the pastoral lesson. The collective unconscious keeps on life support an ecocriticism of self-improvement and a queer theory of reciprocity. The unconscious toward which we orient ourselves clashes with the "Anthropocene unconscious" from which Mark Bould excavates evidence that one cultural text and another cultural text and yet another cultural text is about climate catastrophe, actually.[62] We are reluctant to renew the pedagogical covenant that authorizes Bould's revelation compulsion, for the practice hinges on a rudimentary, totalizing spin on the Freudian mind, one wherein the unconscious is but expression-in-waiting. We instead route our interpretation through an "environmental unconscious" that, as one of us (Swarbrick) has defined the concept in a book titled after it, insists on the incipience of all efforts to know nature: "All of nature's flourishing would thus be driven by a gap, by a failure to translate the enigmatic message and to make matter and meaning stick together."[63] The unconscious, then, "is not simply the result of geometric foreshortening; it is not something somewhere, a space waiting to be uncovered by later readings. The unconscious is, according to Freud, incompletion itself."[64] Rather than a receptacle for the repressed meaning that would save us if only it were released through expression and education, the unconscious affords one terminology for what makes environmental existence unresolvable and unteachable. Seduction affords another.

OUTSIDE IN DESIRE

To seduce means to lead. But unlike education, its etymological helpmate, seduction does not lead out or in; it convolves the two, jumbles them, *mis*leads so that we are left wondering, *which am I?* Seduction is an education in misdirection.

Whereas Freud abandoned the seduction hypothesis as a theoretical dead end—conceptually untenable because ungeneralizable—Jean Laplanche has argued for a general theory of seduction as education, one that is universal to the adult-child relationship in which, structurally speaking, one is "in" language while the other is "outside" it.[65] Of course, "in" and "out" are insufficient topological markers, for it is precisely the inversion of inside and outside that Laplanche theorizes. Although the adult is in language, language implants something alien in the adult. We are, for that reason, outside in language, summoned to speak while remaining incapable of putting into words the unconscious of the other. The asymmetry suggested by the adult-child relationship proves to Laplanche that Freud, who did not have structural linguistics at his disposal, strayed from the trauma that induces our psychosexual being.[66] Invaded by enigmatic signifiers that carry the unconscious sexuality of the other, our mind absorbs this alien other as our own. In Laplanche's paradigmatic words, the unconscious comes from the other.[67] It is a certificate of our ex-centricity.

Laplanche's other is not the vulnerable other of Levinasian ethics, nor is it the other dwelled upon at great length by theories of difference and recognition (from Judith Butler, most notably, writing in the wake of Levinas and Derrida, to the many eco-philosophies now urging us to recognize our earthly cohabitants).[68] Laplanche's other is neither ethical nor recognizable; it is seductive. The other—namely, the adult—seduces us in infancy by flooding our world with "enigmatic signifiers."[69] From the start of its social existence, the child is awash in signifiers that are enigmatic insofar as they introduce loss into the world. The caretaker is forever coming and going. Their look is often elsewhere or distracted. These signifiers do not prevent the child from fantasizing about a full, undivided object. For example, when the child experiences hunger, it fantasizes about the satisfying object: the breast. Fantasy gives the illusion that the object can be had. Language extends this fantasy. It also splinters it.

Going a step beyond the early Lacan, who tended to focus on the symbolic alone as it breaks into and cuts up ("castrates") the infant's, and then the adult's, imaginary world, Laplanche argues that what the enigmatic signifier does, primarily, is seduce the child, setting it adrift.[70] The child before the adult other is confronted primarily with lack. This lack—be it the missing breast, a vacant look, or a voice tinged with desire for what is not the child—reveals an absence in the other and an absence in the self. It is a basic Lacanian idea that the other is the locus in which our image takes shape and finds its coordinates, giving rise to the "I."[71] An empty gaze or an incomprehensible touch makes both the other and the self enigmatic.

To be Copernican, in Laplanche's sense, means answering to this drift—to what in us orbits an unknown center, a center that is not "me," not "ours," one that is ex-centric. This ex-centricity should be understood as, on the one hand, the alien outside inhabiting our relations, making all relations, including those we have to ourselves, nonrelations; and, on the other, the deviational energy of the drives, which have no teacher. "Desire," Edelman condenses, "positivizes the constant and objectless circulation of the drive."[72] The drive's bad education, on the other hand, occasions "a *leading out* from whatever we think 'we' are, even if that leading out is one that 'we' cannot survive."[73] We are fundamentally seduced, which is to say led astray, by the other. The apedagogy that founds sexuality never stops throwing us off-kilter. "We can in no way confuse the domain of the *Triebe* [drives]," Lacan warns, "with a reclassification of human beings' associations with their natural milieu, however new that reclassification may seem. The *Trieb* must be translated insofar as possible with some ambiguity, and I like sometimes to say *dérive* in French, 'drift.'"[74]

As far as we know, Lacan wasn't thinking about ecological drift when he tendered this etymology. Still, the word "drift" is so seductive partly because it ex-centers us with respect to not only the human but also the nonhuman. What if the great Going Astray in psychoanalysis happened, contra Laplanche, not vis-à-vis the human other, whereby every relation either establishes or replays the adult-child couplet, but vis-à-vis the ecological other—the Real that sets adrift all manner of life, from rivers to glaciers, to geologic layers? What if the adult-child seduction were epiphenomenal to the primary seduction happening beneath our feet? The Copernican revolution in psychoanalysis ought to decenter the human subject respective to the alien adult and, as Cahill has shown, respective to the alien in nature, whose traumatic gaps in the symbolic order, or seductions, widen by the day.[75]

Elizabeth Grosz goes farthest in recognizing the seductions of nature. Inspired by Darwin and Deleuze, she deems natural existence excessive all the way down.[76] The Earth's libidinal economy finds outlets for erotic discharge through birdsong, animal and plant architecture, and the very formation of the Earth's strata. See will later insist on this point by making a natural theory of aesthetic experimentation and an aesthetic theory of natural change one and the same.[77] Without adopting a psychoanalytic language—which sets her apart from See, who is friendlier to such a language[78]—Grosz treats reproduction as secondary to the excessive sexuality and becoming-artistic of the world in her theory of sexual selection.[79] There is no such thing as the temptation of biological reductivism, as Grosz would have it, insofar as biology, geology, and life as such are excessive. The Earth sublimates sexuality as art.

This, the matter of sex and art, is where our position and Grosz's deviate. Grosz's Darwinian ontology supplies a sexual pedagogy of the planet. The claim that life is "in excess of systematicity, open-ended, unpredictable" pays no attention to negativity, lack, discord, masochistic desire, or the pathetic satisfaction of the drives.[80] Grosz apprises us of the planet's excessive nature, but her theory of sexuality sanitizes sublimation by substituting art for sex.[81] This aesthetic education of the drive is a misstep. Take lack away, and sexuality goes with it. Sexuality, Freud and Laplanche agree, is masochistic. There would be no seduction, ecological or otherwise, without absence: the true object of sublimation, and the limit shared by all expressions of nature, from birdsong to Beethoven.

Although Freud, like Grosz, was seduced by the desire to educate, his theory has proven wildly uneducable. Seduced by the *che vuoi?* of the other, by the question, *what does the other want from me?* the child begins an education, but an education in ab-sense. The other cannot answer this question. The other, indeed, must not know; such is the nature of repression. Drives emerge as a response—a failed response, but a response nonetheless—to the enigmatic message, which has no referent, no meaning, and thus no answers; it is a question mark and nothing more. For Laplanche, this question mark is the true axis on which relationality turns.[82] Pried loose from the biological and social directives of education, the question mark sets the subject adrift around an impossible object: the unconscious of the other. Nature is the woman's silent other in *The Wall*, and *The Wall* ours. By dispensing an apedagogy wherein there is nothing to teach and nothing to know, the film sets us adrift, away from the certainty that there may be so much as a solution to the pastoral bind.

"It," "the pastoral," "[always] fails," "is [always] absent."

We are, like the woman in *The Wall*, outside in the ecological classroom—schooled by desire, but a desire for nothing nameable. It's time we learned that lesson.

HUMANITY AFTER EXTINCTION

Tragedy befalls the woman as *The Wall* nears its ending. One scene cuts back and forth between the tragic event, in an unspecified past, and the woman's painful recollection, in the present. In the memory, the woman is hiking with Lynx. The camera pans across a tree branch, where dead leaves and dried needles are teeming with ants (figure 10). The woman does not notice this paragon of interconnection and interdependence; she looks strictly down or ahead, and never with wonder. Atop a rock formation, she and Lynx witness something alarming before we do. They rush toward the lodge, and a disembodied axe pierces the alpine skyline (figure 11). Its wielder, whom we discern a few seconds later, is a haggard man; he appears to have attacked the cow Bella. The frantic violence gives way to slow motion as the woman runs into the lodge. The camera pauses on the open door, awaiting her resurgence, rifle in arm. She shoots and kills the man in time to save the cow, but not Lynx. She will eventually roll the man's corpse over one abyss (a cliff) and bury Lynx's body in another (a deep hole).

10

11

This tragedy counts as an event, but it does not resolve, or even fundamentally disturb, the woman's stasis. Instead, the tragedy reinforces that the true horror in *The Wall* is human persistence; it is the residue of a humanity defined by its inability to become-animal. The man's attack, something of a non sequitur, reminds us that even among a human population of two (as far as they and we know), a masculinist logic of devastation and death can prevail. Harrowing isolation does not suffice to shield the woman from the threat of having her world destroyed by a man who says nothing and about whom we know nothing; he's a man, that's all. The tragedy also asserts the pastoral's unsustainability. The scene of multispecies entanglement ought to implode. If the woman won't obliterate it entirely on her own, a stranger, this ex-centric figure whose existence exceeds her vision of the world, will take care of it.

Lynx's subtraction from the woman's inhuman calculation neither slows down nor concludes her descent into negativity. After the violent cacophony, the dreadful silence grows even more remarkable. She muses:

> I sit at the table, and time stands still. I can't see it, smell it, or hear it, but it surrounds me on all sides, its silence and motionlessness is terrible. At heart these thoughts are quite meaningless. I pity animals, and I pity people, because they're thrown into this life without being consulted. Maybe people are more deserving of pity, as they have just enough intelligence to resist the natural course of things. It has made them wicked and desperate, and not very lovable.

She does not exclude the possibility that "life could have been lived differently," that there could have been "a better life" or a "life more bearable," but estimates that "it's too late" for "us" to take the "path" of "love." We abandon the woman on February 25, when, having run out of paper, she is forced to "end [her] report."[83] She vows to go outside and feed the ostracized white crow "waiting there for [her]." Two outcasts, expecting each other, for no apparent reason.

Endings pose a problem for the cinema of extinction. Perhaps no environmental humanists devote as much attention to questions of narrative as scholars of extinction, who routinely proclaim the social and political salience of stories. Their scholarship has this in common with the corporate logic that rebrands marketing as storytelling: a faith in narrative and the way it motivates us to care about certain beings or things and not others.[84] "We Humans Are a Storytelling Species," Lydia Pyne titled the introduction to *Endlings: Fables for the Anthropocene*, echoing the punchy openings of TED Talks and trade paperbacks.[85] The term "endlings" designates a species' last known individuals. Although "endling stories seem so heavily influenced by an English- and a Western-based literary canon," Pyne remarks, "it's worth keeping in mind that many folktales and fairy tales carry with them an arguably 'universal element' to their narratives."[86] She concludes that "we are living in an Age of Endlings, but we might also be living at a point where endling storytelling (in English and non-English) could shape the way we think about extinction. . . . Perhaps recognizing and improving endling storytelling—maybe, just maybe—could offer something other than despair."[87] What evidence, beyond our own trust, do we have of stories' ability to "shape the way we think" and feel?

The body of scholarship labeled "empirical ecocriticism" seeks to answer this question, borrowing methods from environmental communication and psychology to evaluate the "impact of environmental narratives," generally measured through self-reported attitudinal shifts in readers and viewers.[88] Empirical ecocritics believe that the power of, say, a work of climate fiction can be asserted and quantified, so that it is possible to say, with a straight face, that "even a short fictional narrative can have an impact on attitudes toward animals as long as a week after exposure."[89] The chasm between the project of empirical ecocritics and ours cannot be overstated; theirs casts the reader or spectator as a rational and reasonable subject, a subject of self-presence, one devoid of an unconscious, devoid in fact of any and all contradictions. This subject is an abstraction, and a colonial and patriarchal one at that. Very little is empirical about the research that accepts such an abstraction as its unit of analysis. We will not devote much room to contesting the tenets of empirical ecocriticism; it is obvious that we disagree with them. Let us instead focus on what empirical ecocriticism's quantitative and qualitative methods, such as its reliance on surveys, reveal about arguments like Pyne's. The evidence of a text's impact, empirical ecocriticism at least rightly suggests, is necessarily extra-textual. Put differently, a text supplies no evidence of its reception. Claims about the ways stories shape thinking, then, are not about stories but about our faith in them.

This faith's underlying pedagogical assumption is that telling the right story in the right way will yield the right response: a chain of actions powerful enough to reverse the course of extinction, human or otherwise. Stories of multispecies connection and care are thereby positioned as a complex, open-ended rejoinder to other stories, such as total human annihilation, that are by contrast considered simplistic and fatalistic. Is the story of human extinction, however, as straightforward as it is made out to be? Would the eradication of human beings correspond to the extinction of humanity? The woman's post-apocalyptic dwelling in *The Wall* and the anthropogenic transformation of landscapes more generally confront us with a recalcitrant humanity, not gone but static. The problem of the ending, then, has to do with replacing the lone question mark with a period, which is to say, with dropping the curtain on the stasis achieved by crossing into hostile natures. The cinema constitutes a logical medium for working through this problem, for the answers it provides are formal: the muted conclusion of the woman's report in *The Wall*, a more bombastic shift in mode or embrace of the supernatural elsewhere.

One of the most buzzed-about works of formalist film theory in recent memory, Eugenie Brinkema's *Life-Destroying Diagrams* (2022), yearns for a cinema of extinction that would evacuate residual humanity. One chapter in the book spotlights Drew Goddard's *The Cabin in the Woods* (2011), a supernatural horror film that reveals, below the cabin, a lab where employees of The Director manufacture annual sacrificial rites to appease the subterranean deities known as the Ancient Ones.[90] The college student Dana hastens human extinction by refusing to occupy the trope of the slasher "final girl" and to do what neither the zombies above ground nor the various creatures populating the underground lab could accomplish: kill her friend Marty. Annihilation represents, in Brinkema's view, "the positive attestation of a violence that *is* All"—which is to say, "the Anthropocene itself."[91] "Violence," she adds with characteristic recursion, "will not fail to arrive this last time, will not become extinct and die out, run short: what will become extinct, die out, run short, will be human life itself, failing because of dying, failing as disappointed, what is let down, expiring. Being redefined as that which will perish, that which is no longer to be produced."[92] The promise of the film's ending, as Brinkema receives it, "is that the finitude of a violence that is All will constrain and produce a restriction of the play of possibility in its definitive arrival as a violence that does violence to the failed violences, arriving successfully and bringing about an adequate (which is to say: effective) endingness to the ongoingness of the film."[93]

Two shots in *The Cabin in the Woods* seem at odds with Brinkema's totalizing vision of the ending as the "endingness to the ongoingness," and she grants each a footnote. The first shot depicts Dana and Marty, bloodied, slouched, defeated. Dana makes a throwaway observation: "Humanity . . . it's time to give someone else a chance." The second shot, the film's last, shows a giant hand, presumably a deity's but distinctly human in appearance, erupting from the ground to destroy the cabin and—the camera? Us? This hand, like the woman's hand in *The Wall*, arrives at nothing, in this case because the cut to black interrupts the gesture. Both shots in *The Cabin in the Woods* insist on a residual humanity: the existence of "someone else" in the aftermath of extinction, and the involvement of a humanoid hand in the extinguishing itself. This is how Brinkema responds to Dana's remark:

> Dana . . . is absolutely wrong in her interpretation of the scenario at hand: it is not time to give someone else a chance. The endingness of all human life is not *time* (not contained within time—it signals the anarchival and the end of historical time), not for some *one*, not a horizon that admits *someone else*, and not *chance*.[94]

And this is what Brinkema has to say about the hand:

> A project of universalization shown to be feint, given (literal) body *as impossible* in the very particular appearance with which the film ends: the not at all universal anthropomorphic gigantism of a single hand plunging up through the hypotactic world levels with its discernibly national, even New England regional, evocations of a Lovecraftian metaphysics, the hieratic scale of this hand resituating a priority of the human form over the monstrous mutations prevented previously.[95]

Dana isn't wrong. Nor is she right: she is a character. Likewise, toward the end of *The Wall*, the lonely, worn-out woman is not wrong to locate in some mythicized past the possibility of a "better life." Her statement testifies to the pull of the pastoral even in the face of its deflagration. Brinkema's systematic account of *The Cabin in the Woods* codes evidence of humanity's recalcitrance as errors—failures indeed—in what she otherwise describes as the film's surrendering to "the grid," where form and violence are one.[96]

These shots do not qualify as aberrations by our standards. They do not mark self-imposed limits to the film's ability to become its true—purely formal, purely violent—self. Contradictions, such as humanity's concurrent impossibility (as extinction) and inevitability (as "someone else," as a humanoid hand), may be exogenous to the "life-destroying diagram," but they demarcate the province of negative life and the terrain of our investigation. The following chapters continue the practice, modeled in this introduction, of sustaining a granular engagement with individual films. Close reading and close watching, we believe, best attend to contradictions and their formal management.

We could, and at this juncture probably should, provide a road map (i.e., *Negative Life* comprises three main chapters. Their arc is historical: we search for eco-negativity in representations of preindustrial, industrial, and postindustrial moments. The arc is also philosophical: the contradictions of environmental existence erupt as nontransparency, absurdity, and transcendence. Lastly, it is formal: we approach the problem of beginnings and endings from the vantage points of retroaction, non sequiturs, and detonation. Chapter 1, primarily on Reichardt's *First Cow*, seeks alternatives to the nature-as-pedagogue model that nourishes the pastoral lesson and its attendant fantasies. Chapter 2, on Chung's *Minari* and Mathai's *Bhopal Express*, accounts for the afterlife of the familiar and the familial in contexts where catastrophes have constricted existence. Chapter 3, on Schrader's *First Reformed*, turns to melodrama to ponder what it means to intensify or spectacularize environmental contradictions and to subtract oneself from the impossible situation they subtend. Between this trio lie two "interludes" on ecohorror. The interludes take us from one chapter to the next: from excursuses into negativity to the dissolution of the couple and family forms in one case, and from the dissolution of the couple and family forms to melodrama in the other. The interludes accomplish this by compiling cases where the cinema of extinction risks self-parody, converting worldlessness into an overt antagonism between self and world through remarkably repetitive plots and symbolic maximalism) but the truth is: this is a book about being stuck, with nowhere to go.

[CHAPTER ONE]

First Cow at the End of the World

SOMETHING FROM NOTHING

Five years after the seism that was *Beyond the Pleasure Principle*, Freud returned to the question of foundations in his 1925 essay, "Negation."[1] He was unsatisfied, it would seem, with the repetition of the drive he had posited as the groundless grounds of thought. Seeking different foundations if not necessarily sturdier ones, Freud found himself asking once more, *how to begin?*

Logically, anything begins at one. The God of the Hebrew Bible is such a beginning. In the book of Exodus, God says to Moses, "I am that I am" (*'ehye 'ăšer 'ehye*), allowing neither time nor division (Exod. 3:14 [KJV]). Lucretius likewise asserts in *De rerum natura* the one of the atom; it is primary, such that nothing comes from nothing (1.146).[2] The same belief repeats in the anxiety-ridden charge of Shakespeare's King Lear. When he is spurned by his daughter Cordelia, Lear protests, "Nothing will come of nothing. Speak again" (1.1.88).[3] We need only look to mathematics for confirmation that the one inaugurates the set. According to Alain Badiou, the count-as-one founds the order of appearance. While being, concedes Badiou, is mathematically speaking infinite, and thus indifferent to the order of the one, it appears only as one. Or, it is nothing.[4]

Freud's "Negation" intervenes at precisely the point of appearance and disappearance, where being and nothing coalesce. "Negation" is an apocalyptic essay in the strict sense of the Greek *apokalýptein*, "to uncover, disclose, reveal."[5] The birth of thought, Freud insists, is primarily abortive, and revelation, however illuminating, works only by destroying that which it brings to light.

Freud begins "Negation" with patients who no sooner divulge a repressed content than negate it: "It is as though the patient had said:

'It's true that my mother came into my mind as I thought of this person, but I don't feel inclined to let the association count.'"[6] Here, the count-as-one begins not at zero and one but at negative one. Freud elucidates: "the content of a repressed image or idea can make its way into consciousness, on condition that it is *negated*. Negation is a way of taking cognizance of what is repressed."[7] Repression, then, grounds thought and speech. Freud urges caution: the psychoanalytic treatment does not lift repression. Instead, "the outcome of this is a kind of intellectual acceptance of the repressed, while at the same time *what is essential to the repression persists*."[8] Negation lets an impossible content exist, as if through photo-negative, by menacing the count-as-one—menacing, that is, what grounds countability.[9]

How to begin in psychoanalysis? Freud, who goes beyond Badiou in this regard, starts from neither the one (God's "I am that I am") nor the many (the materialist multiplicity that, in the introduction, we deemed a constant variable across much ecocriticism) but the negative. Freud's starting point is the split between "no" and "yes" (no, "It's *not* my mother"; yes, "It *is* his mother").[10] The split uncovered by Freudian psychoanalysis threatens to convert both sides of the equation, such that - is + and vice versa. The result is dizzying. The "'no' is the hallmark of repression, a certificate of origin—like, let us say, 'Made in Germany.'"[11] The presence of such a certificate is undeniable, yet it guarantees nothing: no ground, no origin.

The contradiction in speech suggests a contradiction at the level of the psyche and—though Freud himself does not say so—ontology. We access the most speculative dimension of Freud's essay upon hitting the bedrock of the subject. Just as negative statements add up to positives and positive statements add up to nothing, the subject is, at bottom, split. "The antithesis," Freud writes,

> between subjective and objective does not exist from the first. It only comes into being from the fact that thinking possesses the capacity to bring before the mind once more something that has once been perceived, by reproducing it as a presentation without the external object having still to be there. The first and immediate aim, therefore, of reality-testing is, not to *find* an object in real perception which corresponds to the one presented, but to *refind* such an object, to convince oneself that it is still there.[12]

Thought, for Freud, begins at -1, where something in the order of being has been lost. The activity of thought attempts to "reproduc[e the loss] as a presentation," but that presentation would not be possible without the lost object of perception. Thought loses itself into being.

Although it serves as the foundation of reality-testing, or the ego's recognition of the difference between the external and internal worlds, thought is, according to Freud, foundationless, for it relies on what Alenka Zupančič calls the "missing signifier."[13] This signifier designates the lack in the other from whom we separate in most psychoanalytic ontogeneses. Without the missing signifier, without the minus that marks the radical incompleteness of the other and so installs failure at the origin of subjective life, signification could not begin. Freud thus finds—indeed refinds—negative life at the origin of subjectivity. Henceforth, the aim of reality-testing is not to adequate ourselves, or to match our environment harmoniously. Reality-testing is, per Freud's essay, a hallucination. We might convince ourselves that life adds up, that the count-as-one remains operative, and that the presented object "is still there." Still, the missing signifier haunts thought with negative value.

We begin with Freud's essay in order to welcome the abyssal logic of Kelly Reichardt's filmography, specifically *First Cow* (2019), which, as in Freud's thesis on reality-testing, finds Reichardt returning to familiar ground: the Pacific Northwest she explored in earlier films like *Old Joy* (2006), *Wendy and Lucy* (2008), *Meek's Cutoff* (2010), and *Night Moves* (2013).[14] The U.S.-based auteur is widely recognized for a slow cinema that documents the decreasingly "slow violence" of environmental decay with realist fidelity.[15] Yet a minor strain in Reichardt's visionary cinema, we venture, concerns itself with more, and less, than what Katherine Fusco and Nicole Seymour, in their excellent study of Reichardt's realism, call environmental "emergency"—"a slow-paced realism that highlights the precariousness of contemporary life and emphasizes the everyday, ongoing nature of emergency."[16] To be sure, there are infinite emergences of slow and fast time in Reichardt's work. Piercing this work, however, is something that does not emerge and cannot be counted as one. Reichardt's oeuvre, taken as exemplary of the cinema of extinction rather than ecocinema more broadly, dedicates itself to ushering in what never shows up. Reichardt is committed to realism to the extent that she is committed to reality-testing, but the test's sole objective is to convince the viewer that something radically absent "is still there" and, by extension, that what is present can be so only as absence.

If Reichardt's is a cinema of still-life in both senses—life interrupted, and life ongoing—it strives not to master absence through the representation of imagined fullness prized by ecocritics but, much like *The Wall* and its elevation of engraved trash to the dignity of the lost Thing, to reaffix the emergent properties of life, all the ways of starting at one, to the missing signifier. This foundational absence accounts for the simultaneous splendor and terror of Reichardt's films. The negative life that bothers *First Cow* does more than dislocate the object of ecological reality-testing, the Pacific Northwest and its emergent environs; it dislocates everything that ecological reality-testing takes as its objective ground, its principles. *First Cow* holds our attention in this first chapter because it challenges us, as critics and spectators, to mistrust its title's penchant for origin stories and progress myths so that we may think ecology from negativity. There, philosophy can, as Hegel urges, "beware of the wish to be edifying."[17]

For all our above concern with the question of beginnings, the cinema of extinction, as this chapter's arc will make clear, does not allow us to stray too far from the question of endings, one that the introduction raised with respect to Eugenie Brinkema's interpretation of *The Cabin in the Woods* and its not-quite-annihilative conclusion. *How to begin* and *how to end* are, in many ways, variations on a theme when it comes to the cinema of extinction; both raise the problem of granting narrative form to an encounter with a world that isn't a given (one that isn't there, and can't be had) because it will not stop ending.

We are getting ahead of ourselves. Let us reset, at −1.

ECOLOGY AND THE POLICE

One of the first principles of ecological reality-testing, as we noted in the introduction, is that we—humans, animals, plants, the whole planet—are entangled; we live and die as one. The aim of reality-testing for ecocritics has been to find their complement in a widely and wildly entangled ecology. Companion species of many kinds give the lie to human ipseity; the count-as-one now counts, and counts on, the others (other "ones") we are taught to recognize, live with, and learn from.

The test, as informed by pastoral pedagogy, makes no room for the negative life posited by Freud, which, rather than being subtracted from reality, as are extinct species and various beings with reduced vitality, supports the reality of human and more-than-human entanglements. Theories of entanglement thereby decline to entangle one thing: Zupančič's "missing signifier." Worse than a failure of inclusion, we notice a gesture of exclusion, for one of ecocriticism's founding commandments is to suture the absence that makes our entanglements possible. Before us is a pedagogy that promotes intimacy with more-than-human others but misses the extimacy at its core.

Before turning to Reichardt's cinematic reality-testing, let us consider a joke about the missing signifier. The joke appears in Lacan's reading, in his *Seminar II*, of Edgar Allan Poe's "The Purloined Letter." The joke, like any good joke, contains philosophical insight. Lacan asks why, after their investigation, police are unable to find the missing letter, even though it is sitting in plain sight, undisguised. He offers: "The purloined letter has become a hidden letter. Why don't the policemen find it? They don't find it because they do not know what a letter is. They don't know that because they are the police."[18]

If, as Jacques Rancière avers, the function of the police is to order the sensible, then, following Lacan, we might say that the police fail to locate the missing letter because they are looking for something spatiotemporal.[19] The police officer, like the ecocritic, searches for what appears as one. The missing letter, for Lacan, does not so much occupy as outline space and time, generating reality effects while remaining elsewhere, in and out of existence—or "ex-sistence," to use Lacan's later term.[20] The *ex-* prefix registers something beyond the order of reality that organizes the domain of the police. That the letter belongs to incommensurable registers, the Lacanian Real and ordinary reality, explains why the police miss it. It is the very nature of the signifier to be lost—to be, in Freud's terms, negative—despite our best attempts to believe it is "still there." "Signification as such," aphorizes Lacan, "is never where one thinks it must be."[21]

It would be easier to chuckle at the foolishness of the police, at their inability to see what ex-sists solely in the negative, if the reflex of looking away when confronted with gaps or contradictions were not so prevalent within ecocriticism. Ecocritics have made a habit of correcting a spatio-empirical oversight, presuming that the missing signifier is always somewhere around, able to make reality cohere. Consider the term "Anthropocene," a master-signifier of ecocriticism if there ever was one, which names the beginning of the geologic epoch defined by anthropogenic climate change. The term inaugurates a chain of signification about the geologic human. Soon after this master-signifier entered ecological discourse, alternatives began to circulate. Would not Capitalocene, Plantationocene, Chthulucene, or Plasticene be better signifiers?[22] Perhaps. And yet these valuable attempts at breaking up the Anthropocene by supplementing "Anthropos" with new signifiers and new knowledges borrowed from Black, Indigenous, and proletarian counter-histories overlook that the master-signifier is foundationless; it carries negative value.

The mistake of ecocriticism, and of Poe's police, is to confuse a transcendental absence (the missing signifier) for an empirical one (spatiotemporal oversight). An empirical absence is easy to spot, and detective fiction delights us with subjects capable of filling every last gap with knowledge. By extension, anyone with a copy of the *Communist Manifesto* can see what is empirically missing from our world. A transcendental absence requires a different labor—namely, a labor of the negative—to show what is missing in our spatiotemporal entanglements. It is true that a new master-signifier would be better in many ways: more accurate, more historical, and more knowledgeable. Yet is it not the idiocy of the master-signifier, any master-signifier, that ecocriticism tarries with, like the noir detective who succumbs to an excess of empirical details and misses the Real, or anamorphism, gazing at him?[23]

For all that it gets wrong, the term "Anthropocene" is, negatively speaking, correct, because it universalizes the failure to say all that no binary signifier can mend. The contradiction we call "negative life" orients the ecocritic toward a different way of life than the police's: what, in his play on the French "*manque*," Lacan calls "want-to-be" (*manque-à-être*) or lack of being (*manque à être*). The ecocritical want-to-be has traditionally sought fulfillment, remedying lack via, and in the name of, home, place, composition, worlding, ethics, care, intimacy, kinship, companionship, and love. Such fulfillment is ever-deferred—hence the calls to mourn what has been lost, forgotten, or misplaced. By contrast, the want-to-be of negative life divests from fulfillment, however deferred. This want-to-be masquerades at being and lets its failure be known.

COWED

First Cow plays at wanting-to-be. The main characters play the part of settlers and capitalists in early 1820s Oregon country. When we meet Otis "Cookie" Figowitz (John Magaro), he is working as a cook for a group of ambulatory fur trappers who, angered by food scarcity and motivated by antisemitism, bully him relentlessly. One night, while foraging for mushrooms in the forest, Cookie happens upon King-Lu (Orion Lee), a Chinese immigrant wanted for killing a Russian man. Cookie grants Lu shelter in his tent and watches the fugitive escape across the river the next morning. They meet again soon after, at a fort. Lu pulls Cookie from a bar crawl and invites him to a cabin that the pair will henceforth occupy. It would seem an understatement to designate their living arrangement as homosocial. The arrangement is, at the least, homoromantic. Lu and Cookie owe each other their lives, and they convey their gratitude in care and tenderness. Calling their domestic and economic bond a result of repressed homosexual desire would be beside the point, however, for Reichardt shows no interest in the repressive hypothesis when it comes to sex; there is no homosexuality waiting to achieve its true form through legible expression.[24] Cohabitation, at any rate, involves playing house.

Lu dreams of having a farm, and Cookie of opening a bakery or hotel in San Francisco. For now (a *now* that won't yield a future: more on this later), they settle on a modest, if fast-growing, business venture, selling "oily cakes" at the fort's market. The cakes' tremendous popularity leads to price hikes and bidding wars, eventually catching the attention of the Chief Factor (Toby Jones), who solicits a clafoutis (a crustless tart containing fruit) ahead of a captain's (Scott Shepherd) visit. Cookie and Lu's business venture is a con, and not an especially artful one, so unsubtly concealed is its artifice. Making both the cakes and the clafoutis requires milk that the pair obtain clandestinely from the Chief Factor's cow—the First Cow to be transported to the region, as he likes to boast. Lu dispels queries by telling customers that the cake recipe, which is in reality Cookie's, is a "Chinese secret." Hypnotized by the alchemy of frying and baking, the Chief Factor doesn't bother to ask what goes into either dish. Like the police in Poe's story and Lacan's joke, consumers and patrons, including the Chief Factor, fail to locate what is hidden in plain sight. "Where does he think the milk is coming from?" Lu once asks Cookie, who replies, "Some people can't imagine being stolen from. Too strong." Lu pauses, then concludes, "Let's hope he's one of those."

The film nears the bedroom farce—or the workplace farce; these locations are indistinguishable here, as we've indicated—when the Chief Factor laments that the cow "gives so little" milk, or when he shows her to his guests and she nuzzles Cookie, her familiar. These comedic set pieces stand amid anxieties about the volatility of the capitalist economy. The captain and the Chief Factor, for example, address fur demand: the former warns that the beaver hat trend is waning in Paris, whereas the latter maintains that the Chinese market remains vigorous and that, in any case, the beaver is "too beautiful and supple" to see its popularity irrevocably diminished. And it is due to financial concerns—specifically, to not having enough money, stored in a tree rather than a bank, to take them to San Francisco—that Lu and Cookie milk the cow once too many and are caught in the act. The Chief Factor and captain will embody the police again, ordering their men to find and kill the companions.

The film's title is emblematic of the logic of the master-signifier in that it masquerades in the position of the first and begins the count at one. What the film recounts, however, is not a bovine cinema of firsts but a cinematic reflection on how we as subjects are duped—better still, *cowed*—into the position of the want-to-be who wants nothing more than to stitch together life's lack.

MAN VERSUS MUSHROOM

We take inspiration for our chapter title from Anna L. Tsing's ethnography, *The Mushroom at the End of the World*. Like other texts in the mycological family, such as Louie Schwartzberg's documentary feature *Fantastic Fungi* (2019) and Merlin Sheldrake's book *Entangled Life: How Fungi Make Our Worlds, Change Our Minds & Shape Our Futures* (2020), Tsing's hugely influential book underscores the idiocy of foundation myths, specifically the white, Protestant, masculinist myth of Man's progress over Nature.[25] "Ever since the Enlightenment," Tsing begins, "Western philosophers have shown us a Nature that is grand and universal but also passive and mechanical. Nature was a backdrop and resource for the moral intentionality of Man, which could tame and master Nature."[26] Recent events, however, give the lie to "the moral intentionality of Man's Christian masculinity, which separated Man from Nature."[27] She enumerates:

> First, all that taming and mastering has made such a mess that it is unclear whether life on earth can continue. Second, interspecies entanglements that once seemed the stuff of fables are now materials for serious discussion among biologists and ecologists, who show how life requires the interplay of many kinds of beings. Humans cannot survive by stomping on all the others.[28]

Tsing's opening exemplifies ecocriticism's response to the white Western Man's pretense of ipseity: Man masquerades as the planet's master-signifier, inaugurating narrative progress by taming Nature while ensuring his and the Earth's destruction. Man is, in the Lacanian idiom, the ultimate want-to-be, whose lack of being spells ruin for all.

Tsing trades Man's foundation myth for mycorrhizal interconnection. This mode of relation is emblematized by the fruiting mushroom: "Below the forest floor, fungal bodies extend themselves in nets and skeins, binding roots and mineral soils, long before producing mushrooms."[29] And it is conceptualized by the "assemblage," which Tsing borrows from ecologists and defines as "polyphonic," "ephemeral," and "multidirectional," "the very stuff of collaborative survival," that which is "not a logical machine" but "gesture[s] to the so-much-more out there," all the "entangled ways of life, with each further opening into a mosaic of temporal rhythms and spatial arcs."[30] The mushroom and the assemblage offer alternatives to Man's ordinal beginning and trajectory. Beyond the count-as-one, there are more-than-human, "open-ended gatherings."[31] Mapping these gatherings promises greater empirical and historical accuracy, for assemblages, writes Tsing, "allow us to ask about communal effects without assuming them. They show us potential histories in the making."[32] The paradigmatic mushroom in Tsing's study is the matsutake. Its worth is, in her estimation, not monetary—though it is a pricey delicacy. Tsing invests in the matsutake because of its pedagogical and ethical value. Growing within ecosystems ravaged by human intervention, the mushroom teaches the art of "living in ruins."[33]

In a sharp account of the "mycological turn," Natalia Cecire and Samuel Solomon note that Tsing seeks less to reject than to resolve value under capitalism, with the mushroom serving as something of an antidote to a crisis of social reproduction, or "the means by which life and its social relations are reproduced."[34] They explain that "the representation of fungi as a ubiquitous, renewable, ecologically beneficial source of both use value and value-for-money, something from almost nothing, . . . renders it an untapped resource, 'out there' but also *right here* (under our feet, in the air)."[35] Tsing's "mycoaesthetics" thus sells the idea that "resilience or survivance can—for the right organisms—be the same as thriving and abundance."[36]

Tsing's lesson about assemblages of "lifeways," wherein the being and becoming of what gathers is never settled and always emergent, reminds us of deconstruction's language lesson. For one thing, the being of the signifier, too, appears "indeterminate," "multidirectional," and "greater than the sum of [its] parts," the phonemes.[37] This comparison is instructive for an additional reason. Tsing echoes Ferdinand de Saussure's claim that there are no positive elements in language, no "organisms as the elements that gather" to make meaning, but rather "happenings"—"effects" without causes.[38] Tsing's lifeways are indeed structured like a language, insofar as the diachronic dimension of language holds in nature, or ecologies, as well. Ecologies, for Tsing, are composed of unpredictable potentialities. Put differently, the being and becoming of assemblages are knowable only retroactively (at which point they have already departed the phase we may know them as), just as, for Lacan, the master-signifier (S1) is knowable only from the vantage of a second, temporally belated signifier (S2). The diachronic or retroactive quilting of language not only gives it meaning and structure but also, as Tsing notes, opens it to untold futures. Hence the psychoanalytic dictum: the past comes from the future.

So far, so good. The mushroom exposes the master-signifier Man as a fraud. Its fraudulence is proven by its dependence for meaning and survival on "lifeways," or assemblages of more-than-human happenings, beyond it. But a subtle subreption in Tsing's argument compromises its—and ecocriticism's—ethical entanglements. As Joan Copjec argues in "Sex and the Euthanasia of Reason," the operation of language, in the wake of Saussure's discovery of diachrony, consists in the retroactive assignment of meaning to that which lacks the immediacy of sense.[39] An antinomy—that language requires asynchrony, and thus senselessness, to make sense—is resolved when Saussure says, as he must, that language *is* diachronic. The statement is contradicted when stated as a positive, that is, without further exegetical speech. Instead of standing pat with that contradiction, Saussure ultimately resolves it by recovering language's synchrony.[40] In this second model, S2 assigns meaning to S1 *and*, Copjec illustrates, S1 to S2.[41] In lieu of diachrony: complementarity, co-constitution, and, in the ecocritical parlance, entanglement. S1 and S2 secure each other's position in the signifying chain, bestowing on the other life, direction, and meaning.

Lacan inveighs against and strikes through this complementarity when he proclaims, "There is no such thing as a sexual relationship," or again, "The woman does not exist."[42] Inflammatory rhetoric aside, Lacan's point is not that there are no women but that there is no Woman to complement Man. Against the reciprocal relation of S1 and S2, Man and Woman, afforded by synchrony, Lacan offers no way out of antinomies. Or, more accurately, he shows that antinomies offer the way out on which existence relies. Life, Tsing writes elsewhere, is ghostly; Lacan agrees.[43] Lacan's ghost isn't the specter of empirical absence (say, mushrooms); the absence is transcendental.[44] Rather than fix diachrony by opting for synchronic gatherings where variously individuated members of the more-than-human collective co-compose, we follow Lacan in positing an ex-sistence that insists on the negativity of what lies beyond—impossibly, not just spatiotemporally—the ecological skein.

VAGABONDS OF THE REAL

Agnès Varda's film *Sans toit ni loi* (*Vagabond*, 1985), in which a nameless drifter (Sandrine Bonnaire) moves from place to place (home to home) and group to group (assemblage to assemblage), perhaps best represents the missing signifier's transcendental logic.[45] As Todd McGowan observes, the drifter cannot be included; what is more, her exclusion makes the lives she intersects possible.[46] The film begins with a man's discovery of her dead body, contorted in a ditch. *Vagabond* proceeds through flashbacks to record the zone between two deaths: her biological death and, before that, the social death tied to her estrangement from symbolic recognition. The narrator takes on a detective role, interviewing those with whom she crossed paths: other drifters, a Tunisian vineyard worker, a family of goat farmers, a professor of agronomy, and a maid. Everyone she encountered envied the lack she represented. As the missing signifier, she wanders freely, never becoming-with others, fiercely protecting her lack of belonging (figure 12). This lack registers as the point of impossibility in the film, which others around her cannot enjoy except as proxy, attached as they are to their symbolic identities.

12

The film's retroactive narration ostensibly attempts to restore the meaning of the missing signifier, to give the drifter a name, a place, an occupation, a romantic partner—but no such meaning sticks to her. The film ends where it began, peering into the ditch where the girl's lifeless body marks the nexus of negative life—both the impossibility of inclusion and the enjoyment of non-belonging. The wanderer is the film's empty set: structurally necessary, socially inadmissible. Her death symbolizes the subjective act and the price one pays to enjoy the missing signifier, which her resting place, a gap, physicalizes. There is no complement, no synchronic relation, the film indicates, to fill in the hole that the missing signifier digs. David Lynch's *Twin Peaks* (1990–91) and *Twin Peaks: The Return* (2017) can be accused of attempting just that: FBI agent Dale Cooper (Kyle MacLachlan) searches for a way to repair the trauma of the television show's missing signifier, the dead Laura Palmer (Sheryl Lee), and bends time and space in the process.[47] Varda's feminism, though, is committed to the radicality of the open wound.

Reichardt takes after Varda in this regard. *First Cow* does not, in fact, open in the early 1820s; a morbid framing device will take us back in time. We begin in the present day. The first shot shows an oil tanker, the

Bellemar, off the coast. The tanker cuts through the frame, piercing the picturesque landscape with an 81,448-ton reminder of petrocapitalism's global network of extraction zones, refineries, and pipelines (figure 13). The first assemblage we witness in *First Cow* is not the life-giving assemblage imagined by ecocritics but the capitalist assemblage delivering extinction from and to various corners of the planet. The late-industrial grotesque of a tanker crossing a pastoral landscape intensifies the urge to escape to the preindustrial past.

First Cow follows that urge to its logical destination, one that, it turns out, drifts troublingly far from the comforts of a fuller and more meaningful environmental existence. The next shot features a nameless woman (Alia Shawkat) and her dog scavenging the coastline. She is the film's equivalent of Tsing's mushroom forager, searching among capitalist ruins for alternative lifeways. As though in a wish-fulfillment fantasy, she finds them. Journeying further into the loamy, fungal-rich woods, she and her dog uncover two buried bodies, their identities devoured by the Earth. Shawkat excavates the skeletal remains of men whose friendship and love endure negatively (figure 14). The bones indicate a love that neither became speech in life nor breaks its silence in the afterlife. There is no carbon dating or biographical redress.

13

14

First Cow starts and ends in the same place of unknowing. The film defies its title's claim to firstness by unearthing two relics—two lovers unto death—on whose ex-sistence as the missing signifier the film's realism depends. The journey on which spectators embark consists not in convincing themselves that life and love and more-than-human assemblages go on but in returning to that which, in reality-testing, is never there: the negative life, enduring in a cleft of dirt, that triggers the retroaction of the film, the process of refinding what, one can only hope, is still there.

Reichardt's film belongs to a rich assemblage of anti-pastoral imagery, from Nicolas Poussin's counter-pastoral paintings *Et in Arcadia Ego* (1638; figure 15) and *Landscape with a Man Killed by a Snake* (1648; figure 16), explicated by T. J. Clark in the form of a question—"How much of death and terror can nature contain and still be posited as a value[,] as a world that human beings reach for, steadying themselves?"—to David Lynch's neo-noir thriller *Blue Velvet* (1986), which begins at the level of a picture-perfect American suburb before plunging the camera into the wormy soil and a monstrous substratum (figures 17 and 18).[48] Reichardt neither mythicizes nor sensationalizes deathly encounters. She instead follows Varda's *Vagabond* in tracking the missing signifier's reality effects. In the nineteenth-century Pacific Northwest, manifest destiny, settler-colonial ideology, and racial capitalism combined to attract American explorers dreaming of making it big. Cookie and Lu's social exclusion, due to antisemitism and racism, bars their access to, or inclusion in, such fantasies. *First Cow*'s insight is that their exclusion founds the white colonial fantasy as such.

15

16

17

18

Like Varda's vagabond, Lu and Cookie are figures of non-belonging. As characters who are ultimately excluded from settler sociality but are no more intimate with Indigeneity, they enjoy the missing signifier, the element prohibiting cohesion. Reichardt puts the missing signifier on the side of the dispossessed, for their dispossession reveals an economy of enjoyment radically unlike the one at home within racial capitalism as well as settler and extractive colonialism. Lu and Cookie's is an enjoyment of lack with nothing to teach and nothing to give anyone invested in fantasies of belonging, be it the colonial project of expansion or the ecocritical dream of human and more-than-human entanglement. Enjoyment is epitomized by Cookie's sweets, which, thanks to the secrecy surrounding his recipes, can never be entirely possessed by, or absorbed into, surrounding logics. The men's death, the hidden treasure found by Shawkat's character, attests to the radicality of an enjoyment that could achieve no fate but extinction.

The vector between enjoyment and extinction also orients Katia and Maurice Krafft, the French volcanologists eulogized in Sara Dosa's *Fire of Love* (2022).[49] The documentary feature relies mainly on the abundant footage of volcanic eruptions captured by the scientists. The footage shifts from glorious to ominous when, in mid-career, the couple direct their attention away from the red volcanoes spewing lava and toward the gray volcanoes whose comparatively subdued clouds of smoke conceal a far greater power to destroy. The Kraffts were killed by a pyroclastic flow in the 1991 eruption of Mount Unzen, a gray volcano in Kyushu, Japan. Their bodies melted, and some accessories and pieces of equipment fossilized.

Miranda July's voice-over narration repeats a pair of theses frequently enough to shake our confidence in their veracity: that "this," Katia and Maurice's story, "is a love story," and that their obsession with, and need to be in proximity to, gray volcanoes was motivated by pedagogical and ethical duty. Yes, the film compiles proof of their romantic bond—or, at any rate, of Katia's continued willingness to massage Maurice's fragile ego—in addition to registering the impact of their research on evacuation policies globally. Still, we notice, in the narrator's compulsion to restore futurity's benchmarks (the heterosexual couple, the pedagogy-to-ethics-to-law chain), a defensive response to the overwhelming evidence of the Kraffts' attraction to the negativity of the volcanoes, or the volcanoes' indifference to the world and its meaning. The preserved footage, like the skeletons that remain in *First Cow*, authorizes retroaction; Dosa can order Katia and Maurice to belong—with each other and within civil society. But the footage plots a betrayal that no excess of twee can conceal: the Kraffts' excursus toward negativity must, like Lu and Cookie's, end in destruction.

First Cow follows the structures of *Vagabond* and *Fire of Love* to the letter, excavating the past through flashbacks. After Shawkat's character exhumes the skeleton, Reichardt cuts to a hand reaching out for a mushroom (figure 19). It momentarily seems that the character has resumed her foraging trip. But the hand isn't hers; it is Cookie's. Reichardt inverts the order of things, such that death (the skeleton remains) lies on the surface and life (the mushroom) resides below, in a realm that the film accesses through retroactive narrative. This formal inversion represents the primary way that negative life configures *First Cow*. We are, for the remainder of the film, on the other side of that formal chasm.

19

RETROACTION

Few thinkers have devoted more intellectual labor to narrative's diachronic dimension—that is, to the simple, acausal fact that the signifying chain works in reverse, just as *First Cow*, a film about the hallucinatory role of memory, works in reverse, with a host of S2s trying and failing to suture the latent negativity or nonbeing of the skeletal S1—than the psychoanalyst Jean Laplanche.

Laplanche is best known as the theorist of "afterwardsness," his preferred translation of the German word *Nachträglichkeit*, "delayed action" or "retroaction."[50] In "Time and the Other," Laplanche begins with an example of afterwardsness lifted from Freud's *The Interpretation of Dreams*:

> "I was in the habit," says Freud in *The Interpretation of Dreams*, "of quoting this anecdote to explain the factor of 'afterwardsness' [*Nachträglichkeit*] in the mechanism of the psychoneuroses"; "A young man who was a great admirer of feminine beauty was talking once—so the story went—of the good-looking wet-nurse who had suckled him when he was a baby: 'I'm sorry,' he remarked, 'that I didn't make a better use of my opportunity.'"[51]

There are two protagonists in Freud's story, and two temporalities. There is the child at the breast and the "admirer of feminine beauty." There are likewise two projections of time: progressive and determinate (the child at the breast as a blueprint of adult sexuality, here conceived as entirely evolutionary and genetic, i.e., the child is the father of the man, and so on) and retrogressive and indeterminate (*If only I had known what I know now [adult sexuality]*, the young man regrets, looking back at the missed opportunity). The first is Freudian, resting the advent of sexuality on the biological and somatic blueprint, so that hunger, which is object-specific, results in the pleasure of an empty mouth (sexuality proper); this is Freud at his most Ptolemaic.[52] The second is anti-Freudian, insofar as it denies the relevance of infantile sexuality. "This [retroactive interpretation] is, after all," Laplanche writes, "the position of the young man, who is not Freudian and wants nothing to do with infantile sexuality. He simply puts himself back there: 'If only I'd known!'"[53]

Laplanche tarries with both temporalities, the Freudian and the anti-Freudian. He does so by returning to what Freud, regardless of his Ptolemaic tendencies, centered in his theory of seduction: the enigmatic message of the other.[54] Herein lies the true Copernican basis or ex-centric center of psychoanalysis. It implies neither biological progression nor hermeneutic regression but a foundation of falls, lapses, and absences. It implies, that is, the negative life of the missing signifier from and in the beginning. "The enigma," Laplanche summarizes, "leads back, then, to the otherness of the other; and the otherness of the other is his response to his unconscious, that is to say, to his otherness to himself."[55] Neither a biological script to be unfolded nor a backward feeling, the unconscious, which Laplanche calls the "kernel of our being," is sexual in the sense that it ex-centers our being, or makes being and time *extimate* rather than intimate.[56] We are extimate because of the atemporal kernel coming from the other, one that is implanted from birth and to which we return and return as doomed translators, interpreting "[a] primal to-be-translated," the enigma of sexuality.[57]

Laplanche's conceptualization of *Nachträglichkeit* is on display in Juzo Itami's *Tampopo* (タンポポ, *Dandelion*, 1985), a Japanese film about a struggling restaurateur, Tampopo (Nobuko Miyamoto), who enlists the help of an experienced amateur, Gorō (Tsutomu Yamazaki), to make the perfect ramen.[58] When they succeed, Gorō, the film's pseudo-cowboy, leaves Tampopo and the newly restored noodle shop to continue his journey. Before the film concludes, however, we receive an enigmatic message: a prolonged shot of a woman, hitherto unseen, breastfeeding her baby on a park bench (figure 20). As the credits roll, we watch the mother nurse her child. We are left to interpret the scene's retroactive meaning: whether the child at the breast is, per Freud, the somatic blueprint of the adult sexuality into which *Tampopo* inquires with culinary fascination; or, contra Freud, we, the spectators, occupy the position of Laplanche's "admirer of feminine beauty," and are invited to "put [ourselves] back there," knowing what we know now about the pleasures of the mouth. Progressive or retrogressive? Evolutionary or hermeneutic? The former would make feeding at the breast the source of later culinary and artistic pleasure. The latter would make it merely a missed opportunity.

20

Yet the two options we inherit from Laplanche fail to account for the atemporality of the film's structure. What causes pleasure throughout many comedic entrées into the philosophical realm of the raw and the cooked, the drive and its aim, and the hermeneutic circle is the lack of definitive cause. The ultimate mark of satisfaction in the film is not the first or last sip of well-prepared ramen; it is the point at which the bowl has been emptied and returned to the cook (figure 21). In this vital exchange, both parties are offered not only food, not only stimulation of the mouth, but also "something" absent: the emptiness of the mouth and the bowl—two holes and two rims. The return to nothing repeats in the enigmatic final scene, where the viewer is asked to translate the aporia of the breast.

21

Tampopo counts as a comedy because it, per McGowan's theory of genre, combines excess and lack.[59] The excessive pleasures of eating and of socializing through food redound upon a primordial lack that has no fill—the lack that Laplanche calls the "enigmatic signifier." Comedy brings lack and excess together so that we may enjoy, paradoxically, an excessive lack and a lacking excess. This paradox animates *Tampopo*, nicknamed a "ramen western" after the spaghetti western popularized by Sergio Leone and Clint Eastwood. This paradox also animates *First Cow*, a western occasionally comedic wherein the enjoyment of lack, translated in scenes of theft, cooking, and eating, barely cuts through the temporalities, retrogressive and progressive, of colonial occupation, or "settler time," as Mark Rifkin terms it.[60] Reichardt swaps the child at the breast for the adult at the teat, and in so doing suggests that bovine eroticism is no less relevant to Laplanche's questions about the primal scene: "what object, what consumption, is at issue here? Is it the milk which is to be ingested? Is it the breast which is to be . . . sucked . . . ? Incorporated . . . ? Caressed . . . ? Stimulated . . . ?"[61] In *First Cow*, the answer is all of the above.

I CAN'T BELIEVE IT'S NOT MILK

In his *Project for a Scientific Psychology*, Freud observes that an infant nursing at its mother's breast will hallucinate the breast in her absence.[62] This seems a simple substitution, whereby one object, the milk, is swapped for another, the breast. But Freud rejects this interpretation outright. The milk that satisfies the infant's hunger, he instead offers, is of a different order than the breast, which cannot provide that satisfaction. The breast simply prolongs the desire for the "breast" as a metonym for milk.[63] The signifier "breast," which is already not the milk, makes the breast something other than a source of nourishment: an object of lack. It was never something the infant had to begin with. As Philippe van Haute explains, the objects that Lacan collects under the rubric of *objet a* (breast, feces, gaze, and voice) "are, as it were, 'cut out' of the body ('the effect of a cut') by a relation to the Other that is primarily linguistically structured."[64] The body of psychoanalysis is marked by cuts and gaps. Insofar as it is impossible to mend those, to obtain the object once and for all, life, van Haute argues, is fundamentally maladapted:

> There is an "incommensurability" between the human subject and its drives, such that it can never really live in peace with them, and in this sense, a harmonious relation with oneself and with one's environment is denied to humans in principle. Neurosis and psychic suffering in general thus cannot simply be understood as difficulties "adapting," since the relations of the subject to itself and to its environment are basically marked by the impossibility of adaptation.[65]

Beyond the phenomenality of our object-relations, desire meets a limit where the object of desire dis-incarnates itself. Already a step removed from the original source of satisfaction that is the milk, the "breast" becomes a vehicle for absence.

A similar dynamic of substitution is at play in *First Cow*. The result is both phantasmatic and laden with enjoyment. The film poses the problem of freeing enjoyment from the structure of fantasy—of, in other words, loosening our oral, libidinal, and gustatory fixations from their objects. The film riffs explicitly on the primal fantasy outlined by Freud: the displacement of the milk, the object of nourishment, by a series of fantasy objects. By maintaining the illusion that oily cakes and clafoutis can rise without the requisite milk, Lu and Cookie repeat the primordial separation between the raw and the cooked, which is to say, between the thing-in-itself (the food) and the object of desire. Moreover, they do so surreptitiously, indulging the Chief Factor's fantasy, one utterly disconnected from reality, and letting it, the sweet good, stand in for whatever: home, French cuisine, Europe, sophistication, divine providence, colonial magnanimity, the mother-child romance, and so on. Like Poe's police, the Chief Factor misses the purloined milk because, at a basic, phantasmatic level, the milk is already missing. What he sees and tastes is not what he desires; rather, he desires the empty chain of above signifiers, the *je ne sais quoi* of "God's love" for white, Christian colonizers, mixed and baked into a gustatory token of home comforts. The fantasy obscures Cookie and Lu's transgression, enabling them to take their *jouissance* where they can. This is not to say that they are external to the fantasy. They batter their dreams like everyone else lined up for a taste. And isn't the con artist the foremost American entrepreneur? Still, Cookie and Lu, no matter how much they enjoy the fantasy, never manage fully to buy into it. They know that, at bottom, they peddle not the delicious dough that would guarantee a prosperous future but negative life fried and sugar-dusted.

It is far more enjoyable, *First Cow* suggests, to believe that the milk is absent. The revelation of its presence in the sweet goods make the settler-colonial fantasy of white supremacy, manifest destiny, and firstness symbolized by the cow a sham. The revelation lets spill that the policing and extermination of Indigenous life for God and Man are an obscene, foundationless project, and the colonizer a want-to-be or puppet lacking substance. The Chief Factor at the teat of fantasy finds that it has dried up. What persists is a terrifying Real, the object-cause of his desire. He is left with ab-sense, the senselessness and belatedness that he and the settler-colonial enterprise project onto Indigenous and other racialized subjects. If the fantasy curdles, it's not simply because the Chief Factor gets wise to Cookie and Lu's deception. The Chief Factor eventually comes to terms with the presence of dairy in the concoctions. One night, Lu falls off the tree from which he was keeping a vigil as Cookie milked the cow. An Indigenous worker out to fetch a cat notices the disturbance and wakes the officers, who in turn warn of the likely presence of "attackers" in the meadow. When they locate a bucket of warm milk knocked over, the Chief Factor and the captain, still half-asleep, are wearing white nightgowns—a textbook "the emperor wears no clothes" moment. The deception is but a minor setback, an affront, empirically inadmissible, and therefore fit for the police. Souring the milk is the realization, haphazardly brought about, that figures of authority had been fed by two subordinates, Lu and Cookie.

The statements, *I can't believe it is not milk* and *I can't believe it was milk all along,* carry little descriptive value. Whether the milk is there or not, ab-sense is always at play. Veering from sense gives the fantasy direction while the drive's impossible object, negative life, inheres.

THE GAP OF RACECRAFT

Karen E. Fields and Barbara J. Fields designate the causal chain that supports racist ideology as "racecraft."[66] The concept merges racism and witchcraft to highlight the collusion of racist thinking with folktales and myths, particularly those about an original whiteness. This causal chain conceals a gap, although not an empirical one, for "racecraft originates not in nature but in human action and imagination; it can exist in no other way."[67] The gap of racecraft is not real, in that it does not pertain to some fixable oversight, but Real in the strong, Lacanian sense of a constitutive flaw in the symbolic logic. Consider Fields and Fields's case study of the reformer Martin Luther, who "in adulthood, . . . asserted that a person could steal milk by thinking of a cow":[68]

> Luther's story about the milk-less cow exposes another facet of [racecraft's] suspended causality. As before, he [Luther] begins with a mundane predicament, but rather than ignore the question "How?" he answers explicitly. Reminding his flock that witches "do many accursed things while they remain undiscovered," he gives them a (to us) show-stopping causal sequence: "Thinking about some cow, they can say one good word or another and get milk from a towel, a table, or a handle." Everyone present knows the ordinary sequence (creeping into someone else's barn, scurrying away with a sloshing pail), but the preacher has made it plain that the thievery is not of that order; it is invisible thievery ("they remain undiscovered"). Then and there, cause and effect disappear into the smoky notion of "witches". . . . Like pure races a while ago, Luther's witches enter the world, and come to matter therein, not by observation and experience but by circular reasoning. Neither "witch" nor "pure race" has a material existence. Both are products of thought, and of language. Having no material existence, they cannot have material causation. Strictly speaking, Luther's explanation omitted nothing essential.[69]

Reichardt's cow facilitates racecraft's phantasmatic practice of supplying a missing cause, like God in the Bible or witches in Luther's speculative causation, to explain and justify a desired effect, such as cakes, land grabs, or genocides. Of all the animals we encounter at the fort—a furry cat, a squealing pig, some chickens—the cow most explicitly links European practices of animal agriculture to the Indigenous lands of the Pacific Northwest, smoothing out differences and patching holes in settler-colonial reason. The objective of this causal chain? Theft, killing, the founding of a white, Protestant ethno-class fed on monoculture, and consensus over the notion that firsts are possible, locatable, and "still there." The cow connects the first among all firsts, God's providence, to the bio-racial identity and the temporal project of white supremacy. The film milks the cow for, more than sweet goods, evidence that the retroaction of racecraft scavenges origins for the causes of an obviously unfounded occupation. Henceforth, one can look back on the settlements of the Pacific Northwest through white-colored glasses and see a continuous sequence.

First Cow indulges the retroactive look that, per Fields and Fields, is hallucinatory and akin to witchcraft, but it does so, importantly, from the perspective of a world milking its extinction. The search for causal explanation is triggered by the opening counter-pastoral, mixing the great outdoors with the memento mori of extinct life, skulls, and bones—not to mention the oil tanker off in the distance and the intertextual allusions to the missing signifier of *Vagabond*. Reichardt blends the basic elements of the heist genre with a transcendental meditation on time and narration, coaxing the viewer into a quest for the white supremacist myths founded on theft, or the amnesia around theft, and, behind it all, the gap of racecraft.

The trick of racial capitalism is to ascribe the subject's foundational unknowing, the negative life that Freud finds at the bottom of subjectivity, to racialized others who come to bear a limit, a lack that cannot be stomached and must be disavowed. Lu, Cookie, and the Indigenous characters who inhabit the film's background—whose backgrounding grounds the world of the film—bear negative life so that the fantasy of racecraft can function. Racecraft, that is, functions only when negative life lands elsewhere, at a safe and imaginary distance from racist and colonial ideology. The Chief Factor and the captain are suspicious of Lu, Cookie, and company. The figures of economic and military authority do not know exactly what the other wants, but they cannot imagine that the object of that want would be anything other than what they, themselves, have.

In *Read My Desire: Lacan against the Historicists*, Copjec articulates racial capitalism's enduring fantasy—that the other is deceiving us, that the other knows something we do not know—as a flight from unknowability, the same unknowability that founds subjective life:

> *In* language and yet *more than* language, the subject is a cause for which no signifier can account. Not because she transcends the signifier but because she inhabits it *as limit*. This subject, radically unknowable, radically incalculable, is the only guarantee we have against racism. This is a guarantee that slips from us whenever we disregard the nontransparency of subject to signifier, whenever we make the subject coincide with the signifier rather than its misfire.[70]

First Cow dwells on the perceived coincidence of subject and signifier. The settlers coincide with whiteness, Lu and Cookie more provisionally with aspirational whiteness; the clafoutis is their symbol of intelligibility.

By this scheme, the Indigenous figures occupy the margins of white teleology. Racism, according to Copjec, does not derive from the missing signifier—as though a newer, better signifier could eliminate ideology. Racism ensues instead from the lack of a missing signifier, or from the subject's successful attenuation of its "misfire."

Cookie and Lu's efforts to align with whiteness succeed, up to a point, and for a while. Dressing in the signifiers of colonial success—a new abode, new business endeavors, new dishes, a new bottle of whiskey, new "fancy" boots that Cookie quickly muddies and covers to avoid heckles from strangers—they embody the accumulative spirit. At the same time, they divulge the capitalist gimmick: the capitalist signifier can never coincide with itself because the means of their success, and by extension the means of all capitalist success, are, in their reliance on theft and enslavement, a lie. "Stolen life," Fred Moten's term for the ongoingness of Black and Indigenous dispossession, prevents a life of theft from coinciding with itself.[71] The subject who enacts what Hortense Spillers, in the context of the Middle Passage, calls the "theft of the body," too, is self-divided.[72] This is in part what James Baldwin referred to when, on the occasion of the centennial of the Emancipation Proclamation, he attributed unfreedom to white Americans. "We cannot be free," he unforgettably wrote, "until they are free."[73] For Baldwin, freedom does not equal mending psychic divisions; the disavowal of those divisions, the gap of racecraft, must instead be remedied for emancipation to proceed.

INDIGENOUS APEDAGOGY

Reichardt, like Varda before her, accomplishes the feat, in a film so decidedly oriented toward negativity, of thwarting the glorification of the rebel or outlaw. Lu and Cookie cannot hold the title of heroes for the ecocritic. *First Cow*, indeed, doesn't enable the ecocritic to claim the small victory of holding on to living, and then reanimated, proof that harmonious cohabitation is possible between humans and animals—between, that is, Cookie and a cow more generous toward him than toward the Chief Factor—even en route to further colonial and industrial expansion. The companion-species pastoral is impossible, insofar as the heist offers no interruption from such expansion. Quite the contrary: the theft of the milk may be a victimless crime, but the theft of the land on which the cow resides is not.

We have asserted that *First Cow* frustrates the colonial projection of contradictory fantasies onto Indigenous subjects: first the fantasy that their desires are unknowable, then the fantasy that their desires must be isometric with what the settlers have. This does not mean that the film's Indigenous characters are knowable, let alone that they give Lu and Cookie access to a different way of identifying and belonging. The brevity and circumstantiality of the protagonists' encounters with Indigenous characters testify to this fact. On the run from the Chief Factor's and the captain's men, Lu and Cookie reach a river. Lu jumps, while Cookie hides before falling down a hill. Cookie wakes up in a shack, where an elderly Native couple is tending to his injuries. It would be a stretch to call the couple's gesture one of solidarity. The word "hospitality" might be more appropriate, for there is no political value inherent to the gathering. In any case, Cookie's presence does not coalesce into collective belonging. Like the drifter in *Vagabond*, he soon leaves, providing, as justification, his need to locate his one friend.

Reichardt protects the opacity of the Indigenous life she depicts; neither she nor her protagonists can claim access to its content. Against racecraft and its simultaneous inflation and reduction of Indigeneity into an unsolvable enigma whose solution is actually European civilization, *First Cow* de-dramatizes Indigenous unknowability. If the content of Indigenous life proves inaccessible, it is not because that content is magical or supernatural—though the film does not work especially hard to pull Indigeneity into realism either. Such content proves inaccessible because Reichardt and co-screenwriter Jonathan Raymond do not ask of it that it be otherwise.

Consider the following pair of scenes. In the first, the cow is standing on a pontoon with two characters: an Indigenous individual and a white settler (figure 22). The settler paddles softly to prevent the boat from capsizing. The composition shared by this shot and the opening one likens the pontoon to the oil tanker; historical retroaction reveals that the distinction between the two vehicles is quantitative (they differ in size) rather than qualitative (both transport "natural resources" for the purpose of colonial and capitalist expansion). On the shore, a small group of Native people witness the operation in silence. Their backs are turned against the camera when the cow steps onto the land (figure 23). The Native people witness an origin story unfold in real time. They, however, do not serve as proxies for the spectators; we are not privy to their thoughts or even, at the instant of the landing, to their facial expressions. The witnessing may be communal, but the camera takes no part in the commons.

22

23

The second scene is set at the Chief Factor's house, where he and the captain discuss the punishment—twenty lashes—that the latter inflicted on a man, presumably an enslaved Black man, for mutiny. The Chief Factor finds the sentence "conservative," to which the captain responds that a stricter one would have rendered the man "useless for the remainder of the voyage." The Chief Factor explains:

> CHIEF FACTOR. Here is the rub, you see. When one factors the loss of labor from the punished hand versus the gain of labor from those hands who witness the punishment, a stricter punishment can be the more advisable path. Even a properly rendered death can be useful in the ultimate accounting. It is a highly motivated spectacle for the indolent, let alone the mutinous.
>
> CAPTAIN. Yes, fair enough, but some calculations can never truly be made.
>
> CHIEF FACTOR. Now, there you are wrong, Captain. Any question that cannot be calculated is not worth the asking.

The dialogue is interrupted momentarily by Lu and Cookie's entry, clafoutis in hand. Christopher Blauvelt's camera, more interested in the companions than in the Chief Factor and the captain, had anticipated Lu and Cookie's arrival by panning horizontally across greasy windows. The interruption does not alter the content of the conversation substantively. The two settlers now debate a different mode of colonial propertization: the fur trade. Specifically, as we've previously mentioned, they debate whether Oregon's beaver supply is unlimited, and whether the demand for beaver fur will decrease as new trends seduce consumers. We then notice that another man and his wife, both Indigenous, are present in the room, hitherto excluded from the conversation. Totillicum (Gary Farmer) stands up, inquisitive, while his wife (Sabrina Mary Morrison) remains seated. The Chief Factor repeats, slowly, that he believes the beaver will last forever—an assertion that the Chief Factor's wife (Lily Gladstone), also Indigenous, translates into Chinook. Totillicum chuckles before offering a lengthy reply in Chinook. Anguished by the address's nontransparency, the Chief Factor, his stature squeezed by the 4:3 aspect ratio, gazes at Totillicum (figure 24). The translator chuckles in turn before relaying, simply, "He says he doesn't understand why the white men hunt so much beaver and never eat the tail. The tail is delicious." Once more, colonial ignorance plays out in the gustatory realm. The film derives comic value from the mismatch between the protracted nature of Totillicum's insight in Chinook, with its varied cadence and intonation, and the brevity and flatness of the English translation. Lu, we will later realize, speaks some Chinook;

yet in that moment, he and Cookie stand silently. They aren't in on the joke.

24

In the above scenes, the silence of witnessing and the interference of translation render Indigenous subjectivity nontransparent. This nontransparency departs from the trope of the "stoic" Native denounced, notably, by the American Indian Movement of the 1960s and the Idle No More protest movement of the 2010s.[74] Cari M. Carpenter explains that the sentimental tradition has imposed stoicism—understood as fortitude, as opposed to anger, in the event of dispossession—as the gateway through which Native people could, in the eyes of settlers, trade savagery for nobility.[75] Sentimentality engraves white scripts of emotional expression, but, Carpenter insists, "stoicism cannot simply be dismissed as a stereotype applied to Native Americans; it is also a representation against which many indigenous people have understood and constructed their own resistance."[76] Xine Yao would echo Carpenter a decade later by claiming that "antisocial" practices of "unfeeling"—"not simply . . . negative feelings or the absence of feelings . . . but . . . that which cannot be recognized as feeling"—in fact "provincializ[e] sympathy" by operating as "the constitutive outside to [the] totalizing system" that is sentimentality.[77]

We wouldn't go so far as to hold that subjective nontransparency represents for *First Cow*'s Indigenous characters a tactic or strategy of resistance. In the case at hand, such a statement would require evidence that nontransparency feels like resistance to those characters—something we could assert only by disavowing the very fact of subjective nontransparency. Reichardt's critique of settler-colonialism lies not in an Indigenous characterology but in the obtrusion of interpretive habits dear to that staunchly sentimental tradition: ecocriticism. At its most pastoral, ecocriticism expects its objects to expose readers and spectators to evidence of peril or catastrophe in order to cultivate in them what Seymour identifies as "'proper' environmentalist feelings," and thereby motivate them to adopt new behaviors reflecting an attitudinal adjustment—this is sentimentalism 101.[78]

In its refusal to start at, transit through, or end at −1, ecocriticism tries to fill gaps in knowledge with positive content. By this scheme, the settler-colonial rhetoric, once proven foundationless, must be replaced by Indigenous wisdom. For instance, the chapter on climate violence that concludes Elisabeth R. Anker's *Ugly Freedoms* supplies, as an alternative to the "rational thought and human exceptionalism . . . that grounds freedom in the sovereign will of a logical and reasonable subject who overpowers the limits of nature to dictate her own destiny," a concept of entanglement or enmeshment—specifically, the network of interconnection and interdependence that is the microbiome—substantiated by Indigenous political thought.[79] Even a rigorous effort to "de-idealize" freedom is not impervious, in the end, to a certain idealization of Indigeneity as, per the psychoanalytic idiom laid out early in the introduction to *Negative Life*, a palliative to civilizational discontent.[80]

Reichardt short-circuits the interpretive practices that would expect of Indigenous life that it be fundamentally expressive, pedagogical, and edifying. *First Cow* pushes the ecocritic to a valuable limit, showing that it is no solution to swap the settler subject's violent projection of lack onto the Indigenous subject for an improved fantasy of entangled, multispecies, more-than-human plenitude. It is no solution because the substitution disavows the gap in the signifying chain, positioning an attunement to (a certain vision of) Indigeneity as the sophisticated, enlightened iteration of settler-colonial rationality. In the face of Indigenous nontransparency, the lack at the core of this rationality can don no disguise.

RESTING PLACE

A subtle shift in style is discernible in the film's final moments, which the protagonists spend on the run. Cookie's head injury, especially, draws our attention to a wobblier camera, a composition often obstructed by trees and cottages, and a frame hazy around the edges. We register the pair's exhaustion and accept their fate as they do: the woods are surrounded by simply too many men. The enjoyment of the missing signifier, we've noted, necessarily culminates in self-implosion. True to *First Cow*'s allergy to heroism, this self-implosion is decidedly undramatic. "You lie there, on the needles," Lu instructs Cookie; "I'll keep first watch." Lu looks at Cookie before letting go: he places the bag containing their meager savings behind him and allows his heavy eyelids to fall. "We'll go soon. I've got you," he reassures his friend as they both settle in what will become their shallow grave (figure 25). Play-acting until the last minute, Lu uses the need to rest somewhere temporarily ("We'll go soon") as an alibi for choosing a permanent resting place ("We'll go soon").

25

At the start of *First Cow*, Shawkat's character finds Lu and Cookie in the very position in which they fall asleep at the end. Their bones, that is, have not been dispersed by vultures or other animals, such as her own dog. The skeletons' improbable immutability most firmly positions Shawkat's character as the beneficiary of an ecocritical wish-fulfillment fantasy, as if the preindustrial past were "still there," nearly intact, to dispense insights about environmental existence against a late-industrial landscape split by the oil tanker. We know now that it is not there, and it will not be. The simultaneous cut to black and interruption of ambient noise seconds after Lu lies down excuse us from the compulsion to refind that lost object and seek again to make the past signify. This will not be the last time, in our survey of the cinema of extinction, that we meet the closing credits with relief. The next chapters turn to this problem, that of putting an end to ab-sense. For now, we extend our account of nature's apedagogy in the first of two interludes on the horror of losing oneself to ecological relations.

[INTERLUDE]

The Horror of Entanglement I

In the Earth, Annihilation

TWO EXCURSES

The opening chapter of *Negative Life* assembled a troupe of drifters: the nameless wanderer in *Vagabond*, the pseudo-cowboy Gorō in *Tampopo*, the volcanologists Katia and Maurice Krafft, and of course *First Cow*'s lawless bakers, King-Lu and Cookie. In the first of two interludes on eco-horror, we continue the enumeration which is not one—an enumeration that, we have insisted, vacillates between –1 and 0—as we follow one duo and one quintet in their quest for nothing (more or less). The pair of films we spotlight here, Ben Wheatley's *In the Earth* (2021) and Alex Garland's *Annihilation* (2018), represent excurses toward negativity.

In the COVID-era *In the Earth*, Martin Lowery (Joel Fry) arrives at an outpost during an unspecified pandemic. The outpost leads to an unusually fertile British forest where Olivia Wendle (Hayley Squires), Martin's former romantic partner, is conducting research on using mycorrhizae to increase crop efficiency. The film dares us, once we learn of the characters' shared past, to decode the journey into the woods[1] as an effort on Martin's part to rekindle the romance, or at least to address some unfinished business. Olivia, whose sentimentalism ranks organic form higher than the couple form, believes instead that Martin was pulled by the mycorrhizal mat, which "draws resources to the forest," and does so smartly rather than benevolently, controlling the life forms it subtends "like a brain."[2] It is, by this logic, the call of the wild that Martin answers when he ventures toward the laboratory encampment with Alma (Ellora Torchia), the park ranger assigned to guide him. As they edge closer, they become increasingly exposed to their vibrant milieu, and are unable to sober up amid the prolonged mushroom trip. The wounds they accumulate tear the skin which, as Didier Anzieu has influentially argued, secures psychic integrity.[3] Without the skin-ego as their buffer, the mycorrhizal brain threatens to take them over. Their hike eventually takes them to the totality of a more-than-human entanglement or enmeshment, which is to say nowhere, for this totality may be embraced only through self-annihilation. Another item in *Negative Life*'s archive of apedagogy, *In the Earth* dispenses a non-lesson about what happens when the plurality that pulls you in becomes a totality that melts you down. What happens is: you die, or you try to escape. You'll probably die then, too.

In the Earth clones *Annihilation*'s narrative. Garland's film, too, kicks into gear at an outpost. Lena (Natalie Portman), a biology professor and army veteran, is taken to it after her husband Kane (Oscar Isaac) returns from a special forces mission bewildered and suffers multiple organ failures and internal hemorrhages. This outpost leads to a zone of mutant plant and animal life. This zone is called "the Shimmer," and it has been expanding since the fall of a meteor three years ago. The zone accommodates a journey toward negativity that masquerades as an attempt to heal the heterosexual couple. Lena resolves to reach the lighthouse at the Shimmer's core in order to discover what happened to her husband, and she does. This knowledge, however, does not restore her marriage's coherence. During his own stay in the lighthouse, Kane killed himself by detonating a grenade. The suicide was caught on tape by an alien figure who had taken his appearance—presumably the alien figure who would later exit the Shimmer to live, if tentatively and precariously, as Kane. Lena believes, hopes, that she was not replaced by the clone of herself she confronted in the lighthouse, but in the final scene—the film's second marital reunion—she looks skeptical. The Shimmer gifts self-annihilation, or it gifts self-estrangement. A husband who isn't himself and a wife who now doubts that it is possible to be oneself at all cause heterosexuality's meaning-making machine (reciprocity, love, history, longevity, futurity) to overheat.

Lena, like Martin, embarks on her mission accompanied by others. The psychologist Dr. Ventress (Jennifer Jason Leigh), the physicist Josie Radek (Tessa Thompson), the geomorphologist Cass Sheppard (Tuva Novotny), and the paramedic Anya Thorensen (Gina Rodriguez) are enlisted in the all-female expedition tasked with uncovering not only what the Shimmer really is but also why it has engulfed all but one of the team's male predecessors.[4] (It has engulfed Kane, as well; we just don't know that yet.) They come to the same conclusion that some of their predecessors likely reached on their way to accelerated decomposition and hybridization: that in the Shimmer, everything is becoming everything else. Plurality's drag toward a totality that prohibits individuation: this is what this interlude and the next refer to as the "horror of entanglement."

ECOHORROR, OR FORM

Let us ask the question crudely: How can ecohorror, in a book on the cinema of extinction, be significant enough to inspire two interludes, and not especially brief ones, but not to warrant a stand-alone chapter?

Ecohorror, Christy Tidwell asserts, is misunderstood. Its customary definition, "in terms of 'revenge of nature' narratives in which nature enacts violence on humans in response to the damage caused by human behaviors," is "fundamentally predicated upon a relationship between humanity and nature that does not allow for their interconnectedness."[5] But the human and the nonhuman, corrects Tidwell, "are never truly separate."[6] Ecohorror contests this division and others, including the one between internal and external that organizes theories of embodiment and experience. Tidwell contends that a novel like Mira Grant's *Parasite* (2013)—which "challenges anthropocentrism and human exceptionalism, . . . [develops] a more complex relationship between human and nonhuman, [and] . . . undermines the us versus them logic"—is worthier of the ecohorror label than, say, the plague or disaster narratives, on the page and the screen, which uphold "simplistic separations between human and nonhuman."[7]

We agree that ecohorror dissolves bodily boundaries—the maiming and amputation of *In the Earth* and the decomposition and hybridization of *Annihilation*, for instance, violate the skin-ego—but we would counter that it ultimately estranges human life from an ethics of interconnection and interdependence. In ecohorror, the ecocritical gesture of situating human life in the immanence of relations fails to signal a marriage plot's happy conclusion. Characters cannot keep relations at bay, but neither can they survive ecological incorporation; the web of life thrives on human death. When human beings can no longer externalize nature, nature externalizes them. It either rejects them, as in an organ transplant gone wrong, or accepts them on the fatal condition that they turn into fertilizer. *First Cow*'s corpse-to-mushroom cycle on a compressed timeline.

Tidwell concedes that ecohorror regularly charts relations amid which "we (humans) don't flourish," "connections between human and nonhuman [that] kill rather than simply change us," but ultimately declines to read into those evidence of a design flaw in ecocriticism.[8] Tidwell muses that "reading *Parasite* as new materialist or posthumanist ecohorror means acknowledging the possibilities of connection between human and nonhuman and the power of ecohorror to reveal those connections to us, but it also means acknowledging the fear of such things"; she adds that "*Parasite* asks us to consider—if not necessarily accept—such posthuman, post-anthropocentric, and even post-conscious ways of being."[9] The assumption that dualisms are simple and entanglements complex makes relations and connections permanently available for pedagogical recuperation. Tidwell recovers ecohorror as a good object for ecocriticism, capable of inspiring at least the acknowledgment, and at best the acceptance, of life's complexity. By this measure, the fear that ecohorror instills in readers or viewers should not shake their confidence in the desirability of entanglement. The fear, Tidwell implies, is instructive: it tells us that striving for "posthuman, post-anthropocentric, and even post-conscious ways of being"—or, at any rate, what we, human beings, regard as antithetical or posterior to humanity—is difficult. Difficult but, as ecocritics would have it, necessary.

This reasoning shuttles rather quickly between consciousness and post-consciousness: ecohorror lures us toward a post-consciousness that feels bad so that we may consciously acknowledge or accept the fact of post-consciousness and embrace the versions that, in confirming our self-image as environmentally conscious beings, make us feel better. But horror of the Anthropocene, Sarah Dillon argues, "quite literally . . . gets us nowhere"; it makes "vastation" (desolation, laying waste) the consequence of having found out that "'the world means its malice.'"[10]

The fear we've discussed is key to Tidwell and Carter Soles's account of ecohorror as a genre with ties to the ecogothic, the monster film, science fiction, mythology and folklore (especially significant to *In the Earth*'s iconography), and weird fiction (the designation that has most reliably stuck to Jeff VanderMeer's *Southern Reach* trilogy, from which the novel adapted by Garland is issued).[11] Tidwell and Soles note that ecohorror, as a product of the "self-conscious" Anthropocene, concerns itself primarily with "human fear *of* nonhuman nature" and "fear *for* nonhuman nature."[12] Ecohorror is thus at home within Linda Williams's taxonomy of "body genres," which differentiates between melodrama, pornography, and, of particular relevance here, horror on the basis of the excessive responses they depict and invite.[13] In the case of horror, an excess of violence triggers an excess of fear.[14] Tidwell and Soles's approach categorizes ecohorror as a subgenre of horror in which the object of fear—the object to which we fear to lose ourselves, and which we fear to lose—is nature.

We propose that ecohorror, like the cinema of extinction more broadly, is best understood as a form. "Not genre, never again genre," is one motto of Eugenie Brinkema's radical formalism, which defines horror as "*a formal act of decision*," or that which "regards the body as *nothing but formal material*."[15] Brinkema compresses theories of horror *qua* genre into one word: "neck."[16] The critic-spectator, imagining that the horror film is stepping on their neck, is bound to riff on their experience: "I sense, I perceive, *I feel*."[17] It is clear that we do not live up to Brinkema's exhilarating dogmatism: we have previously contributed to a genre theory rooted in the film experience;[18] and we refer, throughout this book, to the ways we have been shaped or affected by our corpus. Yet we follow Brinkema in refusing to make the spectator's position redemptive. We do not presume spectatorship to be the nexus for the conversion of an enlightening fear *of* nature into an enlightened fear *for* nature.

Jamieson Webster, ventriloquizing Lacan, muses that "the desire of the analyst is for the continuation of psychoanalysis to whatever end, not for any particular end."[19] She then asks, "What kind of desire is this? Is it monstrously inhuman, ethical, or somehow both? How far must one go to find the edge that dissolves everything?"[20] The ecohorror drive sustains life to "whatever end"; it elicits a seduction by "the edge that dissolves everything." Everything includes pedagogy.

The apparent correlation between the language of dissolution employed by Webster and the ecocritical theories of immersion or saturation should not mislead us.[21] What dissolves at the edge is the abundance of human-nature relations turned monolith. It is the impulse to resolve an encounter with horrific alterity into a teachable moment. Webster's dissolution reintroduces difference and rigidity into the world. Neither unthinkable nor unspeakable, the edge, Webster reminds us, authorizes analysis. The Shimmer and the mycorrhiza cannot be deemed analogous to the geometries occupied by Brinkema's radical formalism, such as the grid, the abecedaria, the increment, and the threshold, because geometry demands a limit, a constitutive outside.[22] Pure entanglement, on the other hand, tolerates none. Pure entanglement indeed denotes what Frédéric Neyrat calls an "exophobic situation" of "saturated immanence," wherein the denial of "atopia," the "other of place," grounds every utopian search for a home.[23]

The dualism of human and natural life, one that we associate with the cinema of extinction, is most remarkable in ecohorror, where it manifests as an overt antagonism. This is why we will feel compelled to return to this form. Yet it is also in ecohorror that expressions of this human-nature separation are most repetitive. This is why, to answer fully the question with which we opened this section, ecohorror never graduates from the interlude to the chapter. Spend enough time with ecohorror cinema and its plots lose their edge.

Negative Life's interludes may be said to pantomime the chapters, exaggerating the relational dynamics we observe in our primary anti-pastoral, existential, and transcendental case studies. We turn and return to the narrative uniformity and symbolic maximalism of ecohorror to reinforce the theoretical work that we accomplish elsewhere. Neither beholden to this volume's argumentative progression nor properly digressive, this and the other interlude take the cinema of extinction's most grotesque (outsized, monstrous, freakish) manifestations as an opportunity to return to certain concepts and anticipate others.

TOTALLY ECOLOGICAL

The name *Annihilation* gives totalization—plurality's drag toward "everything"—is refraction. In one of many didactic scenes, Radek explains the Shimmer's behavior. By then, the crew has encountered two supersize, hybrid animals: an alligator-like creature with teeth growing in concentric circles, and a bear-like creature whose scream captures that of its agonizing victims, one of whom is Sheppard. The scene in question begins as the women happen upon hybrids of a different kind: humanoid figures made of twisted branches, leaves, and flowers (figure 26). The figures stand amid tall grasses, like spooky topiaries. Upon examining them, Radek conjectures that "the shimmer is a prism, but it refracts everything. Not just light and radio waves. Animal DNA, plant DNA. All DNA." "What do you mean, all DNA?" Thorensen asks, though she knows. Ventress casually replies, "She's talking about our DNA. She's talking about us." Everything, as we wrote before, is becoming everything else. Let us extend this reasoning: reality in the Shimmer exists in an asymptotic relation to totality. The plant-animal and plant-human hybrids represent phases in a process of transformation—but on the horizon, there is sameness.

26

Consider, as a counter-example, Gilbert Simondon's philosophy of transindividuation. Simondon claims that "the psychical problematic," which is to say the problematic of developing a more or less coherent sense of self or psychic and sensorial life from a world of relations, "cannot be resolved in an intraindividual way."[24] He clarifies: "Emergence into psychical reality is an emergence into a transitory path, since the resolution of the intra-individual psychical problematic (that of perception and that of affectivity) leads to the level of the transindividual; the complete structures and functions resulting from the individuation of the pre-individual reality associated with the living individual are only accomplished and stabilized in the collective."[25] By positing, in brief, that "psychic reality is not self-enclosed," Simondon submits a philosophy of contradiction that is not so different from psychoanalytic theories of the unconscious: there is such a thing as psychic reality (I), yet it emerges relationally (not-I).[26] The Shimmer, by contrast, creeps toward non-contradiction: a total reality that allows for no individuation, psychic or otherwise. It is no wonder that those who dare enter the Shimmer eventually lose their minds. Once all categorical distinctions have been eliminated, we are left with undifferentiated matter that can be only itself—monism on the scales of ontology as well as being.

All of the expedition's members are seduced, in one way or another, by the promise of losing themselves to the Shimmer. Backstories of illness, grief, and guilt are laid out before us. Yet not everyone welcomes the cognitive dissonance of slow fusion, let alone the pain of violent death. Radek accepts post-consciousness, per Tidwell's terminology, but not in any shape or form. She wishes to blend with the milieu on her own terms. Some time after she formulates the refractive hypothesis, and after a spiraling Thorensen meets a fate like Sheppard's and falls prey to the bear-like creature, Radek confesses that she "wouldn't like . . . at all" for her fright or pain to be the "part" of her that survived. As Radek speaks gently, plant stems pierce the scars that self-inflicted cuts have left on her arms. "Ventress wants to face it. You want to fight it," she tells Lena; "But I don't think I want either of those things." These will be her parting words. She skirts around trees and bushes to proceed toward a clearing. Lena, running slightly behind, loses her colleague. Before Lena are the very arboreal figures from which Radek intuited the Shimmer's behavior.

Of *Annihilation*'s characters, Radek stands closest to the figure of the ecocritic who consciously chooses post-consciousness. It is tempting to endorse Radek's smooth, gore-less exit as the right, or good, response to entanglement. By this logic, the Shimmer would occupy a position akin to that of Tidwell's parasite-teacher, capable of demonstrating the entanglements we are right to fear as well as those we ought instead to embrace. But what morality is there in Radek's disposition? *Annihilation* certainly does not exceptionalize it. Her "choice" does not resolve the enigma of life and death in the Shimmer so much as it shakes the foundations of the refractive hypothesis by raising new problematics. Does volition accelerate refraction? If so, is it because the Shimmer thrives on human consciousness, or because human consciousness, once marshaled, could bend the Shimmer's operation? Did Radek really turn into an arboreal figure as she had pictured, or did she become something else? Perhaps something less romantic or melancholic, like dirt? Or something less tangible, like the rainbow glow that saturates the prism? If Radek did lend her body to a human-plant hybrid, what tells us that the preserved "part" of her humanity was serenity rather than suffering? What if this specific hybrid merely muted the agony of transformation of which the bear-like creature at least permitted the expression? We could go on. Our point is that we struggle to identify what, beyond the compelling narrative she submits, distinguishes Radek's hybridization from some of the more recognizably horrific versions cataloged in the film—for instance, the intestines of a crewmate of Kane that wiggle like a snake, or the Rauschenberg-esque assemblage to which the same crewmate's corpse is later appended (figure 27).

27

Whereas with *Annihilation* plurality looks like art (the topiary, the glow, the assemblage) en route to totality, with *In the Earth* "everything" designates an aesthetic category near the sublime. Alma and Martin take a while to approach this sublime. Early in their excursus, they fall victim to an attack. Their tents are raided and their belongings stolen. A shoeless Martin soon incurs a severe foot injury, extending a list of ailments that includes a rash he noticed earlier. Strangers might be responsible for the assault. Maybe it was instead the woodland spirit, goddess, or creature that a local legend calls Parnag Fegg and to which characters refer with pronominal inconsistency. Their assailant may also have been Zach (Reece Shearsmith), the older white man living in a large tent where they seek refuge and are held prisoner.

Zach amputates Martin's leg and shoots an arrow into Alma's back. We understand that he has killed other hikers and deduce that he did so for the purpose of idolatry. At one point, he drugs Martin and Alma to take ritualistic photos in their company. At another, he stitches an amulet and an animal's gut into Martin's arm. These and other, less extreme, actions, such as drawing, represent offerings to the spirit, depicted as an art aficionado in a centuries-old book that Zach adopts as his bible. Zach's compulsive maiming of characters of color—both British actors are mixed-race: Fry has been identified as Black, and Torchia as half-Swiss-Italian, half South African–Indian—asserts his sovereignty. Zach is not the only character to enclose public land: the first utterance we hear from Olivia is a curt warning, relayed by speakerphones, about trespassing onto "private property." *In the Earth* transposes the Oregon-style libertarianism of which *First Cow* traced an economic and military prehistory into a Britain demographically transformed in the twentieth century by migration from colonial and postcolonial nations to the former imperial center.[27]

So far in *In the Earth*, symptoms of the horror of entanglement have been localized (the rash, the wound). They become total when Olivia's laboratory, to which Alma and Martin have managed to flee, is surrounded by a thick mist containing fungal spores. The fog entrapping the trio both recalls and counters the disinfectant mist with which Martin was sprayed upon arriving at the outpost (figures 28 and 29). Going against the mycorrhizal mat's wishes, Alma puts on a hazmat suit as well as a gas mask and tries to traverse the cloud. However, the particles are fine enough to make the filter obsolete. Alma hallucinates, trembles, trips, and crawls. Martin and Olivia pull her back using a rope that they tied to her body. When her convulsions relent at last, she manages to utter, petrified, "It was everything."

28

29

The Kantian sublime is at once alluring and, in threatening to overtake the individual making the aesthetic judgment, terrifying.[28] Monique Allewaert's notion of the "swamp sublime" specifically highlights the blend of curiosity, incredulity, and dread that the hybrid locale, where land becomes sea, inspires in William Bartram's 1791 *Travels*.[29] According to Allewaert, the swamp regions of what are currently Georgia's Sea Islands enabled Black fugitivity, their opacity somewhat protecting the runaways and Maroons from colonial surveillance. In transgressing distinctions between solid, liquid, and gaseous, the Shimmer and the mist represent intuitive analogues of the swamp. Yet Garland's and Wheatley's ideologically haphazard films do not offer anything resembling a coherent aesthetics or politics of Black hybridization as fugitivity. As Rebecca Duncan and Anna Krauthamer have both convincingly argued, ecohorror has generally failed to reflect the asymmetric responsibility for, and experience of, climate and correlate crises, and has instead crafted a myth of the "universally culpable" that, as Duncan puts it, "risks obscuring . . . actually existing socio-ecological inequalities, and so perpetuating these as a result."[30] Radek, *Annihilation*'s only major Black character, partakes in the colonial enterprise that is the expedition. And, as we've argued, asserting a privileged kinship between her and the Shimmer would entail a great deal of projection. *In the Earth*'s fungal mist, for its part, holds the characters of color captive, bound to share a bubble with a white character (Olivia) who, it turns out, is in cahoots with Zach, another one of her exes. The characters cannot transcend the Shimmer or the mist—not as themselves, at any rate—because there is no outside to total entanglement.

ART AND NATURE

Annihilation and *In the Earth* multiply encounters with art or objects reminiscent of it: topiaries, assemblages, drawings, photographs, glow. One art form, performance, fulfills a function consistent across both films, providing something of a palliative to characters experiencing the horror of entanglement. Garland's version of performance exists in the vicinity of modern dance, and Wheatley's of the installation and the happening.

Upon reaching the lighthouse from which the Shimmer emanates, *Annihilation*'s Lena finds evidence of Kane's immolation and replacement by a clone. A tape of the event is conveniently available, along with a video camera that somehow has not been damaged by a refractive process supposed to implicate the nonliving. (For a film so committed to enigma and absence—the zone across which the Shimmer grows is labeled "Area X"—*Annihilation* leaves surprisingly little unsaid and unshown.) After viewing the recording, a panting Lena hears a hum and moves in its direction, through a tunnel and into a crypt. Ventress is sitting there, her eyes gone in one shot and back in the next. She monologues: "It's not like us. It's unlike us. I don't know what it wants, or *if* it wants. But it will grow, until it encompasses everything. Our bodies and our minds will be fragmented into their smallest parts until not one part remains. Annihilation!" Ventress convulses before a stream of golden light pierces her throat and mouth. The expulsion is violent, as though she were fire breathing nonstop. The energy engulfs her and turns into something describable only as a hole. This hole is destructive as well as productive: it births a figure that is recognizably human in silhouette, though it shines like oil or metal. Thus begins the dance, set to Ben Salisbury and Geoff Barrow's similarly metallic score. Back in the lighthouse's main chamber, the figure imitates Lena's every move, falls and gets back up with her, impresses itself upon her (figure 30). Lena manages to stop the choreography just as the figure takes her appearance. She hands it a grenade—or perhaps it hands her one: this possibility cannot be ruled out—and flees before the bomb detonates.

30

Olivia, in Wheatley's film, is not coerced into performance, as is Lena in Garland's. She intentionally develops a practice more rigorously artistic than scientific. Dissatisfied with Zach's plan to appease the creature with artistic offerings, Olivia vows to let the mycorrhiza express itself. To amplify its rhythms, she sets up a network of microphones and other sensors, then connects them to speakerphones and lighting equipment. Like the Icelandic singer-songwriter Björk in some of her recent projects, Olivia appoints herself nature's conductor and engineer.[31] *In the Earth* culminates with a stroboscopic rave, a sped-up nature documentary with footage of plant, animal, and human life flashing in quick succession. Nature expresses everything at once.

Sam See's Darwinian theory of aesthetics avers that sexual selection, or a selection on the basis of taste or feeling that both specifies and negates natural selection, introduces criteria into nature that are untethered from reproductive imperatives.[32] Nature is queer, for See, because it generates abundance or excess through purposeless experimentation—a gloss that also applies to art, and especially modernist art, divorced as it is from realist restrictions.[33] It would appear that ecohorror, better even than modernism, literalizes the becoming-art of queer nature. But the Shimmer and the mist do have a purpose, or at least a destination: total entanglement. Art, then, captures the fantasy of a nature "merely" excessive rather than all-encompassing, a melancholic attachment to a "distribution of the sensible" à la Jacques Rancière, wherein "sensible" denotes both the affective and the intelligible.[34]

If art needs difference for anything like composition to register as such, and if total entanglement accommodates no difference, then ecohorror's artistic performances are nostalgic performances of individuation. They enable characters to mourn a time and a place when and where subjects were subjects, experience was experience, and relations were relations. Art allows characters to move around what Lee Edelman calls the "unbearable—that which we stubbornly "try to subsume to the economy of relation, when it marks, in fact, the impenetrability of what eludes our measure."[35] In performance, characters gain some relief from the experience of losing themselves to the totality of entanglement.

The face-to-face between Lena and the alien reduces the Shimmer's diffuse, invasive alterity to a legible conflict. It also trades the Shimmer's animating principle, refraction, for another one, reflection, which is much easier to cognize. The dance accommodates a narrative of overcoming, an affirmation of post-post-consciousness, to which will necessarily be affixed an asterisk when Lena comes to terms with the impossibility of truly exiting the Shimmer: part of it will remain in her, and part of her in it.[36]

Performance allows *In the Earth*'s Olivia to retain an attachment to pedagogy. When asked what she thinks nature wants to express, she leaps, "I would think that was clear by now, no? How we can all live together without destroying each other." Olivia's motivation for channeling mycorrhizal rhythms is thus to learn what she already knows, or thinks she does. Here also, the dream of a consciousness improved by an encounter with post-consciousness is fleeting. At the end of the rave, Olivia mouths, "Thank you," and collapses. She appears dead. Did the performance disclose the formula for "liv[ing] together without destroying each other"? She certainly seems to think so, given her expression of gratitude. Yet the scene suggests that such a formula, if it exists, does not count human beings as part of the "we." The scene indeed subtracts human life, or a human's life, from "all."

With this operation, −1, ecohorror, and the ecocriticism we have modeled reach "the edge that dissolves everything." The edge reveals that plenitude and abundance are no safeguards against extinction; they withdraw human life. Let us bring up one last, brief example: Danilo Parra's short film *Mushroom* (2022), which, a cynical note from the corporate sponsor tells us, was filmed on a set "powered . . . with Ford electric vehicles."[37] The short depicts a war of attrition between two hikers, an older man (Thomas Bolton) and a younger one (Aaron Macpherson), determined to harvest a giant mushroom that, one of them notes, "is still growing." The war is annulled by an offensive on nature's part. Both men see their attempts thwarted by a violent storm that recalls the rave of *In the Earth*. Their deaths—one is swept by a gust of wind, the other is struck by a tree branch set loose by lightning—play out comedically. An ad for electric vehicles that never actually appear on screen, *Mushroom* might submit a pedagogy about "liv[ing] together without destroying each other." It tells us, basically, to let the mushroom grow, to tame our consumptive cravings.

And yet, whether or not its makers and sponsor are present to it, *Mushroom* also insists on the geometry of a human-nature dualism. Bolton's and Macpherson's characters are not ignorant or blasé consumers; they are outdoor enthusiasts, ecophiles. They approach the mushroom with fascination and excitement and, to secure an opportunity to forage it, camp out on the mycorrhizal mat. The mushroom has no use for them, not alive at least. It thrives when they die. In the last scene, the mushroom, having been cut, tumbles down a slope, finds a new home, and starts growing again. The mushroom and *Mushroom* make plenitude coincide with the subtraction of human beings from the forest ecosystem. For all its limitations when it comes to conveying the asymmetries of ecological experience, and despite the repetitiveness of its plots, ecohorror accomplishes this quite well: it intensifies the compulsion to entangle until the geometry of a human-nature dualism imposes itself. There, at the edge, ethics has to do with what we have called the inhuman calculation: a confrontation with the simultaneous facts of having and not having a world, being and not being of the world.

OVERTURE: FUTURITY'S LATE STYLE

This stage in *Negative Life* marks the end of one cycle and the start of another. The introduction, first chapter, and first interlude corresponded to an anti-pastoral cycle. We embarked on a series of journeys nowhere—prolonged stasis, reckless vagabonding, and excurses toward everything and nothing at once—that have deflated the ecocritical impulse to cast natures and ecologies as fundamentally expressive and pedagogical. What follows constitutes an anti-futurity cycle. In the next chapters and interlude, we further our project of rendering queer and psychoanalytic theories responsive to the pressures of life under climate crisis by turning our attention to the cinema of extinction's severance of life from futurity. The films on our docket are not militantly queer. They do not oppose the heterosexual imaginary so much as make it weird.

Traces of the heterosexual uncanny are visible in *Annihilation* and *In the Earth*. In the former, the reunion between Kane (the alien) and Lena (the human being, probably) happens under the sign not of recognition and reciprocity but of estrangement and alienation. In the latter, the ex-lovers' reunion doesn't look like one: Martin and Olivia display no chemistry and treat each other like strangers. Martin and Alma, for their part, never trauma-bond. In the very last scene, Alma offers, with an eerily deepened voice, to escort Martin out of the woods.

Let us for now close the ecohorror parenthesis and ponder the couple's and the family's late style.

[CHAPTER TWO]

Familiar Afterlives in *Minari* and *Bhopal Express*

A TRAIN PULLS INTO BHOPAL STATION (1)

In the central Indian state of Madhya Pradesh, a train conductor slows down and sounds the alarm when he notices ahead, on the tracks, an agitated man running in his direction. The man, Verma (Kay Kay Menon), waves a flag, white if dirtied by soot. When the train comes to a halt, Verma throws his arms up and shouts in triumph. He's spinning around, visibly relieved, when a second train passes him by, preceded by a thick cloud of coal smoke. The screech of the wheels against the tracks, metal on metal, fuses with the trio Shankar-Ehsaan-Loy's deafening, high-pitched musical score. Verma falls to his knees, begging for this second train to stop—but it's too late. The screen fades to black, then to the title card: *Bhopal Express.*

Mahesh Mathai's 1999 film dramatizes an actual disaster: the Bhopal gas leak. On the night of December 2–3, 1984, a leak at the Union Carbide India Limited pesticide plant exposed the population to methyl isocyanate (MIC) gas, killing at least 3,800 people—according to conservative estimates, others being of the order of 30,000—and injuring over half a million.[1] In Mathai's film, Verma's wife Tara (Nethra Raghuraman) is aboard the Bhopal Express—the second train, which did not stop. This isn't information we hold at first, but it is information we'll have gathered by the time we return, at the film's close, to an extended version of the opening scene. Between this pair of sequences, *Bhopal Express*, like a *First Cow* lacking the limited privilege of historical hindsight, plays out as an extensive flashback, this one relaying the events leading up to and issuing from the spread of the gas. Prior to this spread, Mathai cuts between a dynamic, cinema vérité chronicling of working-class life in Bhopal and an inert witnessing of the leakage. The train's repeated arrival, once unpredictable, then—to spectators—predictable but unpreventable, comes to metaphorize, on the one hand, industrialism's countdown to the next disaster, whereby threats can be managed and deferred but never eliminated; and, on the other hand, the inevitability of being exposed to a toxic gas that has achieved pervasiveness. The Bhopal Express pulls into the station, and Tara and her fellow passengers breathe in the MIC. Yet life goes on, even expands, if only for a minute or two. This chapter addresses normal life's ongoingness in the aftermath of catastrophes that have rendered it impossible.

THE SENSE OF AN ENDING

In the cinema of extinction, how to end constitutes a narrative problem as well as an existential one. Insofar as this cinema speaks to the contradictions of existence within deflagrated environments, the problem of the ending has to do with how a narrative arc might contain incongruities in being and experience that not only prove irresolvable but throw the very chronology of the arc into disarray. In the "futureless emplotment" that is apocalypse, Jessica Hurley suggests, "figuration in the present must remain provisional, for there is no future to serve as meaning's guarantor."[2] What counts as an ending when present activity makes the future a thing of the past?

The challenge of thinking historically about and amid climate change, as Dipesh Chakrabarty has influentially condensed it, has to do with reconciling human and natural history, or "the globe, . . . a humanocentric construction," and "the planet, or the Earth system, [which] decenters the human."[3] Many a critic and theorist has wagered that aesthetic objects hold such worldviews in tension by mediating their social and natural conditions of emergence.[4] For instance, "cinema's Copernican vocation," which James Leo Cahill describes in dialogue with Hans Blumenberg and André Bazin, activates "forms of displacement and recentering," thereby supplying the terms for the human being's disassembly and reassembly in the Anthropocene.[5] In mediating the contingency of environmental existence, the cinema of extinction denotes a late stage in cinema's Copernican vocation, in which human disassembly and reassembly are one and the same. To extend an individual human being's life (biography) is to compress the human species' life span (history): assembly, disassembly. The cinema of extinction's narrative conundrum consists in delimiting and organizing conditions under which the distinction between life and death has eroded, the bridge between present and future swallowed by an ever-widening abyss.[6] This cinema necessitates exit strategies: films must detach themselves from environmental contingency to establish themselves as its artifacts, its indexes—dead things about live things, rather than things caught in the achronological commingling of life and death.[7]

One such exit strategy is to induce a breach in logic. This might mean, in the case of the hazy, drawn-out conclusion to *First Cow* or—as we shall see in the final chapter—the spiraling of transcendental style in *First Reformed*, the eleventh-hour adoption of a new formal grammar. Whether the camera starts to behave erratically or the composition is suddenly disordered, a new cinematic rulebook prevails. In the films we foreground here, *Bhopal Express* and Lee Isaac Chung's *Minari* (2020), the ending constitutes a return to normalcy, rather than a flight of fancy. The gas leak that happens halfway through *Bhopal Express* is followed by overwhelming, chaotic devastation. Still, a peculiarly happy ending awaits Tara and Verma at the Bhopal station, the air of which is saturated by poisonous gas. The reunited newlyweds hold a baby whose mother has died and walk away through the debris as a family. Catastrophe happens later and on a smaller scale in *Minari*. An accidentally sparked fire, a malignant deus ex machina of sorts, engulfs a barn that housed a bountiful harvest promised to a grocer. Here also, devastation restores the family's symmetry, and intergenerational cohabitation proves harmonious at last. Something about these happy endings feels off. The return to normalcy—and normativity—registers as a non sequitur when the forms of life and the modes of living they authorize appear at odds with a milieu now devastated. Freud's tried-and-true formula for the uncanny applies: the familiar made frightening.[8] Or, we should say, the familial made frightening.

The two films take place in the shadow of industrial agriculture's acceleration in the 1980s. In *Minari*, set in 1983, a Korean immigrant family previously based in California lands in rural Arkansas, where Jacob Yi (Steven Yeun) and his wife Monica (Han Ye-ri) secure employment sexing chicks at a hatchery. Whatever time he doesn't spend at work, Jacob spends growing produce on the plot of land they've acquired. Around them, out of focus, the U.S. farm crisis rages. In the 1970s and early 1980s, farmers accumulated debt by purchasing land and equipment to increase output. The Reagan administration and its mismanaged farm program provided no incentives to ease production, and surpluses led to dwindling crop prices, farm incomes, and land values. As foreclosures multiplied, farms were consolidated, with the number of acres operated by single enterprises rising sharply—a trend that extends into the present.[9] The Yis' modest setup isn't so much anachronistic as indicative of a counter-trend, which also extends into the present, toward small-scale, family-run farms that exist, economically and ideologically, on the margins of U.S. industrialization.

When, ahead of the 2021 Golden Globe Awards, the Hollywood Foreign Press Association invoked a substantial amount of dialogue in Korean to classify *Minari* as a "foreign-language film" and bar it from competing for best picture honors, commentators were quick to assert that the semi-autobiographical film told "an authentically American story."[10] Chung's fellow director, Lulu Wang, tweeted, "I have not seen a more American film than #Minari this year. It's a story about an immigrant family, IN America, pursuing the American dream."[11] Those certainly are the stories America enjoys telling about itself. *Minari* also conjures a more fraught, "authentically American" history: that of overworked and underpaid Korean farm laborers. In the late nineteenth century, as Coleen Lyle recounts, "U.S. industrialization began to depend upon the importation of transnational Asian labor and capital expansion into the Asia-Pacific."[12] The Chinese Exclusion Act of 1882 made way for the first significant wave of Korean immigration, which began in 1903, when SS *Gaelic* passengers arrived in Hawaii (annexed five years earlier, in 1898) to work on pineapple and sugar plantations.[13] Over the following years, Korean communities established themselves in the continental United States, primarily in California. The history of Korean immigration to the United States, then, was tethered to farming, and specifically to undervalued farm labor. If *Minari* inspires fewer somber acknowledgments of that history than passionate odes to the "American dream," it is largely because the film defies the expected geography of Korean American life. *Minari* is not a California story; in fact, it starts after its characters have left that state.[14] Chung inverts the frontier myth. Having traveled East, not West, the Yis can, on the land they own, become the "self-made Yis." And they do. They also come to terms, through the illogical fire, with the material and semiotic instability of that self-making.

Whereas in *Minari* the Yis grapple with the uncertainty of independent farming on the margins of industrialization, the characters in *Bhopal Express*, set one year later, directly absorb industrialization's fallout. MIC, the gas produced at the Union Carbide plant, is used to generate carbamate-based pesticides of the kind sprayed by U.S. corporations to extend crop yields. Verma works as an assistant supervisor at the plant. His best friend Bashir (Naseeruddin Shah) has quit his job there due to unsafe conditions and now drives a rickshaw. Reaganism echoes even louder in *Bhopal Express* than in *Minari*. In Mathai's film, the U.S. president represents one of several topics of conversation that characters broach as they signal their membership in the so-called global community of the late twentieth century. In both films, Asiatic figures are not offered the benefits of the global world order of which the U.S. imaginary considers them emblematic.[15]

Bhopal Express's characters, who fall victim to the global trade of pesticides necessitated by industrial agriculture, constitute paradigmatic subjects of "late industrialism," an era in which, as Chloe Ahmann and Alison Kenner note, industrialism's systemic harm is brought into sharp relief.[16] It is due to the Bhopal gas leak, among other catastrophes, that Kim Fortun symbolically locates in the year 1984 the beginning of late industrialism's "deteriorating industrial infrastructure, landscapes dotted with toxic waste ponds, climate instability, [and] incredible imbrication of commercial interest in knowledge production, in legal decisions, in governance at all scales."[17] The Union Carbide factory, says Fortun, was "underdesigned for safety and . . . already set for decommissioning. The market was saturated."[18] What makes the leak not just evental but epochal, according to Fortun, is its ongoing effects: "The exposure continues. The Union Carbide factory in Bhopal hasn't operated since 1984, but the waste produced by it remains on site, underground, and in open ponds. Nearby water wells, still used by local communities, have high chemical as well as bacterial contamination."[19] In capturing the intensification of industrial agriculture and its repercussions on marginalized populations, *Bhopal Express* and *Minari* present themselves as, more than period pieces, tales about the making of the present—or, per the narratology we shall lay out, tales that send us, the spectators, on a necessarily frustrating quest for the present's causes. Our question resurges: How to end?

We contend that the endings of Mathai's and Chung's films mark the partial absorption of existential threat by the couple and family forms. The resulting relations, wherein norms look more or less like themselves but perhaps don't feel as such, constitute an idiosyncratic iteration of non-oppositional eco-negativity. Before us isn't queerness so much as heterosexuality, undead. The films' characters adhere to ideals of unity, growth, and futurity that, in the wake of agrarian misfortune and chemical catastrophe, are no longer accommodated or supported by the milieux they occupy.

Jacques Lacan queries the uncanny family when he asks, in his lectures on the psychoses, "Why does this," the familial relapse, "which Freud gave us in the Oedipus complex[,] retain its irreducible and yet enigmatic value for us? And why privilege the Oedipus complex? Why does Freud always want to find it everywhere, with such insistence?"[20] If the Oedipal drama recurs, Lacan estimates, it is not because Freud overestimated paternal power. Rather, the familial is the nightmare from which we try to awake and whose horror the Oedipus story contains. The Oedipal drama installs "the quilting point between the signifier and the signified" and, thus, retroactively makes sense of the ab-sense that characterizes the child's sexual researches.[21] By acceding to the law emblematized by the father's "no," the Oedipal child halts, albeit temporarily, the senseless sliding of the signifier that characterizes the psychotic world and "knot[s]" the loose threads that precede it. The Oedipal drama, for Lacan, makes sense of the delirium that comes before it, much like a quilting point (*point de capiton*) pins the upholsterer's loose fabric, holding it in place: "Everything radiates out from and is organized around this signifier, similar to these little lines of force that an upholstery button forms on the surface of material. It's the point of convergence that enables everything that happens in this discourse to be situated retroactively and prospectively."[22] The quilting point creates a beginning and end where there would otherwise be none. The beginning and end emerge retroactively, not progressively, in response to the rupture or break to which we refer here as the non sequitur.

Bhopal Express and *Minari* both quilt the traumatic non sequitur by relapsing to the Oedipal family.[23] The gesture establishes a narrative time that proceeds organically from start to end. Yet, as exemplars of the cinema of extinction, these films also insist that their own efforts to mend the non sequitur through kinship are too little, too late. The family cannot prevent disaster—in *Bhopal Express*, it has already happened; in *Minari*, it is unpreventable—and neither can the family grant disaster meaning.

The simultaneous affirmation and negation of the evolutionary program is frightening in at least two ways. First, it tells us, spectators and environmentalists, that we are, much like Mathai's and Chung's characters, mistimed. The train has left the station—or, in Mathai's split structure, the train has entered the station delivering death, and we are too late to stop it. We apprehend the beginning only after the end, once life and death have merged. The ultimate denial by both films of a fruitful progression from cause to effect does not take the appearance of a multiplication of causes that, in ecocriticism, has to do with accommodating a wider range of human and nonhuman actors. The cause is not so much animalized or vegetized as subtracted. *Bhopal Express* and *Minari* posit an absent cause in the historical sequence.[24] The non sequitur induces a spectator who must suture the acausal event after the blow (*après-coup*), for disaster in the form of a break in logic is a fait accompli. The only action available is retroaction, and the backward search for the cause of family reunion will amount to nothing.

Second, the image given to us at the end of *Bhopal Express* and *Minari* is, as noted above, uncanny. So out of sequence with what comes before, so quaint a conclusion to the horrors of a generalized combustion of sense, the family persists. This persistence is what concerns Lacan in his reading of Freud: the Oedipal family lives on and haunts everything. It is to be feared, in his example, as one would fear God. The quilting point may give spectators the sense of an ending, it may convert, in Frank Kermode's kairetic words, "humanly uninteresting successiveness" into "a significant season,"[25] but it does not ensure happiness. Endings are happy, per Lee Edelman's queer theory of the Child as the conservative version of *kairos*, when they are properly destructive—though, of course, this destruction often announces itself as repair.[26] "Resolution," Hugh S. Manon observes, "is the marker not of wholeness per se but a wish for the possibility of wholeness. It represents the softening of a hard reality, seducing viewers to accept the fundamental lie of human subjectivity: that satisfaction is possible."[27] In *Bhopal Express* and *Minari*, happiness seduces without successfully concealing the lie of resolution.

Many ecocritics faced with an absolute ending, that of multispecies life on Earth, turn to narrative to see what has hitherto been missed, such as animal and plant storytellers. These critics' backward look does nothing to change the narrative of apocalypse; instead, it fills the gaps of causal sequence.[28] Mathai's and Chung's familial endings, for their part, point to something beyond life, sense, and norms: they attest to the fulgurating event of the non sequitur. The rupture to which they maintain fidelity could be read as the secular form of grace in the cinema of extinction—the "immanent exception," in Alain Badiou's words, breaking in on the contagion of a progressive emplotment.[29] Still, "grace" is too positive a word. While Badiou would no doubt recoil at familial conclusions that appear to conform to the heterosexual and otherwise habitual relations that he, to his credit, seeks to escape, we, in this chapter and throughout *Negative Life*, attest to the contradictory forms of fidelity that Badiou and fellow Lacanians tend to disavow.[30] It is not clear to us why an immanent exception must produce radical results—why, for instance, the familiar and familial outcomes of the Bhopal gas leak and the incineration of a family barn wouldn't count as fidelity to traumatic events. What excludes the status quo from the category of the evental?

For Badiou, the answer is simple: the event cannot inhabit the ordinary situation, and must therefore be affirmed by radical subjects who destitute that situation. Still, Badiou doesn't escape the residuum of habit. His love-event and the forms of fidelity it produces, Mari Ruti observes, cling to a model of love that is shockingly traditional: "Badiou's scathing critique of the pragmatism of our society's romantic culture does not keep him from advocating relational longevity. On this issue, he often sounds so quaintly (or suspiciously, depending on one's perspective) traditionalist, . . . in part because the accent on longevity comes too close to old-style heteronormativity."[31] As Freud knew well, old habits, including the heteronormativity he saw as the true mystery of human sexuality, die hard. Badiou's old-style heteronormativity "seeps into his analysis like rain water into a damp basement."[32]

Our version of negative life is less optimistic than Badiou's and other iterations of queer negativity. Disrupt, void, and reset the status quo as it might, negative life does so in ways that are neither exculpatory nor emancipatory, nor affirmative. Negative life isn't a pure outside we might embrace by martyring ourselves from the everyday (if only). Negative life isn't a shapeless, fluctuating time-space of vivifying entanglement unstained by teleology. Negative life, though it answers to nothing and proffers nothing, isn't wholly external to ostensibly normative situations; more often than not, it metastasizes *as* normative situations. As we see it, and as a theorist of the queerly normative like Rebekah Sheldon has seen it before us,[33] the normative is already negative, and the negative is less positive (progressive, wild, oppositional) than some radical theorists would like. This insight into the contradictory nature of negativity doesn't free us from the responsibility of elaborating events. It is a simple reminder that events won't always be salutary, and that the elaboration might look a lot like the ordinary, boring, conservative family structures we find in *Bhopal Express* and *Minari*. Negative life isn't only a bulwark against the pastoralism of ecocriticism but a brake on the crypto-pastoralism of radical negativity, which, taken to its logical extreme, mirrors its opposite: anodyne positivity.

The non sequitur is how *Bhopal Express* and *Minari* formalize contradiction. It designates the correlation, or impossible correlation, between the disaster and its resolution, which is to say, between the revelation of environmental existence as empty at best and malign at worst and the relapse to the couple and family forms. These films both do and do not quilt reality, undermining the normative impulses they nevertheless repeat. Negative life, in the present chapter, has something to do with the family unit's unnatural *after*life, or its survival in milieux made precarious by toxicity (in Mathai's film) and a misfortune (in Chung's) exacerbated by structural inequalities. The non sequitur, then, is tied to uncanny survival but is irreducible to it. It designates what remains negative in the happy ending and inscribes itself as an exception to the chemical causality of environmental pollution and narrative progression alike. That the shock of the disaster lasts despite the happiness reveals not so much a failed ending, swappable for a better one, as an ending that assigns an abortive meaning to whatever precedes it. There would be only the banality of an unfolding chemical chain, gas cloud, or ideology, only the human animal's emplotment by place, if it were not for the non sequitur, which breaks and brakes the train of narrative logic long enough to allow a gap to appear before history's "and thens" take over. The gap and its suture by the heterosexual unit install a happy ending only to imperil it.

Happy endings in these films mark a shift not in ideology or style but in mode. *Minari* comes to occupy a mode that we call the "agrarian absurd," affirming agrarianism in light of the inconvenient truth, revealed by the barn disaster, that threats to life and livelihood can always materialize, unaccounted for by calculation and speculation. *Bhopal Express*, for its part, comes to inhabit a mode, no less absurd, that we more specifically call the "toxic supernatural," inflating figures of futurity like heterosexual marriage and family in a context that doesn't guarantee survival, let alone reproduction, so that these figures take on an otherworldly quality.

BURNING BARNS WITH STEVEN YEUN

The Yis alight in Arkansas as a fragile unit. Refusing Jacob's help, Monica struggles to climb into an anonymous mobile home elevated on wheels and cinder blocks. Upon seeing its interior, darkened by wallpaper and wood paneling, she shakes her head: "It just gets worse and worse."[34] "Isn't the city better?" she will later ask her daughter Anne (Noel Kate Cho) as the two burn the trash. Monica finds no promise in rural life. She advocates moving to a nearby town where they would enjoy a mall, good schools, and maybe "a Korean grandma" to babysit the children. In that town, she bargains, the family could cultivate a garden. But Jacob dreams in acres; he wants not a garden but land, vast and unenclosed. The causes behind the family's exit from California are never satisfyingly addressed. Instead, they hover just below the surface, implied in every expression of resentment. It's suggested that Monica sexed chicks too slowly by Californian hatchery standards. More significantly, the family's upward mobility appears to have been thwarted by Jacob's commitment, as the eldest son, to sending his Korean family remittances. What Jacob sees as the "new start" for which they were both yearning, Monica sees as a nonstarter. "If this is the 'start' you wanted," she says, pausing as if to register the gravity of her hypothesis, "maybe there's no chance for us."

Jacob and Monica showcase clashing styles of response to existential threats that could tear the family apart. Some of these threats are climatic (after a tornado narrowly misses the area, Monica meets with indignation Jacob's reassurance that "we worried for no reason"), ecosystemic (when the well dries up, Jacob reroutes the irrigation system and exhausts the domestic water supply—a disruption that Monica endures quietly, for a while), or economic (a Memphis grocer retracts an order that Jacob was ready to deliver, leaving him discouraged). Other threats are health-related. Jacob and Monica's son David (Alan Kim) lives with a heart murmur that invites constant monitoring. Monica warns David against intense physical activity and regularly listens to his heartbeat with a stethoscope. One night, as Monica is shampooing Jacob's hair—a welcome truce—he concedes that perhaps she and the children should return to California, where they would be in greater proximity to medical care. Alert to the idea that David's heart "could stop at any moment," the Yis are perpetually bracing themselves for a tragedy.

A health-related crisis does befall a family member, but that member isn't David. In fact, near the end of *Minari*, a doctor announces that David's condition has improved and recommends sustaining a lifestyle that involves frequently disobeying the parental ban on physical exertion. It is Monica's mother Soon-ja (Youn Yuh-jung) who suffers a stroke a few months after moving in with the Yis. The event, which she survives with impaired movement and speech, comes as a surprise. Soon-ja may be elderly, but her vitality surpasses anyone else's in the household. More than once, David laments that Soon-ja "is not a real grandma." Her humor is juvenile. When her grandson replaces Mountain Dew with urine and serves it to her, she ultimately advocates clemency on the basis that the prank "was funny." And when she teaches the children to play the card game Hwatu, she doesn't grant her opponents special treatment. Giddy and mischievous, she showers the baffled children with insults. The stroke exposes this seemingly invincible character as mortal.

Soon-ja is recovering alone on the farm when the film reaches its climax. The Yis, for their part, are away, in Oklahoma City. Jacob, who has been growing "Korean produce" to serve the immigrant market, strikes a deal with a grocery owner, and the two agree to begin shipments the next week. The deal should bring relief. "Now we can make money and live without worries," Jacob proclaims outside, by the shipping gate. Monica isn't so sure. As the children wait in the car, she communicates one long-held grievance after the other: "You chose the farm over our family"; "So you're saying, we can't save each other, but money can"; "Things may be good now, but I don't think they will stay that way. Things won't end well, and I can't bear it. I've lost my faith in you. I can't do this anymore." Jacob pauses a few seconds, as if to scan for a path forward, before concluding, "Okay. It's done." Monica's intuition that "things won't end well" isn't entirely correct, but a catastrophe does await the family on its way to a happy ending.

At the farm, Soon-ja is cleaning the barn that stores the produce to be supplied to the Oklahoma City grocer. When she burns the trash—an activity that has come to symbolize Monica's skepticism toward rural life—a piece of paper flies off, setting the hay ablaze. Flames quickly swallow the barn as a powerless Soon-ja watches in silent agony. Chung cuts back and forth between the couple's fight in Oklahoma and the fire in Arkansas, but the events are not concurrent. The former takes place during the daytime, and the latter after nightfall. By the time the barn catches fire, Monica, Jacob, and the children have almost completed their car ride home. They rush to the farm when they smell the smoke. Jacob enters the barn, followed by his wife moments later, in an attempt to salvage the produce. Their efforts prove futile: there are simply too many crates of vegetables in the barn, and fire has already spread to every corner. Jacob assists Monica in exiting the barn as they cough vigorously. They collapse on the grass, holding each other; a vertical pan reveals the height of the flames (figure 31). Like Soon-ja moments before, they bear witness to a destruction they cannot contain. Meanwhile, David and Anne run to catch up to their grandmother, who, confused, has walked away from the farm. "Please don't leave, Grandma. Come with us," David instructs. The trio hold hands as they return (figure 32).

31

32

The next section addresses how the fire makes the Yis feel at home again within forms of marital and intergenerational intimacy. For now, let us attend to the cinematic and literary trope of the barn burning from which *Minari* partially departs, one wherein fire typically harms both the production of meaning and the reproduction of norms pertaining to the couple and the family forms. *Minari* is, incredibly, not the only film in Yeun's filmography to dramatize the incineration of structures for growing or storing produce. In Lee Chang-dong's *Beoning* (버닝, *Burning*, 2018), released two years prior to *Minari*, Shin Hae-mi (Jeon Jong-seo) returns to Paju, South Korea, with the mysterious Ben (Yeun); the pair bonded when a bombing stranded them at the airport in Nairobi, Kenya.[35] One night, Ben makes a confession to the protagonist, a young writer named Lee Jong-su (Yoo Ah-in): every two months, Ben burns an abandoned greenhouse. He adds that multiple greenhouses exist in Jong-su's rural neighborhood, to which the latter had to return when his father, a cattle farmer, became entangled in legal affairs. Ben warns that he will strike again soon, near Jong-su's house. In the days that follow, Jong-su scans his surroundings. No greenhouses burn down. One day, while inspecting a structure, he receives a confusing call. Hae-mi is on the line. The call cuts off before Jong-su can gather any information. Suspecting that Ben has killed Hae-mi or that Hae-mi has escaped Ben—theories supported by evidence of Ben's abusive behavior—Jong-su summons Ben to the countryside. There, Jong-su stabs Ben before dousing his body and car in gasoline and setting them on fire. Jong-su tosses his own bloodied clothes into the fire, returns to his truck, and drives off. The camera, affixed to the truck's hood, lingers on Jong-su, nude and shivering. The blaze is both behind and before him: in the distance, yet reflected in the windshield, blurred by snowflakes, droplets, and steam (figure 33).

33

Two instances of combustion bookend *Burning*: the offscreen bombing that precipitates Ben's arrival into Hae-mi's life and by extension

Jong-su's, and the onscreen incineration of Ben and his car. Between the two fires, only one greenhouse is seen burning down. In a flashback or a dream sequence, a figure (possibly a young Jong-su) stands, at least partially nude, before a greenhouse in flames (figure 34). Apart from this short scene, which anticipates the ending, the burning of greenhouses remains a threat rather than a reality. But it's a threat with immediate consequences, one that upends Jong-su's life and likely conceals Hae-mi's death. At the very least, Ben's arrival upends the nascent sexual and romantic intimacy between Jong-su and Hae-mi. Who they are to each other and what future awaits their relationship become open-ended questions. Ben's arsonism also throws agrarian semiotics into disarray. The burning of greenhouses, even abandoned ones, precludes future growth.

34

We would be wrong, however, to cast Ben as Edelman's "*sinthom*osexual," or as what one of us has called the "*sinthomo*-environmentalist."[36] Yes, Ben "asserts [him]self *against* futurity, *against* its propagation," staging "an impasse in the passage to the future."[37] And yes, his destructive habit forcibly unburdens rural areas from the symbolic labor of guaranteeing the future. But in Ben's posture we see no shattering, no self-loss. Ben imperils certain norms (coupledom, growth) to assert others (masculinist domination through misogynistic violence and environmental destruction). Since it appears that, for Ben, burning greenhouses euphemizes killing women, Jong-su opts for the killing and burning he deems morally good to mitigate his complicity.

This loop of an ending—with Jong-su adopting Ben's pyromaniacal habit to neutralize the threat that the latter embodies—represents *Burning*'s most significant deviation from one of its sources of inspiration, Japanese writer Haruki Murakami's 1983 story "Barn Burning." The story's beats are essentially the same as those of Lee's film,[38] save for the men's final encounter, which isn't a showdown but a casual chat; an action such as Jong-su's would be at odds with Murakami's predilection for passivity. The narrator recognizes the woman's companion at a coffee shop, and the two initiate a conversation:

> "Say, by the way, how's your barn doing?" I braved the question.
>
> The trace of a smile came to his lips. "Oh, you still remember?" he said, removing his handkerchief from his pocket to wipe his mouth. "Why, sure, I burned it. Burned it nice and clean. Just as promised."
>
> "One right near my house?"
>
> "Yeah. Really, right by there."
>
> "When?"
>
> "Last—when was it? Maybe ten days after I visited your place."
>
> I told him about how I plotted the barns on my map and ran my daily circuits. "So there's no way I could have *not* seen it," I insisted.
>
> "Very thorough," he gibed, obviously having his fun. "Thorough and logical. All I can say is, you must have missed it. Does happen, you know. Things so close up, they don't even register."[39]

The analogy between burning barns and killing women is so obviously laid out in Murakami's story as to qualify as an equation. Yet the narrator, like the police in Lacan's reading of Poe's "The Purloined Letter," brought up in chapter 1, seems to miss it. When he reroutes the conversation toward the woman's disappearance, it isn't to interrogate her former companion. The man says he has been unable to get a hold of her, and the narrator, curious but nevertheless reluctant to find out anything that would require him to act, doesn't probe his interlocutor further. The narrator will later muse, "She'd disappeared," accepting as an explanation the absence of one. In suggesting that the woman ghosted him, the narrator can indeed acknowledge a mystery while relinquishing the inconvenience of solving it. *Burning* neutralizes its central threat by setting it ablaze; Murakami's story does so by deflating it. The narrator either denies or disavows the disturbance brought about by the self-proclaimed barn burner, aligning himself with the casualization of misogynistic violence. The woman's life is but a memory.

The threat of setting greenhouses on fire in *Burning* also opens up a discursive space wherein anxieties about class transgression are negotiated. Ben is coded as upper-class; even his name, Americanized, positions him as something of a global citizen. The practice of burning greenhouses thereby constitutes interclass tourism. Ben visits the working class intentionally and sporadically, leaving a trail of destruction behind him. In *Burning*, Lee and fellow screenwriter Oh Jung-mi invert the vector of class transgression drawn in William Faulkner's 1939 "Barn Burning," the story to which Murakami's owes its title.[40] One barn burning, carried out, puts Faulkner's late nineteenth-century-set story in motion, and another, thwarted, concludes it. In both instances, Abner Snopes, a tenant farmer, is rebelling against upper-class families in the American South. While Abner's son Sarty does not initially betray him—or, more accurately, isn't given the opportunity to do so in court—the boy eventually publicizes his father's plan, leading to the latter's probable death.[41] In defiance of the law, including the law of private property that Locke deems "natural," which is to say unalienable and foundational, Abner's barn burnings, both planned and enacted, violate class distinctions and shatter the family unit.[42] *Minari*, another "all-American tale," may be the anti-"Barn Burning." The accidental barn burning in Chung's film, even as it reveals the instability and precariousness of the Yis' project of self-making, merely slows down upward mobility, and it fortifies the family. We now ask why.

ECO-EXISTENTIALISM

As farmers and immigrants, the Yis must, in order to survive and thrive, engage in constant risk calculation and constant speculation concerning their actions' possible outcomes. In doing so, they appeal to various systems of beliefs and values. In the planning stages of the irrigation infrastructure, Jacob teaches David how to determine the ideal location for a well by "using [their] minds." David gathers that clustered trees indicate access to underground water—"cause trees like water." When, after the fire, the ritual is performed again, scientific reasoning makes way for prophecy. Jacob's employee Paul (Will Patton), a devout Christian known to bear a cross on Sundays and to speak in tongues even more frequently, uses a water dowsing stick. This time, Jacob, who was previously reluctant to endorse Will's superstitions, goes along. The Yis' livelihood depends on more than their ability to wield the right agricultural techniques; it also hinges on striking a balance between assimilation and integration. Participation in the majority-white church's activities grants them access to a community and its related benefits, such as emergency childcare. But whereas they seek to blend in locally, they seek to stand out regionally; the marketing of produce as Korean necessitates a certain commodification of racial and cultural difference.

Chung's characters are caught in what Angela Mitropoulos calls an "oikopolitics": an episteme that "valoriz[es] . . . contingency," "re-found[ing] decision—posited as a condition of property in [oneself]—under conditions of uncertainty."[43] The term "oikopolitics" synthesizes the Lucretian understanding of uncertainty as *fortuna* (the universe and its floods and plagues are governed by chance) and the Machiavellian alignment of the household and the polis (decision is valorized as "auto-teleological production"—property in oneself—under conditions of uncertainty).[44] Subjects climb the oikopolitical hierarchy not by eliminating *fortuna*, which would require overcoming what Joshua Schuster and Derek Woods identify as capitalism's "extinction scenarios," but by granting it value.[45] Oikopolitics, for Mitropoulos, upholds a statistical rationality in which the distinction between gain and loss is absorbed by an ongoing calculus of risk codified by forms like the contract and the insurance.[46] As a marginalized subject committed to a project of self-making, Jacob is made to valorize risk. He takes out loans, for instance, to secure equipment and aid productivity. When in an emergency he uses the domestic water supply, it's because the gravity of one possible outcome (a ruined harvest) outweighs that of the other (a temporary lack of running water in the household). Class mobility for the Yis would manifest through the ability to derive greater benefits from risk.

The barn burning proves momentous, for it imposes a limit on the valorization of contingency. The Yis might have secured insurance, but compensation would represent for them value replaced, not value added. Jacob could not have accounted for the barn burning in his risk calculus; it *befalls* the family, much like a Lucretian plague. Just as the fire reveals an unpredictable, even unknowable destructive force, its aftermath reveals a *productive* force unaccounted for by Jacob's calculation. Early in the film, Soon-ja suggests planting the *minari* seeds she has brought from South Korea. Jacob says he'll think about it but fails to follow up. She plants the seeds regardless, by the creek, where crops require little to no attention. In the ultimate scene, Jacob and David happen upon the peppery vegetable, which now covers the damp gully (figure 35). "Grandma picked a good spot," Jacob recognizes. His own efforts to grow Korean produce were not directly rewarded, but the produce that did grow unattended reminds him that all was not lost in the barn fire.

35

The film's characters inhabit the mode we call "agrarian absurd" when they must bear the fact that their lives are shaped by productive and destructive forces which exceed what they might account for through speculation, be it informed by agricultural science or by superstition. The barn burning doesn't fracture the Yi family because its members become oriented, together, toward absurdity. It is not the case that nothing worse could happen; something more catastrophic very well could. And yet the Yis, present to this possibility, keep going, united. The ending of *Minari*, as we see it, thus preserves marital and familial geometries by undergoing something of an existential turn. The Yis' survival and persistence are Sisyphean.

Albert Camus memorably appeals to the myth of Sisyphus to synthesize his philosophy of the absurd: the "confrontation between the human need [for meaning] and the unreasonable silence of the world."[47] Knowledge of life's meaninglessness, Camus insists, cannot be retracted or relinquished: "A man who has become conscious of the absurd is forever bound to it."[48] Suicide, the "one truly serious philosophical problem," would qualify as "acceptance at its extreme."[49] One must keep living in order to revolt against absurdity; "revolt" here stands in opposition to both disavowal and acquiescence. "It is essential," writes Camus, "to die unreconciled and not of one's own free will."[50]

Sisyphus, who for cheating death was condemned by the gods to roll a rock repeatedly to the top of a mountain from which it would inevitably roll down, represents for Camus the paradigmatic absurd hero: "He is, as much through his passions as through his torture. His scorn of the gods, his hatred of death, and his passion for life won him that unspeakable penalty in which the whole being is exerted toward accomplishing nothing. This is the price that must be paid for the passions of this earth."[51] Sisyphus earns his hero status in the state of suspension between the trip up and the trip down the mountain, as he returns to a labor he knows to be endless and purposeless:

> At the very end of his long effort measured by skyless space and time without depth, the purpose is achieved. Then Sisyphus watches the stone rush down in a few moments toward that lower world whence he will have to push it up again toward the summit. He goes back down to the plain.
>
> It is during that return, that pause, that Sisyphus interests me. A face that toils so close to stones is already stone itself! I see that man going back down with a heavy yet measured step toward the torments of which he will never know the end. That hour like a breathing-space which returns as surely as his suffering, that is the hour of consciousness. At each of those moments when he leaves the heights and gradually sinks

> toward the lairs of the gods, he is superior to his fate. He is stronger than his rock.
>
> If the myth is tragic, that is because its hero is conscious.[52]

As Sisyphus walks down, "contemplat[ing] his torment, silenc[ing] all the idols," his faith belongs to him, not to the gods, and not to the rock, now merely "a thing." [53] "One must," concludes Camus, "imagine Sisyphus happy."[54]

Minari's ending counts as happy by existential standards. Instead of achieving narrative closure by restoring meaning to agrarian work and family life, Chung's film hints at the persistence of characters who are, in Camus's idiom, "unreconciled."[55] Jacob, something of an absurd hero, enjoys a successful harvest (the Sisyphean climb). Then, the marital fight severs the link between economic stability and family unity, and the fire destroys the link between production and product (the Sisyphean descent). Yet Jacob persists in defiance of an existential absurdity spectacularized by a catastrophe that resists absorption into schemes of valuation (the Sisyphean climb, again). Granted, Chung's tale of persistence doesn't map exactly onto Camus's Sisyphean existentialism. For one thing, the familial, the marital, and the normative more broadly clash with an individualist ethics like Camus's that locates freedom in the affirmation of one's senseless fate. But again, what binds the Yis once *Minari* has adopted the agrarian absurd is less an adherence to norms than a common orientation toward the absurdity of the existence to which norms would typically ascribe meaning. In offering this distinction, we don't claim access to the characters' psychology. Our reasoning instead pertains to narrative structure: the fire confronts characters with the absurd, so that a consciousness of the absurd ought to be presumed in the wake of this tragedy.

As existentialism's importance to this chapter suggests, our survey of the cinema of extinction gets, with *Minari* and *Bhopal Express*, as close as it ever will to the question of authenticity. Far more than *The Wall* or *First Reformed*, for instance, the two films at hand display a commitment to imagining something like an authentic relation to environmental contradictions; there is very little cynicism or nihilism to be detected in these marital and familial fables. Our own commitments are more formal than moral. We aren't interested in attesting to the authenticity of the Yis' ultimate disposition. We are even less interested in condemning their disposition as inauthentic, for such a condemnation would imply the existence of authenticity elsewhere. What makes *Minari* and *Bhopal Express* so uncanny, and so interesting, in our eyes is that they register the crisis of meaning brought about by negative life but package it into shapes—marriage, family, and work as traditional guarantors of futurity's meaning and materiality—inherited from a world that no longer exists.

In *Minari*'s absurd happy ending, whereby characters persist in a milieu that has disrupted the coherence of their life and livelihood, we decipher, more specifically, an emergent eco-existentialism. Deborah Bird Rose has developed an ecological existentialism inspired by the philosophy of Emmanuel Levinas in response "to the two big shifts in Western thought that define our current moment: the shift into uncertainty and the shift into collectivity."[56] While we agree with Rose that the uncertainty of contemporary life begets a return to existentialism, however antiquated this philosophy might appear, we insist that this uncertainty resists polishing. The ecological is made to perform an ameliorative function in Rose's proposition: ecological existentialism is existentialism made better. "Against existentialist loneliness," Rose writes, "I propose that our condition as a co-evolving species of life on Earth, our kinship in the great family of life on Earth, situates us in time and place. We are still creatures for whom there is no predetermined essence or destiny; we are a work-in-progress."[57] Rose recognizes uncertainty only insofar as it opens onto "the rich plenitude, with all its joys and hazards, of our entanglement in the place, time, and multispecies complexities of life on Earth."[58] While they concede, via María Puig de la Bellacasa, that not "all interdependency is good," Schuster and Woods maintain that "the embodied, entangled, engaged, ecologically interrelated conditions of existence" constitute a "better way to begin" when it comes to existential thinking.[59] With Rose, and to a limited extent with Schuster and Woods, multispecies entanglement untangles existentialism, evacuating the recalcitrantly existential from existentialism. Absurdity is thus salvaged and recuperated by the plane of meaning and meaningfulness guaranteed by "a kinship of becoming: no telos, no deus ex machina to rescue us, no clockwork to keep us ticking along."[60] But for absurdity to remain absurd, one must stay open to the possibility of a deus ex machina or, as we have called the fire in *Minari*, a malignant deus ex machina. Existentialists continue to affirm their fate knowing that illogic might reroute it. "It is always easy to be logical," Camus sums up; "It is almost impossible to be logical to the bitter end."[61]

If eco-existentialism cannot realistically resolve existentialism into the pastoral of harmonious, multispecies co-living, it can at least remind us that ecological thought necessitates a notion of contingency as external. So claims Frédéric Neyrat in a "manifesto for a radical existentialism."[62] Neyrat deems contemporary theory—specifically some eco-adjacent trends especially popular in the late 2000s and early 2010s, such as new materialism, speculative realism, and object-oriented ontology—guilty of "exophobi[a]," a refusal to confront "the externality of nature."[63] "When everything is inside," Neyrat reasons, "when each real distance is considered a sacrilege, when everything is re-thought beginning from substance, when the anthropological hierarchy that stems from a privileged 'access' to being disappears, everything can equally be said to be an 'object.'"[64] What results from such exophobia is a condition of "saturated immanence," "a world immunized against the outside," wherein "the undamaged . . . [is turned] into a contagious substance, susceptible to being found in anything and anyone."[65] What Neyrat views as a contagious substance would correspond, in Rose's philosophy, to the ontologically undifferentiated immanence of multispecies entanglement.

Yet, Neyrat explains, to exist is to be oriented toward alterity: "The verb 'to exist' is made up of *ek-*, outside of, and *sistere*, to be placed—*sistere* coming from *sta-*, to be standing. By extension, to exist means to live."[66] Life represents "an 'exit' from infinity, a necessary eccentricity," "the dismissal of being."[67] An eco-existentialism would thereby be conjured by a "peripheral medium" who "occupies no center but can bring about—starting from eccentricity—a certain number of mediations, a certain exercise of consciousness extended as *non-place of passage* toward metaphysical lands."[68] The agrarian absurd concept we have elaborated with respect to *Minari* echoes Neyrat's eco-existentialism to the extent that we imply a nature that resists absorption into the imminence of relations. Nature is more than can be cultivated; it is also a force that introduces illogic into a calculus of risk that otherwise appeals to agricultural science and superstition. The normal life to which *Minari* returns in its ending is a life of eccentricity, to borrow Neyrat's term, but it doesn't defy the laws of physics or chemistry. We adhere to Frank Kermode's thesis on the retroactivity of endings: that they affix meaning by making time move backward, just as a period fixes the meaning of a sentence by quilting its free-floating signifiers, amplifying, in turn, their abortive and self-mutilating logic.[69]

The ending, per Kermode, is totalizing, like the apocalypse. He compares the ending to the sound that we humans attribute to the clock: "We ask what it *says*: and we agree that it says *tick-tock*. By this fiction we humanize it, make it talk our language. Of course, it is we who provide the fictional difference between the two sounds."[70] In other words, we organize a meaningless succession of sounds into a significant duration: "*tick* is our word for a physical beginning, *tock* our word for an end. We say they differ," and "what enables them to be different is a special kind of middle."[71] Between *tick* and *tock*, there is a totality in the making: *tick* produces *tock*, and *tock* confirms the meaning of *tick*. The *tock-tick* interval, however, loops incongruously, *ad absurdum.* The ground of meaning, *tock*, provides no stability for the figure *tick* to emerge. In Neyrat's, and our, eco-existentialist verdict, the end gives meaning, but a provisional, Sisyphean meaning to the senseless drift that precedes it. We are, with Sisyphus, no sooner up than running down that hill—again.

The cinema of extinction gives new weight to Kermode's insight that "*tick* is a humble genesis, *tock* a feeble apocalypse," because it ratchets up the absurdity, the inharmony, that the ending is supposed to contain.[72] If endings are minor apocalypses, unveiling what could not have been seen before they quilted a "special kind of middle," the endings of *Bhopal Express* and *Minari*, in particular, expose the nothing that Kermode, following the existentialism of Martin Heidegger, Jean-Paul Sartre, and Camus, describes as the absurd yawn enabling human existence. The ending, Kermode's ending, purges existence of "simple chronicity, of the emptiness of *tock-tick*, humanly uninteresting time," and supplants it with significance: "*chronos* becomes *kairos*," a point in time "charged with a meaning derived from its relation to the end."[73] Try as they might, Mathai's and Chung's endings offer no such purgation of meaninglessness. Nor do they entirely convince us that the desire for narrative is the desire for an end, as Peter Brooks contends.[74] Instead, their endings demand the implausible suturing of a dehisced temporal structure wherein the pastoral absurd not only relapses but prolapses.

That the family unit lives on in these films doesn't soften their formal logic; instead, it dramatizes that logic by showing that every end is also a *tick*, that is to say, an absurdity. *Bhopal Express*'s nervous tick—its symptom, if you will—is most apparent at the end, in a family unit that not only persists but insists after death; here, as in neurosis, the normative is what is most discordant. The negative life on display is haunting. The next sections return to *Bhopal Express* to consider an unreconciled existence that persists only by occupying a supernatural register.

A TRAIN PULLS INTO BHOPAL STATION (II)

Pramod K. Nayar deems *Bhopal Express* exemplary of the "Bhopal Gothic," a loose genre that comprises various media and cultural representations of the Bhopal gas leak.[75] "Bhopal," Nayar explains, "is an ongoing nightmare, a persistent haunting, and much of this revolves around poisoned bodies, genetic codes and the environment."[76] The uncanny in the Bhopal Gothic stems from two forms of hybridization: the forced encounter of body and toxicant, and "the global asserting/ingratiating itself into and uniting itself with the local."[77] The Bhopal Gothic designation highlights a supernatural aspect even in the disaster films that do not inscribe themselves in a science fiction lineage. There is no shortage, across disaster cinema, of paternal figures who defy the laws of physics to save the day.

Whereas audiences may be used to interpreting the restoration of the marital and familial units afforded by heroic feats as evidence of a threat's containment, *Bhopal Express* locates the supernatural in the solidification of those units despite the protagonist's failure to perform the heroic gesture that might have temporarily limited some Bhopal Express passengers' exposure to MIC. A threat must go away in order to resurge in the event of, say, a sequel. And even if Verma had gotten the right train to stop, the gas wouldn't have been contained. Verma, then, isn't a triumphant hero or even an absurd one; he is a pathetic hero, his actions inadequate to the scale of the massacre. One could conjecture that *Bhopal Express* naively embraces the worn-out tropes of marital and familial unification in order to grant narrative closure to a film that captures a disaster horrifying in its ongoingness. We instead note that the intensified attachment to the couple and family forms that the characters display as they incur chromosomal damage from their exposure to the gas makes the normal and the normative otherworldly.

At the level of content, *Bhopal Express* depicts an environmental catastrophe that could have been avoided had better safety measures been in place, and workers' rights been upheld. At the level of form, Mathai's film suggests that the negative life or senseless gap into which the ending-before-the-beginning throws us is inevitable. The delay between this ending-before-the-beginning and the ending's resumption derails causality by introducing a cut: the conclusion does not evolve organically from what came before it. Evolutionary telling cannot explain the film's retroactivity, its beginning *après-coup*. Why?

There is more to the causal sequence than chemical reactions leading to chemical death, or filmic reactions leading to narrative completion (what Gilles Deleuze, in *Cinema 2*, calls the clichéd movement of ordinary time);[78] there is, in addition, a cut or break that *Bhopal Express* must work over and repeat, no matter the consequence. Mathai's film introduces the cut early, as if to say the wound comes first, even if its magnitude may be recognized only at the end. Something is subtracted from the start. We begin with negative life, which the film visualizes through the rails, an image of which Lacan himself was fond. These tracks emblematize the signifying bar that cuts into the human animal, subtracting its enjoyment while producing the very objects that slide across it. As a barred subject, Verma is precisely where he should be, where he must be: on the rails, hoping to arrest their movement. However, the sliding does not stop, as the appearance of the second train—the intended train carrying his beloved, Tara—reveals. Verma misses the mark, tragically.

We might say that the end fails to be the end Verma had wanted; in metaphorical terms, beginning and end fail to come together due to the metonymic slippage that displaces the desired object. In this sense, the end is never quite the end because of the restless negativity that keeps the train, or the signifier, sliding beyond reach. This interpretation only gets us so far, however, for it ignores what the film does successfully.

Verma, insofar as he is barred, misses the intended object, the one that, metaphorically speaking, would complete his trajectory. Nevertheless, the film hits on something else: the barred object that, despite all movement, all coming and going, all chronicity, synchronicity, and locomotion, stays in place. This unmovable object is, simply, the place of the drive with its repetition compulsion, automatism, and enjoyment in returning to the site of rupture. All this the film enacts at the level of form, where the disjunction of the narrative causes the film to proceed backward. As in a noir, we start when death is guaranteed. Where Verma fails, the film succeeds by derailing forward progress and returning to negative life.

MIC production, the gas leak, environmental racism and other forms of inequality, worker immiseration, extractive capitalism and colonialism: these are but a few of the causal matrices we have inventoried in this chapter that underwrite the film's ending. *A* leads to *b* leads to *c*, and so on. Yet form cuts against the causal matrix that saturates subjects in manufactured death. An ending told twice disrupts the logic that would see Verma's tragedy as a consequence of cause alone. To harken back to Kermode's kairetic thinking, we would say that the film proceeds as history does: not like a clock, but broken and in reverse.

Let us entertain the standard ecological reading: *Bhopal Express* allegorizes varieties of slow violence that unevenly distribute harm and injustice on individuals and populations. We could add, following posthuman causality, numerous interacting agencies, supernumerary causes that are nonhuman (chemical, geological), exerting their dizzying force on the weak human vessel. Lastly, we could try to recuperate this subject bombarded by multicausal forces and say: at least there is entanglement, at least we have stories like this one to teach us how to learn and live going forward.

Such causal heuristics ignore the contradiction between pollution and redemption, two causal logics. No matter how multifactorial the intersecting timelines of postmodern cinema may get, these are stories that tend to proceed from start to end. And, of course, *Bhopal Express* does not. Loosened from time, Mathai's film discloses something in excess of the causal network that narrative, including environmental narrative, adopts even when it multiplies the number of actors deserving attention. The film, that is, discloses what Ruti calls subjective "destiny."[79] Speaking apropos of the repetition compulsion, Ruti uses a train metaphor:

> One might say that the repetition compulsion functions like a train that has been placed on a highly specific set of rails that control its trajectory. This train always aims at its designated destination. . . . These stations, which house the subject's most symptomatic fixations, are likely to carry names such as Anxiety, Depression, Disenchantment, Weariness, Sorrow, Bitterness, and Misery. . . . As much as the repetition compulsion disturbs the smooth unfolding of our lives, its obliteration might have even more catastrophic consequences in the sense that we would be left without our customary moorings; we would, as it were, lose the comfort of knowing our destination (or destiny).[80]

Destiny, here, does not consign subjects to a predetermined fate. Neither does it reduce subjectivity to a mere effect of multiple, yet fully knowable, causes, as ecocriticism does. Ruti's destiny subtracts the subject's causal foundation. It is this lack of foundation, negative life, that compels a repetition that gives the subject a semblance of consistency.

It isn't too much to say that ecocriticism disavows the absent cause of the subject. While ecocriticism posits a multiplicity of agents, causes, objects, quadruple-objects, networks, and entanglements, all of which situate, contextualize, and historicize the subject as an effect of contingent relations, these contingent relations mask the subject's destined repetition, which is contingent only in the mundane sense that each subject repeats trauma differently. An eco-historical reading of *Bhopal Express* would receive the traumatic accident as the outcome of contingent causes and Verma's response to their contingent yet traceable effect.[81] Historicism is, at bottom, the belief in forward action, no matter how varied or how conditional the action. Ecocriticism repeats this faith in a prime mover, giving readers an infinite regress of evolutionary causes in a narrative of more-than-human vibrancy and fragility. No doubt, the events of *Bhopal Express* could have been otherwise. The same is true of our time of mass extinctions. However, it is only from the perspective of the end that this "otherwise" takes on meaning, and the contingency of our more-than-human relations snaps into place. *Bhopal Express* imposes retroactivity not to repeat the progressive line that the past informs the present; no. The film begins at the end to elevate it to its kairetic destiny: the end, in Mathai's film, causes the past. *Bhopal Express* halts history's "and thens" with a compulsory, unmoving void that, for the duration of the film, we must occupy.

ALREADY DEAD

We have argued that *Bhopal Express* moves along two tracks: one progressive, concerning Verma's attempt to stop the train carrying his beloved from reaching its destination; the other retroactive, regarding the past from the perspective of the end, that is, the perspective of destiny. The first is phenomenological; it issues from Verma's experience, his being in time. The second, by contrast, is purely formal, issuing from a break in time and returning to that break as per the repetition compulsion and its fixation on loss and absence. Accordingly, there are two losses: first, the loss of a habitable ecology and, by extension, the threatened loss of the family, and second, the loss of narrative continuity. The latter, we've submitted, constitutes the film's greatest achievement because it formalizes the drive's crucial derailment of evolutionary timelines, both conservative and environmental. Whereas other films, such as *Terminator II: Judgment Day* (1991), *12 Monkeys* (1995), and *Tenet* (2020), feature heroes, typically paternal, time-traveling from the future to stop an environmentally destructive past, *Bhopal Express* offers no such overcoming of contradiction.[82] In Mathai's film, the contradiction between progressive hope and the intractable negativity of the drive is final. Verma misses the train. He was always going to miss the train. The end.

This conclusion and our emphasis on intractable contradiction sound like a recipe for political quietism. Freud acknowledges the accusation leveled against psychoanalysis in "Analysis Terminable and Interminable" when he grants that the analysand's investment in unconscious repetition, their unwillingness to let go of a painful and debilitating symptom, is never-ending.[83] All the psychoanalyst can hope for in the end would be to reconcile the analysand to their psychic suffering. Freud admits that this is a grim conclusion unlikely to inspire political optimism. *Negative Life* declines to trade entanglement for some other positive content worth rallying around. As we admitted in the preface, our quest to get ecocriticism unstuck implies a stuckness of a different sort: the atemporality of repetition compulsion. Todd McGowan nonetheless argues that sustaining contradiction is itself a radical act, for it upsets the logic of temporal progress.[84] Radicalism demands an outside of the kind on which our ecocriticism of contradictions insists. Without one, we must satisfy ourselves with garden-variety reformisms, such as the immanent ethics of home, place, composition, worlding, ethics, care, intimacy, kinship, companionship, and love.

The political act imagined by *Bhopal Express* appears not in Verma's desperate yelling but in the silent, rhythmic, and inexhaustible formal cut. The cut alone disrupts the temporal progression of the film and the phenomenological movement of the characters to show, after the fact, that the past and present are radically contingent. In Darwinian and Bergsonian theories of creative evolution, the past causes the future. Against this conception of cause, and in contrast to narratives and theories concerned with the novelty of the future, *Bhopal Express* reconciles thought—the thought of the film—to negative life, that which estranges thought from itself, interminably.

We have discussed the agrarian absurd in *Minari*'s non sequitur. *Bhopal Express*'s own final, absurd minutes take on supernatural qualities as they quilt chromosomal damage by pervasive toxicants to the afterlife of the family. Against all logic, Verma and Tara survive. Their survival is not simply a case of improbability. This, in any case, is how Amitav Ghosh defines the ecological uncanny: as the recognition of improbable forces, such as tornadoes, breaking in on human affairs (*fortuna*, in Mitropoulos's Lucretian lexicon).[85] The uncanny, for Ghosh, confronts readers with nonhuman protagonists. It makes the familiar, anthropocentric narrative unfamiliar: we have always been upstaged by more-than-human actors, though we have not always accepted it. This version of the uncanny still operates within the world of recognition. Ghosh hopes—and he is not alone in this—that an upsurge of unfamiliarity, when recognized, will lead to newer and better stories of human and nonhuman cohabitation.

Mathai swaps recognition for repetition: first as tragedy, then as absurdity. *Bhopal Express* embraces repetition and, we might say, binding—not the binding of nature lovers but that of extinction. "Extinction," writes Ray Brassier, "is real yet not empirical. It is transcendental yet not ideal, since it coincides with the external objectification of thought unfolding at a specific historical juncture when the resources of intelligibility, and hence the lexicon of ideality, are being renegotiated. In this regard, it is precisely the extinction of meaning that clears the way for the intelligibility of extinction."[86] Brassier adds that "senselessness and purposelessness are not merely privative; they represent a gain in intelligibility. The cancellation of sense, purpose, and possibility marks the point at which the 'horror' concomitant with the impossibility of either being or not-being becomes intelligible."[87] When thought thinks about the end of time—absolute extinction by solar death—thought necessarily stumbles; it exceeds all Kantian modesty by exceeding the limits of sense. Still, senselessness for Brassier, and we would add in *Bhopal Express*, is not without merit since it represents the breaking point between being and not-being, and between thought and its negation. "Thus, if everything is dead already," from the perspective of the end, "this is not only because extinction disables those possibilities which were taken to be constitutive of life and existence," such as sense, direction, prospection, and introspection, "but also because the will to know is driven by the traumatic reality of extinction."[88] When thought binds itself to contradiction by thinking of its impossibility, it "achieves a binding of extinction," which is to say that thought succeeds, in Freud's words, at "transforming . . . hysterical misery into common unhappiness."[89] This transformation only happens at the end of thought, where and when it self-destructs. The "adequation" of thought to the end "constitutes the truth of extinction," Brassier writes.

"But," Brassier crucially amends, "to acknowledge this truth, the subject of philosophy," or film, or ecology, "must also recognize that he or she is already dead, and that philosophy," or film, or ecology, "is neither a medium of affirmation nor a source of justification, but rather the organon of extinction."[90] The promise of both philosophy and Freudian psychoanalysis is not to reconcile thought with the whole (of narrative, of space and time) but to reconcile thought with the hole (of narrative, of space and time). That reconciliation, that kairetic moment, is the quilting point from which we determine that time stops, and we live with the consequences thereof. At the end of *Bhopal Express*, time stops for Verma; he is out of time. Before the train arrives again, viewers were left to endure mere chronicity, with one thing, one blind event, leading to the next. One breath, one death, after another. Tick-*tock*.

Hurley contends that apocalyptic imaginaries are, at least in the twentieth century, planned endings; that is, the "infrastructures of apocalypse" produce the fearful ends that films like *Bhopal Express* and *Minari* capture, all the while obscuring the structural causes that make apocalypse ordinary and mundane.[91] Hurley turns to narratives that "defamiliarize the present, estranging us from the everyday world that we inhabit in the idea that it is nonnuclear and nonapocalyptic and revealing the most quotidian elements of our everyday lives—the highways, the air travel, the industrially produced food, the toxic environments, the daily roster of species extinctions—to be saturated with nuclear logics, an apocalypse in progress."[92] The present, Hurley shows, is an apocalypse in the making. This argument, however persuasive, thinks in terms of narrative progress. It uses one sequential chain (narrative defamiliarization) to postpone another sequential chain (nuclear apocalypse). But is one progressive outcome truly perturbed by another progressive outcome? We take apocalypse—the end of sense and purpose—as a fait accompli. The end is irreversible. What is reversible, however, is the meaning accorded to that end and the progressive chain tying us to it.

From the start, *Bhopal Express* has patiently bound the viewer to the end, enabling us to relive a trauma that, for Verma and thinkers of the accident, happens; the event befalls. But *Bhopal Express* is not interested in the ontology of the accident;[93] it is concerned, formally speaking, with the ontology of the recalcitrant—how, in other words, to think the repetition compulsion, the subject's innermost derailment, as the only possible brake in what is otherwise a series of chronic accidents emblematized by the train's unyielding movement. How might we brake not apocalypse per se but life's deadly causation, even if it means breaking or cracking up formally and subjectively? From the vantage point of the end, the past looks less determinative, less sequential and meaningful, and the totality of our polluted planet less totalizing, since these determinates cannot account for the acausality of a negative life that appears in the oscillation and fulguration of a non sequitur disrupting from within, devoid of cause or sequence.

What *Minari* formalizes through the non-sequential cut, *Bhopal Express* formalizes through dilation. When the dilatory narrative reaches its destination in chromosomal damage, a peculiar thing happens: Verma lives. Not only that, but Verma and his wife Tara, whom he finds sheltered in a telephone booth (the one place where the teleology of chemical death does not telegraph), live on together. They find each other at the end, in a landscape strewn with corpses. The film does not bother to explain their strange persistence. It hyperbolizes their existence by granting them a child. Soon after reuniting, they find a baby nursing at the breast of its dead mother (figure 36). A visual reminder of the end of *Tampopo*, the breastfeeding child feasts on the mother with vampiric tenacity. As we saw in the first chapter, for Laplanche, the child at the breast de-links sexuality from vitality and spins off sexual fantasies with no vital connection to the material world. *Bhopal Express* goes further, de-linking vitality from life. The vampiric child affixed to the corpsified breast, feeding on chemical death, registers a "surplus vitality,"[94] one that is, in Lacan's words, "indestructible" because it embodies the contradictory and parasitic life of the drive: dead on arrival, but ongoing.[95]

36

It is not clear that *Bhopal Express* intends to end as a horror film, but intention, we know from Mathai's formal severing, is beside the point. The family persists but in a deracinated form, feeding and destroying itself, polluting sense with ab-sense (figure 37). The family's supernatural absurdity exceeds our ability or energy to queer it, abolish it, or redeem it, queering, abolishing, and redeeming all being in their own way progressive projects. Before us is another relapse to the family unit. Whereas in *The Wall*, whose source material was received as a tale of nuclear apocalypse in post-World War II Austria, the wall shields its protagonist from radiation, in *Bhopal Express* the couple and family guarantee no refuge from MIC. Humanity is depleted in one case and zombified in the other. Would not a more radical ending to *Bhopal Express* remain faithful to the event's detonation of the heterosexual family as the *point de capiton* of environmental catastrophe? Perhaps. And yet Mathai's film, like Chung's, remains faithful to the contradiction of the ending, all endings.[96] Mathai severs the formal repetitions of the drive from the forward movement of desire—a cut it enacts through contradiction. Negativity cuts in at the exact moment when the status quo divulges that it is already self-external: negative life.

37

Verma, Tara, and the vampiric adoptee they name Bashir, after the former plant employee whose rebellion against industrial capitalism couldn't protect him from its fallout, do not escape the fantasy of life's persistence but follow it to its end point, where it becomes otherworldly. They remain faithful to the event in its sickly achronicity—faithful not as positive embodiments of the event's radical design, as Badiou would have it, but as negative embodiments of the gap in every design. That the films discussed in this chapter feature immigrant, subaltern, racialized, urban or rural, and working-class families, rather than the white, middle-class, suburban unit we have come to associate with ideological resolution, casts the characters' drive to repeat the trauma at the end as itself a type of fidelity to the event. The return of the repressed keeps the traumatic event alive by confronting viewers with the obscene enjoyment of life's ongoingness—life, that is, as it is preserved and casualized, sustained and extinguished; life as it goes on and on in the pages of ecocriticism, where numerous family arrangements (animal, vegetal, and mineral) spring forth to quilt life's tattered threads in a totalizing pattern of mutual recognition.

The life that lurches forward at the end of *Bhopal Express* is retroactive in the precise sense that it causes us to see the past not as a flowing continuum but as a dehisced or divided middle. The contradiction of the end, when the survivors are living dead, causes us to see that we are dead, too. The challenge posed by Chung's and Mathai's films and their two agrarian and supernatural versions of the absurd is to take the remainder, or the return to the status quo, as the most traumatic point of each film. It is a traumatic point because it causes the past, and thus every linear narrative of life's progressive flowering, to rupture. The cinema of extinction makes reproductive futurism comfortable only when it bends backward.

[INTERLUDE]

The Horror of Entanglement II

Antichrist, Lamb, X

THE PHILOSOPHER AND THE VOICE

In *The World Viewed* and related studies, including *Pursuits of Happiness* and *Contesting Tears*, Stanley Cavell returns to the problem of skepticism by investigating the visual and auditory means by which film represents the world to us. Cavell restages the skeptic's problem of philosophical doubt as a theatrical confrontation between, on the one hand, the world of vision and, on the other, the world of sound, which he identifies as a lost world occupied by madness, melancholia—and, notably, women.

Women embody the melodramatic mode in Cavell's theater of philosophy. Giving voice to a world that no one will hear marks "evidently a mad state," one that "seems to be reserved for the women of the opera."[1] Because sound communicates that "we may leap, as it were, from a judgment of the world as unreal, or alien, to an encompassing sense of another realm flush with this one, into which there is no good reason we do not or cannot step," Cavell contends that "singing, . . . above all the aria, [expresses] the sense of being pressed or stretched between worlds—one in which to be seen, the roughly familiar world of the philosophers, and one from which to be heard, one to which one releases or abandons one's spirit, and which recedes when the breath of the song ends."[2] Within this Orphic economy of loss and redemption, the aria hovers between the finality of reason (the "loss of the world" under skepticism) and the quest for spiritual reunion (the romantic's wish for unity and coherence).[3]

Melodrama, for Cavell, designates this state of suspense, which hovers, as does the aria in opera, between comedy—the mode of reconciliation—and tragedy. Cavell maps "Kant's vision of the human being as living in two worlds" onto roughly the "two general matching interpretations of the expressive capacity of song: ecstasy over the absolute success of its expressiveness in recalling the world, as if bringing it back to life; melancholia over its inability to sustain the world, which may be put as an expression of the absolute inexpressiveness of the voice, of its failure to make itself heard, to become intelligible."[4]

The significance of voice in opera and film is that it links the two worlds separated by skepticism even in its failure to do so. In *The World Viewed*, Cavell observes that

> it is the nature of hearing that what is heard comes *from* someplace, whereas what you can see you can look *at*. It is why sounds are warnings, or calls; it is why our access to another world is normally through voices from it; and why a man can be spoken to by God and survive, but not if he sees God, in which case he is no longer in *this* world. . . . Yet this seems, ontologically, to be what is happening when we look at a photograph: we see things that are not present.[5]

Cavell's belief in the fidelity of sound bears a striking resemblance to the relationship between Echo and Narcissus in Ovid's *Metamorphoses*; in fact, Cavell will often refer to the theatricalization of sound in opera and film as an act of metamorphosis, typically performed by women. In that story, Echo is tasked with repeating the young boy Narcissus, who, like the philosopher, cannot see beyond the remit of his senses. Everywhere Narcissus looks, he sees only himself. Derrida reads this Ovidian episode as an allegory of a democracy to come, in which Echo "lets be heard [*laisse alors entendre*] by whoever wants to hear it, by whoever might love hearing it, something other than what she seems to be saying."[6] Echo's repetition of "Come!" "Come!" lies at the "intersection of repetition and the unforeseeable"; her fidelity to Narcissistic words returns in the form of the unknowable, "and this fidelity, always trembling, risky, would be faithful not only to what is called the past," Derrida argues, but "to what remains to come and has yet neither date nor figure."[7] Cavell's interest in sound resembles Derrida's interest in the "risky" nature of the "unforeseeable" (the *to come*), which both thinkers deem necessary to the democratization of reason by sexual difference. Sound for Cavell "comes *from* someplace," that is, from "another world"; it is a world occupied by women. This world can be accessed or heard only at the risk of a "spiritual derangement" to which Adriana Cavarero also alludes when she equates Echo's "revocalization" with "desemanticization."[8]

If opera reserved the "mad state" for women, it is because women, according to Cavell, represent "that philosophical self-torment whose shape is skepticism," in which the desire "to become intelligible, expressive, [and] exposed" competes with "the absolute inexpressiveness of the voice, of its failure to make itself heard, to become intelligible."[9] Cavell suggests that what distinguishes the "comedy of remarriage" from the "melodrama of the unknown woman" is precisely this willingness on the part of the protagonists to converse, that is, to transform what is unknown about themselves (their privacy and isolation) into something known.

The play on knowing as a sexual innuendo is not accidental to Cavell's project. In *Pursuits of Happiness* and *Contesting Tears*, Cavell maps the fragile "*connection* between a photograph and what it is a photograph of" sustained by film, the medium, onto the scene of marriage.[10] In each film, the question for Cavell is whether or not a married couple will "face the music" of their separation through *re*marriage. "Remarriage comedies begin or climax with the threatened end of a marriage," Cavell writes, "that is to say, with the threat of divorce; the drive of the narrative is to get the original pair together *again*."[11] What defines marriage in Cavell's reading is nothing other than the conversation that exists or fails to exist between a man and woman.[12] The comedy of remarriage stages or theatricalizes the private self's isolation via the breakdown and reconstitution of the married couple's conversation. The exaggerated emotion contained in these films thus represents the woman's struggle to make what is unknown about her desires known again. Just as the philosopher, under skepticism, is tormented by the world's silence, the comedy of remarriage is tormented by the silence or incommunication of the married couple. This genre responds to the problem of radical doubt, reimagined here as the problem of the heteronormative couple, by translating sound and fury—the stuff of melodrama—into intelligible conversation.

In the final, dense pages of the introduction to *Contesting Tears*, Cavell asserts: "I am led to stress the condition that I find to precede, to ground the possibility and the necessity of, 'the desire to express all,' namely the terror of absolute inexpressiveness, suffocation, which at the same time reveals itself as a terror of absolute expressiveness, unconditioned exposure; they are the extreme states of voicelessness."[13] Absolute expression and absolute inexpression represent the extreme states of the woman's voice in opera; in film, they are the conditions of melodrama. We allude to melodrama now, but shall defer the bulk of our investigation into this mode until the next chapter, *Negative Life*'s last.

We witnessed in the preceding interlude and chapter a heteroromantic and heterosexual unit made weird by ecologies that, by entangling all, apotheosize relation as a horrifying totality. *In the Earth* reveals the fungal network beneath our feet, where thinking, feeling, playing, and resource-swapping organize life. A documentary feature like Louie Schwartzberg's *Fantastic Fungi* (2019) represents the fungal brain as our next of kin: a companion, and a teacher. The mycorrhizal ground is, to Eduardo Kohn and many other ecocritics, a massive, supercomputing intelligence covering the Earth, calling us to expansive belonging-with the more-than-human *everything*.[14] The mycorrhizal summons, in Cavellian terms, invites reunion. *In the Earth*, by contrast, estranges the couple and renders relation horrifying, as do *Minari* and, to even a greater degree, *Annihilation* and *Bhopal Express*. The latter film, we saw, inscribes chemical disaster into the chromosomal ongoingness of the family form. The horror of entanglement aligns neither with the comedy of remarriage nor, as we shall see, with the melodrama of the unknown woman, for, in it, conversation yields no conversion.

HORROR KNOWING

Although an object-oriented ontologist (OOO) such as Timothy Morton would no doubt fault Cavell for believing that "meaning is only possible between a human mind and what it thinks"—the belief known in OOO as "correlationism"—both Morton and Cavell share an interest in the object's capacity to withdraw from human relation.[15] Morton follows Graham Harman in positing a strange world in which all objects are essentially withdrawn: "Around 1900 Edmund Husserl discovered something strange about objects," Morton remarks; "No matter how many times you turned around a coin, you never saw the other side as the other side."[16] The withdrawn object provides a strange confirmation of the Kantian two-world paradigm, which Cavell associates with skepticism. What separates Morton from Cavell is that the latter seeks ways, evidenced in the remarriage comedy, of repairing the gap created by skepticism between the phenomenon and the thing. In contrast, the former seeks to de-anthropomorphize this gap by replicating it at every level. For the object-oriented ontologist, objects relate to other objects in the same way that humans relate to objects; all objects are subterranean, that is, withdrawn from their relations to other objects. "It is Kant who shows," Morton notes, "that things never coincide with their phenomena. All we need to do is extend this revolutionary insight beyond the human-world gap. . . . . We are not going to try to bust through human finitude, but to place that finitude in a universe of trillions of finitudes, as many as there are things—because a thing is just a rift between what it is and how it appears, for any entity whatsoever, not simply that special entity called the (human) subject."[17]

For Morton and Harman, the way out of correlationism, or the privileging of the human-world gap, is not so much to transcend this gap as to multiply the distance between things at every scale of existence. The idea that strikes terror in the heart of the skeptic in Cavell's philosophy—the idea that we are all isolated and withdrawn from our relations—becomes a salutary condition in object-oriented ontology, insofar as the object's isolation names the very way things are, all things whatsoever. According to OOO, the real problem of existence is not how to remarry phenomenon and thing, but how two things—essentially unknown to one another because they are withdrawn—can ever relate in the first place. How can one substantial thing call unto another substantial thing? Despite their methodological differences, Cavell and Morton see the gap between things as fundamental to post-Kantian thought. Formulated in Cavellian terms, OOO's response to skepticism is not to overturn it but to theatricalize its structure. OOO would thus prove to be yet another version of melodrama.

The unknown woman of melodrama and the unknown object of correlationism are horrifying, Cavell and OOO argue, because they testify to a limit, one requiring education and conversion through sexual difference, the other the dethroning of human mastery. But Morton is more sanguine about this limit: they, like Cavell, assume that the desire to know is fundamental to human subjectivity and that the limit posed by the shy object curbs human mastery. The will to knowledge and the will to power are crucial to Cavell's and Morton's respective views of human subjectivity, and only an aesthetic reeducation of and by women (Cavell) or objects (Morton) can check the post-Kantian subject's horrifying will to know.

In the ecohorror that scales up and down between the totalizing sexual couple and ecological totality, we recognize no such desire to know. We recognize only "a horror of knowing," rather than a "desire for knowledge," after Lacan, who theorizes the subject not as a subject of knowledge but as a subject of desire.[18] According to Lacan, desire, rather than knowledge, is horrifying because it confronts the subject with an internal limit or X factor. We desire to know in order to avoid knowing the X that Lacan calls *jouissance*, or unconscious repetition. This X factor is not an ordinary limit mappable onto Hollywood gender norms, nor is it ethical in the sense suggested by OOO, which imagines a flat ontology where hierarchy is obliterated. The limit theorized by Lacan thwarts intersubjective and interspecies progress and feeds unconscious repetition in ways that cut against self-interest. Power, from this perspective, is not the problem—apologies to Nietzsche, Adorno, Heidegger, and Foucault. Enjoyment is. There is both too much and too little enjoyment in ecohorror, specifically in Lars von Trier's *Antichrist* (2009), Valdimar Jóhannsson's *Lamb* (2021), and Ti West's *X* (2022).

What links these examples is the horror of knowing the X factor from which ecocriticism retreats as it instead chooses the neutered landscape of flat ontology, the domestic space of heterosexual reunion, or both. Here, the lessons imparted by Cavell's film philosophy and OOO's withdrawn object falter. Neither reunion nor divorce, totality nor multiplicity, can explain the outcomes of these films, which are horrifying because they extrude something that ex-sists, or exits, the ecological couple. They extrude the −1, negative life, that surfaces in *Antichrist* and in *Lamb* as sodomy, or something like it: an alignment of adult orgasm with child suicide that in turn dislocates reproductive futurism from marital sex in the first case, and the displacement of reproductive futurism onto an extramarital scene of bestiality in the second. In the less inhibited *X*, negative life shows up as the undead life of the drive, the proverbial X factor. These films tease the happy ending exemplified by the sexual couple in nature—not subtracted from an urban crowd but excessive to its fertile environs—in order to expose the obscene enjoyment that subtends it.

THE SODOMITIC UNIT: *ANTICHRIST* AND *LAMB*

In "Acts against Nature," Elizabeth A. Wilson positions "the negativity and inhumanity that queer theorists such as Leo Bersani, Lee Edelman, and Jonathan Goldberg have so lovingly exhumed from sodomy" against new materialist readings of nature or biology that we might call, in the nomenclature proper to our study, "pastoralizing."[19] In insisting on nature's inherent perversity, Karen Barad makes sodomy an act of nature rather than one against nature. Rather than threatening all social order, sodomy thereby authorizes a better one, opening onto an ethics of "connections and commitments."[20] Wilson doubts that nature can be, so straightforwardly, "an ally for progressive sexual politics."[21] As she reminds us in terms we have echoed throughout *Negative Life*, "the capacity to productively reconfigure and rework is constituted through violations that make the ground on which political and conceptual and ethical claims are made perpetually uncertain, and fundamentally negative. The vicissitudes of sodomy will always spoil our capacity to do good with nature and to do good by nature."[22] *Antichrist* and *Lamb* prove Wilson right by representing whatever comes after sodomy as unsustainable. Sodomy deflagrates the pastoral landscape, exhausts life, however committed characters may be to connecting in its wake.

Recent accounts of sodomy in queer studies have excavated its capitalist and colonial histories. Christopher Chitty and Andil Gosine have both described anti-sodomy legislation, one dimension of the regulation of sexuality, as an instrument of capital accumulation, bourgeois rule, and colonial domination. Legislating the practice proved necessary to hegemony, Chitty explains, because sodomy cultures, in their cross-class pollination and public-private indistinction, challenged republican experiments.[23] Gosine, for his part, observes that a sodomitic imaginary separating the sexual practices that make one human from those that make one animal—or that involve animals—provided one framework, the pathologization of Indigeneity, for the civilizational enterprise.[24] Whereas Chitty concerns himself primarily with male homosexual practices in the major cities of Renaissance Europe and Gosine with a range of practices, including those that fall under the rubric of bestiality, they agree that sodomy is made to stand in, metonymically, for nonreproductive sex and the danger it poses to sociopolitical coherence. *Antichrist* and *Lamb* dramatize the repression of sodomy integral to white fantasies of order and progress that, here, take the form of marital healing and familial inheritance. In these films, the fact of sexual transgression is not spoken, not for a while at least, but it is known. Repression achieves no suppression. The pastoral of white, heterosexual domesticity eventually collapses onto sodomitic foundations that were always exposed anyway.

Antichrist and *Lamb* begin with evidence of sexual transgression. Von Trier, ever the miserabilist, opens his film in an operatic mode, with a black-and-white, slow-motion sequence of child suicide—or is it infanticide?—set to Handel's "Lascia ch'io pianga" (in English: "Let me weep"). A woman (Charlotte Gainsbourg, to whom the credits refer as "She") and a man (Willem Dafoe, "He") are having sex, first in the shower, then on a washing machine, then in bed; they knock multiple objects over on their way from one location to another. Their young child Nic (Storm Acheche Sahlstrøm) wakes up, gazes at his parents, and walks in the opposite direction, a faint smile visible on his face. He clears the contents of a desk, climbs onto it, and jumps out the window, holding on to his stuffed bear, then letting go of it. The boy and his inanimate pet fall slightly faster than the large snowflakes populating the frame. Gainsbourg's character appears to orgasm, followed by Dafoe's, whose face was largely concealed until now.

The jump cuts enforce causality, with Nic's death leading to the orgasm; it is implied that she's reacting to Nic's movement and noise. We're thus made to interpret the sequence not as an example of dialectical montage but as a narrative insistence on the debt pleasure owes to death. The orgasm is authorized by the child-to-leave, instead of the child-to-come. We will later learn that, having internalized the literature on witch hunts and other instances of gynocide to which her abandoned thesis research had pertained, she previously harmed Nic by repeatedly forcing him to wear the wrong shoe on each foot. But the revelation is redundant: the opening scene's editing has already ascertained her guilt. *His* guilt, Dafoe's character's, is more ambiguous. Von Trier has never given male interiority much thought. In his films, men make women suffer, or watch them suffer. The female leads have reported a similar dynamic on set.

One of *Antichrist*'s compositional registers is the genital grotesque. In the prologue, Dafoe's character's erect penis penetrates Gainsbourg's character's vagina—again, in slow motion. She will attempt to return to the scene of penetration on multiple occasions, amid episodes of acute panic. When she grabs her husband's sex and directs it toward her own, she isn't quite seeking relief from grief; we are instead dared to interpret the gesture as a bid to relive the sadism of letting Nic die. For a while, he resists her advances, for intercourse would interfere with the patient-therapist configuration that he is determined to impose at a remote cottage within a Washington forest nicknamed Eden. When the exposure therapy goes south—which is to say, when she fails the ecocritical test, once exposed to nature, of converting her ecophobia (her fear of "the woods") into ecophilia (Eden)—she smashes a block of wood into his groin before she masturbates him, and he ejaculates blood. She later mutilates her own clitoris using a large pair of rusty scissors. Genitality demarcates the terrain on which the drama of heterosexual aggression and dissolution plays out. What makes sodomy a relevant analytic is the "misuse" of the sexual organs, which renders all sex explicitly morbid. Even in the prologue, before sperm is traded for blood, sex appears nonreproductive, for the orgasm enjoys greater proximity to child mortality than it does to childbirth (the *petite mort* coincides with the *mort du petit*).

A birthing scene happens early in *Lamb*, but not before a breathing scene. The camera adopts the perspective of an entity whose loud respiration sounds not quite human, yet not entirely animal. Late on a snowy day in rural Iceland, the entity walks toward a barn, spooking a herd of horses. The entity, it is suggested, is the bipodal ram-man hybrid who will return at the end of the film to seize the similarly bipodal child-lamb hybrid that our central couple, María (Noomi Rapace) and Ingvar (Hilmir Snær Guðnason), have been raising as their own. The entity likely fathered the infant María and Ingvar name Ada, after the human daughter they have lost. It remains a possibility, however, that the entity starts haunting the family after Ingvar impregnates the sheep that will give birth to Ada. In any case, however tempting an explanation the Christmas carols and twinkle lights make immaculate conception, the existence of any of the hybrid beings indicates that bestiality has happened. Proof of bestiality, whether it took place recently or one generation ago, lives and breathes in the domestic sphere. Sodomy brings together a couple who, before Ada's delivery, seemed estranged. Although it takes Ingvar a while to warm up to the infant, the arrival and subsequent expulsion of his troublemaking brother Pétur (Björn Hlynur Haraldsson), with whom María previously had a proto-incestuous affair, solidifies the marital unit, for a while.

Evidence of sodomy doubles as the horror of entanglement: a terrible hybridity that María and Ingvar, like good, future-oriented ecocritics, commit to loving, and do so successfully largely because they see themselves, or the better parts of themselves, in the mirror that this hybrid figure holds up. Much of *Lamb* plays out as a comedy of manners—*My Fair Lady* for the zoological enthusiast—in which María and Ingvar raise Ada in their image. Whereas in *Antichrist* the child's death causes the couple to spiral, in *Lamb* María and Ingvar simply recast with a not-quite-human understudy the role of the child they lost under circumstances about which we know nothing. Each adult personifies the want-to-be, eager to dress up life's lack. Inhabiting humanity, here, has to do with recognizing oneself naked without a second coat of wool in the form of a knitted Nordic sweater. Like *First Cow*'s Lu and Cookie, María and Ingvar play house, but here the stakes are higher: everything, from a meal to an impromptu dance party, has to feel like the most natural thing in the world.

In typical ecohorror fashion, the ending of *Lamb* inflicts the punishment, or collects the price that must be paid, for the enjoyment of transgression. It is not the case that nature takes back what it is owed: the ram-man hybrid, although nude, is unnatural, for he is able to pull a firearm's trigger. The scene in which the entity shoots and kills Ingvar is a callback to others. Most obviously, the scene mirrors another in which Pétur walks away from the house with a rifle in one hand and Ada's hand in the other (figure 38). Pétur decides against shooting Ada, and for their next outing takes her fishing, ratifying not just her domesticity but her humanity (figure 39). Unlike the family's cat, for instance, she must use tools to fish. The murder scene also reverses an earlier one in which María shoots and kills Ada's birth mother, the former driven to agony by the latter's baaing. In the film's final minutes, María embraces her deceased husband before standing up and, in turn, miming death. She closes her tear-filled eyes, looks up, and draws a labored breath that sounds like a swan song. *Lamb*, like *In the Earth* and *Annihilation*, concludes by subtracting human beings from processes of hybridization.

38

39

In *Antichrist*, too, a major character dies, though not at the hands of some extra-human entity. Dafoe's character, partially dismembered, strangles Gainsbourg's before dumping her corpse onto a pile of branches, dousing it in oil, and setting it on fire. The strangulation is unbearably long and graphic. The immolation that follows, though, happens in just a few seconds, as if fast-forwarded. The murder fulfills the gynocidal prophecy to which Gainsbourg's character came to subscribe. She inferred from the feeling of the ground burning that nature was evil (it is "Satan's church" because "it is everything," she once says, echoing *In the Earth*'s Alma) and that women, who are of nature, were evil as well.

Antichrist accumulates quasi-biblical signs of nature's evil: acorns that pelt the metal roof and keep "falling, and falling, and dying, and dying"; swollen ticks that cover Dafoe's character's hand like pustules one morning; a self-disemboweling red fox that warns him, "Chaos reigns"; a stillborn deer attached to its galloping mother's birth canal; and so on. This iconography doesn't substantiate a woman-nature equivalence per se, but Gainsbourg's character avers one. When given the choice between two systems of interpretation, two symbolic orders against which to test reality, she favors a misogynistic theology over medical models of grief pathology and female hysteria, which are also misogynistic.

An epilogue follows the immolation of Gainsbourg's character. It is, like the prologue, a black-and-white, slow-motion sequence set to Handel's "Lascia ch'io pianga." Dafoe's character limps toward the top of a mountain, accompanied by hundreds of docile, nude, faceless women (figure 40). It is hard to receive the ending as anything other than a farce about the masculinist triumph of scientific rationality over the dangers of nature. When entanglement becomes too horrific, the cynical punchline goes, there is always—for the white, bourgeois, American, heterosexual, male character—mastery. The succession of Edenic fall and ascent confirms that neither exposure therapy nor talk therapy could repair the marriage and, in Cavellian terms, the integrity of the worlds inhabited by its members. There can be no pedagogy of reunion in *Antichrist* or *Lamb* because sodomy teaches nothing, and it wasn't hidden well enough to begin with. The next section flips this script by turning to a film whose very title functions as a placeholder for that which it vows never to reveal.

40

WHERE HORROR MEETS SEX: *X*

We terminate our series on ecohorror with *X* not because it is an obvious example of nature cinema—though it does feature a predatory animal within a Gothic landscape—but because it slashes its way *out* of this cinema. The infanticidal orgasm we saw in *Antichrist* returns in the homicidal *jouissance* of *X*. Whereas Cavell's film philosophy tries to give voice to the X factor, and ecocriticism tries to entangle it to the point of suffocation, West's film enables the X to contaminate the voice and, with it, the sexual relation. The film *X* is horrifying because it refuses sexual complementarity.

What makes *X* an ecohorror movie to a genre theorist is its citation of 1970s horror films' own citations of Southern Gothic tropes. In *X*, grotesque, elderly characters display transgressive impulses and dark humor in a setting where nature proves lethal; for instance, an alligator spies on one character and devours another. Tropes like this one are filtered through 1970s slasher films, especially *The Texas Chainsaw Massacre* (1974), *X*'s closest kin.[25] *X*'s aesthetic throwback earns its retro status—its status as self-reflexive rather than merely imitative or kitsch—through its association with A24, a production and distribution company celebrated for a prestige horror catalog that also includes *Lamb*. What, for us, ties *X* to the ecohorror form is more significantly its absorption of human life into a mathematics of inhuman desire.

The plot of *X* is simple: six adult filmmakers go to a farm in rural Texas in 1979 to shoot a sex film, where they are terrorized by their homicidal hosts: an old man, Howard (Stephen Ure), and an old woman, Pearl (Mia Goth). Howard, we learn, is unable to satisfy his wife's, Pearl's, sexual urges due to a heart condition. Pearl satisfies her sexual appetite any way she can, if not through coitus, then through murder (repeated stabbings and a pitchfork through the eyes of her victim will do just fine). By refusing to pastoralize sex, *X* refuses an easy temptation: seeing pornography as a denatured intimacy. Instead, the film denatures sexual intimacy and, with it, the pastoral setting.[26]

The film is, perversely, sex-positive: the old man and woman who haunt the frame, whose bodies would be the reanimated flesh or the zombified undead in a lesser horror film, are, in the end, sexual beings, and terrifying for that reason. They are not frightening because they possess supernatural abilities or traffic in the tropes of ageism and ableism. They instead are frightening because they put the spectator in the position of the drive with its unyielding, age-defying persistence. While all else ages, mortifies, rots, and dies, the drive is eternal; in Mari Ruti's words, it is the "immortal within."[27] *X* does not frighten viewers with deathly figures intent on robbing life of sexual pleasure; it frightens viewers with deathly figures who are petrified by sexual pleasure.

At the center of the film's gangrenous lust is a young woman, Maxine Minx (also played by Mia Goth), an aspiring porn actress who, all in the film argot, has "the X factor." As the bearer of this X, the negative life that horrifies and attracts others, Maxine is, within the heavy-handed Christian iconography of the film, a pseudo- or porno-Christ: the final shot is of Maxine fleeing the scene of the massacre in a truck, silhouetted by the dark cabin interior, driving with a crucifix dangling from the rearview mirror. The crucifix appears to levitate (figure 41), at once elevated and debased, martyred and worshiped. Maxine is preyed upon because of the X; she also survives because of it, because of the "something more" in her that triggers others' desire—and their horror.

41

Maxine moves through the film like a walking partial-object: breasts half-exposed by overalls; body and voice mutilated and recomposed by the pornographic film within the film; aroused breathing abstracted from Maxine's body and repeated rhythmically, hauntingly, as the film's score. Maxine examines her freckled face in the mirror at the film's start as she says to her imaginary double: "You are a fucking sex symbol." She is. But as a sex symbol, Maxine symbolizes more (>) and less (<) than a sex *object*; she symbolizes the object-X, the inscrutable void that does not appear on screen, that appears only absently in a vacant image or sound, *the partial object*, partial because it echoes the subject's initial self-sacrifice and the emergence of the phantasmatic X.

At a critical juncture, the porno filmmakers' film within the film gets underway, and Maxine rides cowgirl for the camera, her back facing the cabin room's window. The filmmakers had chosen the rural location for its isolation, privacy, and the rustic thematics it could lend their porno film's thin plot and shoestring budget; they also chose it for the transgressive thrill of sinning in God's country. Still, they are discreet, not wanting to upset their conservative hosts. Howard warns them to keep their distance. He does not explain why, leaving it to the pornographers' and our imagination. It is not, however, the farmers' delicate sensibility or Christian morality they risk treading on. It is instead the horror of an abyssal lack that Maxine and others awaken in Pearl.

As Maxine undulates for the camera, all eyes fixate on her, including Pearl's. Pearl has been stalking Maxine up to this point and now peers through the cabin window at the object-cause of her desire (figure 42).

Beyond fetishistic spectatorship, beyond the male gaze, or, more potent still, the rape of the pornographic eye, as Andrea Dworkin puts it,[28] there is, *X* shows, the unmasterable and masochistic absence that Maxine gives her audience to enjoy, and horror at, unknowingly. Maxine has the X factor, but the word "has" is misleading since neither she nor anyone else, for that matter, can truly possess it; what arouses her spectators is the masochistic thrill of repeating the sacrificial act that inaugurated their sexual and subjective life, the sacrifice, namely, of the X (*objet a*). Sacrifice, not mastery, and loss, not possession, typify sexuality in *X* and make sex the true object of horror, for the X severs sex from sense, compassion, tenderness, or rapport. Howard and Pearl will stop at nothing to get the X, and murder serves their lust just as well. What is a bloodied corpse, if not the partial object par excellence? In this sense, the film *X* performs the horror version of psychoanalytic ethics, at least as it is adumbrated in Lacan's *Seminar VII* via the story of Antigone, who attaches herself to her brother's mutilated corpse and acts on behalf of the sacrificial body, the object-cause of her militancy.[29] In *X*, the mutilated corpse serves no higher function than the repetition of loss, and each blood-soaked kill is the murderer's encounter with the immortal within.

42

And yet frenzied gore is not all we get. Like the Christ-event in Badiou's *Saint Paul*, Maxine's evental sex scene divides along two axes: there is the body before the spectator, and there is the purified, senseless, and disembodied event that bequeaths to all not the Holy Kingdom but a different kind of eternity: the object-X. This is the *fabular* element in the pornographic scene.[30] Unlike Saint Paul's fabulation, "Christ is resurrected," Maxine raises the sexualized body not once but repeatedly to the dignity of the Thing, with each thrust and each pendulation of the body disclosing the transcendental X that the clap of bodies disincarnates for the eroticized spectator. In fact, the sex is brief. What lasts is the X, primarily as it—the X as point of subtraction—inheres in sound.

As Pearl watches Maxine from outside the cabin window, a distortional element occurs, delaying, modulating, and misaligning sound and image. The voice, including the moan and breath emanating from Maxine's throat, disconnects, taking on a life of its own relative to the image. It becomes objectile, though it has no substance of its own. The film automates Maxine's voice into an orgasmic murmur that replays throughout. But the voice itself has no connection to the screened body, sexual experience, or the material reality of the film. The voice-object exsists bodies, experience, and the material reality of the film.[31] This irreal element, diegetically unlocatable, physically unobtainable, obtrudes in the film and, worse still, in the desire of Pearl, whose spectatorial position the film viewer inhabits. The eruption of the object-X as an invocatory, repetitious sound implicates the spectator's desire *in* the image, thus denying the spectator any safe distance from which to master the sexual scene. Horror, according to *X*, is the affective correlate of our involvement in a scene that entangles us not with "bodies and their pleasures"[32] but, more importantly, with bodies and X: the voice-object. Because the latter is torn from place and person, it can function as a sacrificial object, an acoustic object, and a reminder of the primordial objects sacrificed at the subject's entry into language. The voice-object is the phantasmatic echo of the lost invocatory object that Lacan contends we sacrifice, that we indeed must sacrifice, at the dawn of subjectivity as we relinquish the nonsense of sound and the *jouissance* of *lalangue* (a mixture of sound and libido) for the order of symbolic meaning.[33] Looking over Pearl's shoulder as she pays fidelity to the special X that Maxine reveals, we become, like the geriatric voyeur, spectatorial embodiments of the death drive's recursive, unstoppable, and satisfyingly unsatisfiable return to nothing.

X outlines four basic procedures one can adopt in relation to the unknowable X factor. It does so with a butcher's eye for detail, cleaving each scene with ruthless accuracy but never arriving at the X—the impossible object that inhabits the film, the lover, and the dismembered corpse. There will be, interspersed with the carnage, or coextensive with it, a good deal of sex. The film delineates bodies into partial objects—breast, gaze, voice—sometimes in parallel with the murder spree, sometimes as one and the same. For instance, a knife wound to the chest and a burst of blood against an adjacent car headlight mimic, or instead become, as in *Antichrist*, the money shot, the signature release of the pornographic "frenzy of the visible," in Linda Williams's words, registered in sanguinary showers (figure 43).[34] There will be blood, bone, sex, and death, but there will never be the X factor. The film can isolate the mouth, neck, and chest; the killer can uproot the lungs from the chest, splay them out, or cut them into bits; and the pornographer can reproduce the moan, heavy breathing, and ecstatic purr of sex, but no one, neither the lover nor the madman nor the artist, can capture the X. It, the X, is akin to Kant's "object = *X*," but is worse, far worse, for the X does not inhabit a noumenal beyond;[35] it insists in the diegetic scene while remaining irreducible to it. *X* refuses to make any formal distinction between murder and sex. Both are time-honored ways of re-creating the sacrificial object-X that inaugurates desire.

43

In the film, the object of desire remains enigmatic. Its calling card, the X factor, spurs desire but also makes desire horrifying, its operations of dissection (<, >, ∧, ∨) akin to the vivisections of the murder's knife, which dehisce the body to reveal the beatific X, the trace of loss that ignites the murderer's, and the lover's, flame. As to the question, *What am I for the other?* the answer *X* gives is a horror equivalent to the ethics of the sublime: *less than nothing*.

X formalizes desire as the *desire for less than nothing* and conducts its truth procedures at the zero-degree difference between sex and death. Lacan's formula of desire $<>*a* provides the matrix through which the subject or spectator relates to the object-X. The formula is simple: barred subject + diamond + *objet a*. The object-X (*objet a*) is the limit or gap around which the entire sensory spectacle turns. Structurally speaking, the object-X inexists the image, ex-sists sound and sense, yet its absence from all of the above makes all the above possible. One can, consequently, never obtain the X because missing it is integral to sense. With the insertion of this diamond <>, Lacan forbids the complementarity of subject and object and transposes Kant's (and Cavell's and OOO's) outer, noumenal limit *into* the desiring subject. As Lacan formalizes it, desire is internally inhibited by the *objet a*, or the impossible object of desire. The *objet a* is, for Lacan, the object we sacrifice in order to become subjects, but it does not exist before that act of sacrifice. Strangely, we lose the *objet a* into existence by separating from it. We lose it, and in that act of losing, we make it an object of desire.[36]

The *objet a* thus functions as the X factor of desire, orienting our wants, yet also limiting our wants, for it exists only as missing. We must approach it obliquely.[37] *X* formalizes this approach and, in the process, eschews a central cliché of both ecohorror and ecophilosophy: that what frightens spectators most is the encounter with death.[38] *X* downplays being-toward-death. What is truly horrifying, the film theorizes, is being-toward-sex.[39]

The following are *X*'s four formulas for remaining faithful to the X factor—formulas that Badiou, though he would grimace at their nature, would call "truth procedures."[40]

Lesser ($<*a*): a long shot from a second-floor window; Pearl, haggard, looks down at a sprightly Maxine who, sensing the other's stare, looks up at a shadowy figure obscured by curtains. Later, at ground level, Maxine finds herself in the old woman's line of sight and, sensing her prying look, returns the gaze (figure 44).

Greater ($>*a*): a close-up in bed; Maxine sleeps on her side, facing the mattress edge, her back bisecting the middle of the frame; the crepuscular Pearl who had kept her distance before slides into bed next to her, the one a figure of death, the other, a sexual beatitude. Sex and death share a bed, are as close as close can be, and yet they do not share the same frame—the close-up isolates one or the other, but never both. Distant or near, the X escapes (figure 45).

Over ($∧*a*): an aerial view of Maxine swimming out into a lake; on land, she was hunted by the $< and $>; here, in the water, she is hunted by another solitary predator, an alligator. The overhead shot remains static, giving only the surface of the water and the horizontal race between hunter and prey. Maxine swims in a straight line from right to left toward the pier, unaware that the animal is close behind. When she leaps from the water to safety, the geometric contest ends, and so does the $∧. Neither spectator nor beast is any closer to the X (figure 46).

Under ($∨*a*): a ground shot of Maxine, whose special something (the X factor) has spared her a gruesome death; she hides beneath a squelching and undulating mattress. Her pursuer, Pearl, and Pearl's husband, Howard, fuck above her. Pearl wants the X, and Howard, risking heart failure, aims to give it; he dies soon after. We are, at ground level, beneath the murderer's mattress, weighted with the full horror of the sexual. Maxine confronts, from the vantage of the $\$\vee$ she now occupies, the drive in all its horror; the drive as it pursues her, morcellates her, and, in the loving manner unique to the drive, elevates something in her (something more than her) to the status of the X. Maxine discovers, to her horror, not that she is an object for the other's gaze but that she herself contains the gaze, the object-X that triggers the other's bloodstained devotion (figure 47).

44

45

46

47

At a formal level, *X* is not about infernal houses, eerie landscapes, or sex-crazed serial killers, though it offers all of these and more; it is about the formal truth procedures enabled by $<>*a* and the death-driven ethics of remaining faithful to the X. The blood-soaked carnage of *X*, that is, discloses an ethics formalizable in the framing of the sex-event as lesser, greater, over, and under, but never equal to the event as such. Whereas *Antichrist* and *Lamb* introduced yet another set of marital and familial units who made doomed bids to extend normalcy and normativity beyond catastrophe, *X* relays an effort to usher in catastrophe, or cut across totalizing pastorals of sexual and ecological entanglement. An elderly character played by Mia Goth, for instance, tries—and fails, but tries anyway—to kill a young character also played by Goth, putting a slasher spin on *Bhopal Express*'s chromosomal damage and its denial of lineage. The next chapter, *Negative Life*'s last, turns to melodrama proper to consider the implications of refusing the world, or losing it on one's terms, by subtracting oneself from environmental contradictions.

[CHAPTER THREE]

The Queer Impossibility of *First Reformed*

QUEER ECOCIDE

On April 14, 2018, David S. Buckel, a prominent human rights lawyer, gay and trans rights advocate, and environmentalist, doused himself with gasoline and set himself on fire in Brooklyn's Prospect Park. A passerby who saw the smoke reported it to the police as a brushfire.[1] In a 1,276-word letter he had sent to media outlets and left on the scene of his suicide, Buckel drew a parallel between his death and the disastrous impact of fossil fuel dependency. "Pollution," he wrote, "ravages our planet, oozing [un]inhabitability via air, soil, water, and weather. Most humans on the planet now breathe air made unhealthy by fossil fuels, and many die early deaths as a result—my early death by fossil fuels reveals what we are doing to ourselves."[2] Buckel's act did more than spectacularize the impossibility of sustained life in toxifying atmospheres. He sought to detoxify these atmospheres by making his combustion his ultimate carbon emission. He explained: "It may be clear that staying in the world is doing more harm than good. . . . A lifetime of service may be preserved by giving a life."[3] To live, as Buckel noted, is to make waste, and, so too, to lay waste to the worlds we wish to protect. Buckel's deoxygenated remains figured the species extinction they were meant to defer.

On April 23, 2018, nine days after Buckel took his own life, Dennis Dickey, a border patrol agent, ignited a wildfire that spread to the Coronado National Forest in Arizona. Dickey had invited family and friends to a "gender reveal party," a ritual in which expectant parents announce the gender to be assigned to their future child. His plan was to shoot a rifle and hit a target containing Tannerite, a highly explosive substance whose detonation would produce pink or blue powder. The fire that ensued ravaged 47,000 acres.[4]

The first tragedy pertains to a person's death (while evoking mass extinction). The other pertains to an ecosystem's decimation. Both locate queerness in proximity to environmental peril. Buckel's suicide, which according to his husband was inspired by the self-immolation of some Buddhist monks, belongs to a queer genealogy of direct action that frames death as protest.[5] Buckel reduced himself to cinder and ash in public. Similarly, in the 1990s, ACT UP members scattered the ashes of individuals "murdered by AIDS and killed by government neglect" on the White House lawn.[6] Buckel's death also extends a morbid strand of queer theory's antisocial thesis—a strand, developed in part by Lee Edelman, which figures politics from the refusal, and in this case the impossibility, of reproduction and futurity.[7] Buckel's self-annihilation points to a contradiction that environmental politics too often straightens out: that to live today is to accelerate extinction. Queer theory has long recognized that by saving life we work to destroy it. What makes Buckel's action disturbingly timely is the link it draws between queerness and a general intensification of the antisocial thesis by climate change.

Whereas Buckel's immolation merges intentionality and inevitability through the synthesis of individual suicide and species extinction, the Coronado National Forest wildfire highlights the immeasurable environmental cost of flippant acts of destruction. The latter case differently fuses sex and death. Rather than adopting queerness as an orientation toward death, Dickey used lethal explosives to protect the integrity of the gender binary. But his attempt to label a child "naturally" female or male unleashed the queer negativity it had attempted to repress; his turned out to be an "*act against nature*."[8] As the wildfire melodramatized, reproduction kills; each newborn comes with a carbon footprint that threatens the planet. While queer theory's antisocial thesis makes the "*sinthomo*sexual" and the "gay outlaw" exceptional to the demands of reproductive futurity, all the while figuring futurity's inner unraveling, environmental destruction raises the bar considerably.[9] It is now the case that reproductivity, on the Left and the Right, makes life lethal. Whether the Tannerite is pink or blue, the queerness of it all is that, like it or not, we are all standing in the burn-zone—though structural inequalities unevenly distribute the consequences thereof. Narratives of the good (among environmentalists) and narratives of sustainable growth (among conservatives and progressives alike) all collapse under the weight of environmental existence's queer nature. Whereas a previous iteration of queer negativity figured the death drive through an atomistic politics of individual refusal, the intensification of queerness within toxic environments makes unwitting *sinthomo*sexuals of us all. Edelman's "fuck Annie" has become a collective planetary emission.[10]

This chapter concludes our investigation into how queer negativity might help us think, or, more accurately, might confront us with our inability to think, about the experience of environmental destruction. Neel Ahuja claims that "queer theory has always been a theory of extinctions."[11] Ahuja draws an analogy between late-carbon liberalism's parasitic relation to the Earth—a systemic reproduction that elicits destruction—and late-twentieth and early twenty-first-century figurations of queer subjectivity as epiphenomenal to the circulation of HIV/AIDS. Ahuja argues that in the face of extinction, we should de-fetishize the transcendental space of queer negation and instead pay attention to the "casual reproduction of the forms of ecological violence that kill quietly, outside the spectacular time of crisis."[12] In what follows, we attend to public acts that do not fit neatly into either of the temporal categories delineated by Ahuja. These acts of self-destruction, of which Buckel's immolation is exemplary, synchronize, if momentarily, the slow temporality of human extinction with the instantaneous temporality of individual annihilation.

The impossibility of narrative closure brought about by futurity's undesirability or unlikeliness goes by several names in queer theory: from the death drive, to the *jouissance* of narrative incompletion, to queer failure. Chapter 2 tested the idioms of the absurd and the supernatural to come to terms with the continued sale of futurity's iconography past its expiration date. To address a version of the cinema of extinction that does not so much quilt reality as tear it further, we now return to a term brought up in the second interlude: "melodrama." The melodrama that interests us here is not so much that of not-yet-being-known as that of knowing that knowledge doesn't repair or redeem. In *Melodrama: An Aesthetics of Impossibility*, Jonathan Goldberg echoes Gilles Deleuze's description of modern cinema by pointing to a queer "excess" or "Truth" that melodrama makes contradictorily available to the seer: "The bearer of Truth [in melodrama] may insist on the Truth but is nonetheless powerless to make it happen. Rather, Truth must be witnessed and recognized, and thus hailed by the very forces that seek to deny it."[13] This is a time of the seer, not of the agent, says Deleuze, who conceives of time (and cinema) in terms felicitous to our aims here as a "fossilization" of thought by a truth too "intolerable" to be borne.[14] Deleuze characterizes his cinema books as a great "martyrology" of those who have seen but cannot act within the world as constituted.[15] These martyrs embrace annihilation as the only possible act, thus making narrative impossibility the living testimony to lives reduced to ash.

We conclude *Negative Life* by turning to *First Reformed* (2017), written and directed by Paul Schrader, to track the convergence of these melodramatic forces as they bear on characters confronted with the truth of unlivability. The film takes place in the fictional town of Snowbridge, New York, where the protagonist, Reverend Ernst Toller (Ethan Hawke), tends to the First Reformed Church in the months leading up to its 250th-anniversary reconsecration. Abundant Life, a megachurch nearby, is orchestrating the celebration, underwritten by Ed Balq, an oil magnate with an abysmal environmental record. At First Reformed, Toller meets Mary Mensana (Amanda Seyfried), a parishioner, and her husband Michael (Philip Ettinger). Mary is pregnant. Michael, a radical environmentalist who believes that bringing a child into a doomed world is unethical, kills himself and requests that his ashes be scattered at a toxic waste dump later revealed to be tied to Balq Industries. Visibly transformed by Michael's death, Toller plans his own suicide to coincide with the reconsecration. All three protagonists in *First Reformed*—Reverend Toller, Mary, and Michael—self-destruct. Michael commits suicide. Toller puts on a suicide vest, which he replaces with barbed wire. Mary, still pregnant, cuts herself when she passionately embraces Toller. These acts of self-destruction made in the name of environmentalism read as queer: Michael refuses heterosexual reproduction; and Toller and Mary's lacerative embrace makes both romantic and religious passion jarring. Casting reproduction as the ultimate force of destruction, these acts preempt extinction in the name of pushing it away.

First Reformed imagines a queer obliteration of the ego that does not reorganize itself into impersonal kinship. According to Leo Bersani's theory of "homo-ness," in sex, individuals narcissistically extend themselves into the world, misrecognizing difference as "a nonthreatening supplement to sameness."[16] Suddenly in excess of itself, the ego is shattered by its illusory mastery—a process it repeats masochistically. For Edelman, shattering is brought about by the death drive, an urge to return to an inorganic state that opposes forms of social viability.[17] Nicole Seymour proposes that self-shattering and antisociality open out onto a "queer interest in the natural world."[18] "After all," Seymour explains, "a measure of self-renunciation and anti-sociality is central to many if not most forms of environmentalism, including ecocriticism; the renunciation of anthropocentrism and the adoption of biocentric or ecocentric viewpoints are veritable prerequisites for participation in either."[19] Where Seymour sees humility, Edelman and Bersani see an inflated humanism: in the latter's version of queer theory's antisocial thesis, it is in order to find traces of themselves in the world that individuals push themselves beyond their limits and imperil their egos. Taken together, these theories of self-shattering suggest that the humility and narcissism motivating Michael and Toller in *First Reformed* are two sides of the same coin. The characters seek to return to the Earth so as not to encroach on the survival of other species at the same time as they view their planned deaths, megalomaniacally, as emblematic of human extinction.

First Reformed, we propose, stages self-destruction to melodramatize the contemporary intensification of negativity by ordinary toxicity and pollution. Schrader suggests that life amidst climate crisis is configured by what Goldberg, after the filmmaker Douglas Sirk, calls melodrama's "impossible situation"—that is, a relational impasse from which there is no way out without loss.[20] To exist is to contribute to environmental destruction and thus to pose an obstacle to any ethical project rooted in futurity, reproduction, or even survival: such is the impasse of the present, as *First Reformed* inhabits it. The "metaphysical location of the impossible situation," Goldberg explains, is "a relationship between the absolute opposition of life and death," an identification "with something impersonal, not living and not dead"—here, an identification with extinction.[21] Rather than dwell indefinitely in the impasse, *First Reformed* has recourse to self-annihilation, an event that spectacularizes the combustion of ethics. Reading with scholarship on cinematic ontology, we further claim that Schrader's film, part of a broadly religious tradition he calls "transcendental cinema," problematizes the conflation of intentional and inevitable self-destruction amidst environmental catastrophe through the collapse of representation. What results is a cinema wherein narrative shattering signals both the fossilization of thought by time and the intensification of queerness within disastrous environments.

DESTRUCTIVE MELANCHOLY

Near the beginning of *First Reformed*, Toller, in voice-over narration, dictates the inaugural entry in a diary. He is to write entries in longhand, as factually as possible, for exactly one year. "I will keep this diary for twelve months," he recites, "and at the end of that time it will be destroyed. Shredded, then burnt. The experiment will be over." The protocol lays out a combustible askesis eventually echoed by Toller's and Michael's ideations and performances of self-destruction. Before he reaches the twelve-month mark and gets to shred and burn a catalog of his innermost thoughts, Toller follows Michael in planning his own death—an act that, as we will see, challenges thinkability. Michael's last name, Mensana, lays out a paradox: his suicide issues from *and* eliminates *mens sana*, a sane or healthy mind.

Toller's journal is a coping mechanism in the face of grief. His son, whom he had convinced to enlist in the army, died in the Iraq War.

This tragedy contributed to the dissolution of Toller's marriage. The object of Toller's grief evolves throughout the film. Its scale balloons to become planetary: Toller comes to mourn a doomed Earth—a planet that has already died but keeps being desecrated. He assures us, in voice-over, that he hasn't lost his faith. Instead, he believes that the planet's destruction exceeds the category of redeemable sins within a Christian paradigm. Early in *First Reformed*, Michael asks Toller, "Can God forgive us? For what we've done to this world?" After Michael's death, Toller confronts Balq with the same question: "Will God forgive us for what we are doing to his creation?"

Pairing the rubrics of queerness and ecology, Catriona Sandilands observes affinities between practices of grieving the ungrievable in the contexts of HIV/AIDS and environmental collapse.[22] The populations lost to HIV/AIDS as well as extinct species and ravaged ecosystems qualify as ungrievable for two reasons: their existence is trivialized by homophobia or by capitalist systems of extraction and exploitation; and their disappearance constitutes a loss of almost unthinkable magnitude. Whereas in grief, per the Freudian model, the individual manages to overcome loss, in melancholy the individual, rather than giving up the lost object, internalizes it. Freud: "So by taking flight into the ego, love escapes extinction."[23] Sandilands insists that melancholy isn't merely a denial of loss. Melancholy may be a politicized way of preserving a "life . . . already gone" within a culture that doesn't recognize this life's significance.[24]

The politics of melancholy has a long standing in queer theory. From the racial melancholy of David Eng's *Racial Castration* to the queer-of-color melancholy of José Esteban Muñoz's *Disidentifications*, the psychoanalytic theory of melancholy—of losses turned inward—has become a linchpin of anti-normativity.[25] Melancholy's uptake in queer theory owes to the melancholic traffic between heteronormativity and its genealogy of abjection, exemplified by Judith Butler's ironic claim that "the 'truest' gay male melancholic is the strictly straight man."[26] From the perspective afforded by Butler's gender melancholia, the strictly straight man only becomes so due to heteronormativity's foreclosure of same-sex attachments. The strictly straight man preserves his attachments against loss by turning them inward, making the ego the sedimentary effect of unavowable losses. It is because melancholy reverses the inside/outside paradigm on which heteronormativity's foundations are built that queer theory prioritizes a melancholic politics of preservation. We are, the queer melancholic intones, everything we abject.

One popular offshoot of queer melancholy is Timothy Morton's "dark ecology," which they also brand as a "queer ecology."[27] In a statement on environmental destruction that they explicitly tie to Butler's theory of gender melancholy, Morton writes: "It is strictly impossible for us to mourn this absolute, radical loss. It is worse than losing our mother. It resembles the heterosexist melancholy that Butler brilliantly outlines in their essay on how the foreclosure of homosexual attachment makes it impossible to mourn for it."[28] Morton adds in parentheses: "(In general, a partnership between queer theory and ecological criticism is long overdue.)"[29] Indeed, this "partnership" makes immediate sense, given that dark ecology, like queer theory, "undermines the naturalness of the stories we tell about how we are involved in nature."[30] Similarly to Butler's gender melancholic, queer ecology "preserves the dark, depressive quality of life in the shadow of ecological catastrophe."[31] As others have since argued, queer ecology spells the end of Nature construed as radical exteriority.[32] Melancholy entails that everything that was once deemed outside, including our abjects, is brought inside. Ecological politics becomes "claustrophobic precisely because what is *outside* it is now *included*."[33]

In contrast with this Butlerian-ecological view, which has, since Morton's writing, become the mainstream of queer and ecological criticism (no longer dark indeed), we contend that it is precisely because what is outside is now inside, via the inward turn of melancholy, that ecological thought becomes impossible. We are living in an age that Frédéric Neyrat calls "saturated immanence," when the very thought of the outside, of what escapes the immediacy of our relations (transcendence with a lowercase *t*), is rendered unthinkable or suspect due to the conviction that every outside is a projection of desire turned inward.[34]

Although an insistence on the traffic between inside and outside was necessary to avoid normative splits like nature/culture and sex/gender, we end up with a dearth of real differences to think with. All differences are now inside the gender-culture matrix, which means that queer and ecological theories have reproduced the very inside/outside split that melancholy was supposed to deconstruct. No wonder, then, that queer and ecological paradigms converge today in melodramatic acts. As Goldberg argues, the subject of melodrama is *subjected to* a "Truth" that is unbearable because it is outside the immanence of our relations.[35] Melodramatic truth does not exist but rather *insists* by punching holes in the immanence of relations turned inward.

If, as both Butler and Morton argue, the truest gay male melancholic is the strictly straight man, then the truest gay male environmentalist could be the border patrol agent, Dennis Dickey, who set fire to a national forest in the name of gender conformity. By this logic, a gender reveal party would be a melancholic act of preservation gone awry: by preserving one attachment ("natural" genders), he, Dickey, unintentionally destroys another (nature). Herein lies the difficulty of melancholy politics as it is currently theorized: it is far too sweet. For both Butler and Morton, melancholy is a way of coping with unavowable losses and of turning loss into a politics of preservation. Although losses structure our existence, they are made contingent by melancholy: homosexual and ecological attachments that are foreclosed in one arena become the bedrock of the psychic-social field. Yet reading melancholy as preservation only accounts for one half of the melancholic turn. The problem, as we see it, with a model where relations are turned inward is that it obscures another, simultaneous turn outward. As Elizabeth A. Wilson points out, queer theorizations of melancholy tend to overlook melancholy's sadism—its "aggression turned outward."[36] Wilson writes: "As well as attaching to things that are damaging us, we are also trying to damage the things to which we are attached"; "shouldn't gay melancholia entail, beyond the logic of strangulated affect and public catharsis, a hatred of the object it has loved and lost?"[37] Wilson's argument is that theories of gay melancholia have centered too narrowly on modes and objects of repair without acknowledging that repair itself is structured by animus.[38] I love you/I hate you: these statements are braided. The very structuration of reparative politics is a sadistic cut: between the worlds we want and the worlds we abject. Through the lens of Wilson's "aggression turned outward," then, a gender reveal party in Arizona that decimates 47,000 acres of forest in the name of the gender binary seems less like an example of preservation gone wrong—a way of framing melancholy that diminishes environmental destruction as merely contingent, a friendly fire. We propose a different interpretation: when nature burns, as it did so spectacularly for Dickey, then and only then has the queer melancholic reached their sweet-sadistic mark. A nature loved/a nature destroyed.

This opposition between a politics of repair and a politics of destruction collapses not only in instantaneous acts of willed combustion, whether queer acts of refusal or ecological acts of dark, Gothic despair, but also gradually, unexceptionally, and garishly, in pink and blue, across the political spectrum. Within this impossible representational space that we call melodrama, queerness appears less sweet, and less righteous, than it typically does; and this is no less true of the queer representational space of *First Reformed*. A sentimental, child-centered politics certainly transpires throughout the film,[39] but it is ultimately sacrificed to something else, something queerer. This queerness is at play in Toller and Michael's conversation, and it manifests in a suspicion of reproduction, and the notion that human beings ought to be subtracted from any equation pertaining to the planet's future.[40] There is a fundamental queerness to the contemporary experience of awaiting, and by the same means contributing to, extinction. Instead of folding the ego's destruction into a realm of intra-psychic, non-normative preservation, queer ecocide in *First Reformed* calls for an irrecuperable abolition of the individual—its subtraction from the act of thinking sociality.

VOICE AS OBJECT

Toller is exposed to Michael's worldview in a conversation that takes place at the Mensanas' residence, an austere house in shades of gray and brown, with creaky hardwood floors. Toller meets Michael on Mary's advice. Not long ago, Michael returned from Fort Providence, in Canada's Northwest Territories, where he was arrested while advocating with an organization called the Green Planet Movement. The two characters sit face to face, as if in a Socratic dialogue. Emphasizing their initial schism is the door frame that stands between them. The aperture leads to the living room, where sunlight scarcely passes through the diaphanous curtains (figure 48). "Mary says things have gotten you down," Toller offers in a bid to move beyond small talk. Michael brings up Mary's pregnancy. Congratulations and thanks soon give way to a thought experiment. "How old are you, Reverend?" Michael asks. "Forty-six." "Thirty-three," Michael reciprocates, pointing to himself, before continuing, "That's how old our child will be in 2050. Five years older than I am now. You'll be eighty-one. Do you know what the world will be like in 2050?" Michael draws for a bemused Toller a portrait of the planet's dire future: "The Earth's temperature will be three degrees centigrade higher. Four is the threshold. 'Severe, widespread, irreversible impacts.' And when scientists say stuff like that—the National Center for Atmospheric Research, Lawrence Livermore, the Potsdam Institute . . ." In voice-over, Toller ventriloquizes Michael: "By 2050 sea levels two feet higher on the East Coast. Low-lying areas underwater across the world. Bangladesh, twenty percent loss of land mass. Central Africa, fifty percent reduction in crops due to drought. The Western reservoirs dried up. Climate change refugees. Epidemics. Extreme weather." The voice-over narration, which probably relays the journal entry that Toller is to write later that day, suggests that he has metabolized, or will metabolize, Michael's message.

48

When Toller internalizes Michael's message, he takes in an object that is and is not of a piece with the reality represented. As Freud notes in "Mourning and Melancholia," the melancholic does not know what they have lost in the object. The melancholic's vocalizations, which are ritualistically self-blaming, remind us that loss is internalized to be replayed.[41] The ecological melancholy of Michael's speech, though well-meaning, automates this unconscious wish to repeat loss as desire's sole aim. Put differently: what appears as the inward turn of melancholy (preservation) is at the same time the outward turn of sadism, a sadism that refuses to let go of the object "nature" once and for all because having is a prerequisite for losing, and losing is deeply satisfying.

To preserve his attachment to the planet, then, Toller internalizes its destruction in the form of a vocative object. This object takes on an enigmatic quality in its reenactment. Not only is it difficult to place the voice-object diegetically, but it is unclear to what extent this object's purpose is strictly preservative. The voice-over shatters the scene of representation. Does the voice belong to Toller or to Michael? Does it belong in the present moment, in the near future of Toller's journal-writing, or in the speculated future of extinction? This shattering is the enigmatic, sweet-sadistic core of the voice-over itself. The voice-over is ostensibly Toller's, but it has taken on a life of its own. The voice-over is an instance of the Lacanian *objet a*, which Slavoj Žižek glosses as the vocative remainder of unconscious *jouissance*: "the voice as object . . .

cannot be attributed to any subject and thus hovers in some indefinite interspace. This voice is implacable precisely because it cannot be properly placed, being part neither of the diegetic 'reality' nor of the sound accompaniment (commentary, musical score), but belonging, rather, to that mysterious domain designated by Lacan as 'between two deaths.'"[42] Toller's voice-over carries a deadly refrain that cannot be placed, either narratively or acoustically, and so it jeopardizes the representative space of the film by repeating an impossible situation. In Goldberg's impossible situation, intentionality and inevitability coincide: the subject of melodrama bears a "Truth" (the truth of extinction) that cannot be brought about in part because the melodramatic subject is constituted by impossibility. To save life, Michael and Toller internalize the voice of inevitable destruction. Yet this voice *qua* autonomous object threatens the scene of life by taking the voice away from the living. Toller's voice repeats, and with this repetition we are confronted with an impossibility that is neither life nor death, but a melodramatic suspension of the two. Ultimately, it is subtraction that both Michael and Toller elect in response to the ecocidal mania of reproductive futurism.

Whether Toller adopts Michael's worldview during or after their conversation is unclear. In the heat of the moment, Toller, visibly panicked, tries to mute Michael's operatic pessimism. Toller asks Michael whether he has considered harming himself. Michael doesn't respond directly and instead asks Toller, "How can you sanction bringing a girl—for argument's sake, let's say my child is a girl, a child full of hope and naive belief—into a world . . . when that little girl grows to be a young woman and looks you in the eyes and says, 'You knew this all along, didn't you?' What do you say then?" Toller resorts to anti-choice rhetoric by suggesting that abortion's immorality supersedes reproduction's. Mary is notably excluded from this conversation about the ethics of her own pregnancy, making her a mere discursive object: a synecdoche for an imperiled and perilous future (we return to Mary's role as a symbol, more than a character, later in this chapter). Michael rejects Toller's relativistic suggestion that "throughout history" humans have experienced sorrow. The present environmental catastrophe, Michael insists, denotes a historical shift: "This is something new." He brings up martyrdom—a change of topic that, as we eventually learn, isn't a non sequitur. In the remainder of *First Reformed*, Michael and Toller fashion themselves as ecological martyrs, choosing to die to slow down extinction.

DEATH AS PROTEST

Michael has, in fact, been thinking of harming himself—and possibly others. Mary asks Toller to come over when her husband is at work. She guides Toller to a clapboard garage. A wooden crate hidden under stacks of junk contains an explosive vest, which Toller promises to dispose of. The next day, Toller receives an ominous text message from Michael: "Meet me at the Westbrook Park Trail. East entrance. The red diamond trail. Come alone." When he reaches the site, Toller discovers a gruesome scene. Michael, dead, is lying face down next to a rifle. His head—*mens sana*—is partly blown off. Blood stains the snow. At his request, Michael's ashes are scattered at Hanstown, a site turned into a toxic waste dump by Balq Industries. At the service, which Ed Balq later condemns as a "protest funeral," the Abundant Life youth choir sings an acapella version of Neil Young's "Who's Gonna Stand Up," whose chorus goes, "Who's gonna stand up and save the Earth? / Who's gonna say that she's had enough? / Who's gonna take on the big machine? / Who's gonna stand up and save the Earth? / This all starts with you and me."

Toller doesn't inform the police of the suicide vest's existence. While his silence ostensibly aims to protect Mary's privacy and Michael's memory, we later realize that Toller holds on to the vest so he can wear it himself. Detonating the explosive device at the reconsecration would signal the absurdity of the event's financial ties to a corporation responsible for environmental wreckage. On the day of the event, Toller solemnly buttons the vest, hidden under his cassock. He writes his journal's final entry, which, uncharacteristically, isn't relayed in voice-over, and he connects the vest's wires. Although his plan is derailed by the sight of Mary entering the church, Toller's suicide bombing clearly aims to realize the stunt that Michael, deprived of his vest, couldn't stage.

In addition to figuring accelerated, human-caused extinction, Toller's planned suicide preempts a death that already appears imminent due to a high risk of environment-caused illness. Michael's death as well as a head-to-head with Balq prompt Toller to research Balq Industries' EPA violations. Strikingly, footage of Toller's research accompanies a voice-over narration in which Toller addresses health complications: "I can no longer ignore my health. I've postponed my checkup too often." Throughout the film, Toller coughs. His urine is bloody. A doctor recommends a gastroscopy, hinting at a stomach cancer diagnosis. Like Richard Powers's novel *Gain*, which juxtaposes the history of a chemical conglomerate with the story of a woman with ovarian cancer living near the headquarters, *First Reformed* suggests a correlation between Toller's symptoms and environmental toxicity without confirming causality.[43]

Pointing to the oblique relation between toxicity, symptom, diagnosis, and cure, Michelle Murphy explains that the measurement of certain chemical exposures and not others, motivated by corporate and other special-interest groups, has delineated domains of perceptibility and domains of imperceptibility.[44] Elizabeth A. Povinelli echoes this point while ratcheting up toxicity to the scale of the global carbon cycle, where geochemical processes press inexorably on life itself.[45]

Refracted through biospheric and geochemical enmeshment, intentionality runs aground with inevitability as the two terms map the scarred terrain of "geontology," Povinelli's word for the distributions of life (*bios*) and nonlife (*geos*) under late liberalism.[46] For Povinelli, this division between biology and geology underlies Western ontologies: the question of Being—from Aristotle to Heidegger to the Dakota Access Pipeline—prioritizes life, understood as intentional, self-organizing, purposive, and enclosed, over its so-called opposite, nonlife, understood as unintentional, desultory, and inert. And while it is true that geology extrudes life, an uncritical theory of life has rendered imperceptible not only the countless viral relays between biology and geology but also, on a macro scale, geochemical disturbances to the planetary carbon cycle, histories of fossil fuel extraction, and the onset of anthropogenic climate change. Jane Bennett's assemblage theory marks one of the better-known attempts to puncture life's enclosure by obviating theory's myopic focus on the biological body politic.[47] Bennett instead traces assemblages of organic and inorganic matter that range across differences of intentionality and inevitability, cause and effect, and life and death.

Still, something of nonlife's vitiating force falls out of the picture of Bennett's vital assemblages. While the neologism "geontology" is meant to signal not so much a sublimation of as a *confrontation* with nonlife, the neo-vitalist turn to assemblages avoids that confrontation with its focus on "lively matters."[48] Bennett cuts through the red tape of geontopolitics only to claim that all things are animate—not alive per se but vibrant or vibratory. This argument concedes too much to an image of life as lively and dynamic, thus falling under the sway of a covert biontologism. Queer theory can make a difference here. Equally suspicious of the biontologization of life as purposive and self-organizing, queer theorists such as Edelman and Bersani posit a "real" that is neither life nor its opposite, biological death, but nonlife.[49] Edelman calls it the "rock of the real."[50] The point is not that this rock, or this real, is life-like; rather, the point is that life tries falteringly to knit together, to assemble and reassemble, this geontological tear in reality, becoming lifeless as a result. By harnessing life's vitiating force, queer theory collapses life's metabolic narrative in upon itself, like a collapsed lung. This is what is happening now at a planetary scale as human intentionality and the narratives thereof queer themselves from within by choking on life's abject remainders (CO_2). Hence Povinelli's question: "Where is the human body if it is viewed from with[in] the lung? The larger, massive biotic assemblage the lungs know intimately—including green plants, photosynthetic bacteria, nonsulfur purple bacteria, hydrogen, sulfur and iron bacteria, animals, and microbes—is now what is thought to produce the metabolism of the planetary carbon cycle, which may be on the verge of a massive reorganization due to human action."[51] Scaling down from the outer atmosphere of the planet to the inner atmosphere of the human lung, Povinelli shows that the metabolism of the human body maps the metabolic and geographical coordinates of a planetary system on life support. "These excisions [of scale]," Povinelli adds, "are becoming more difficult as the carbon cycle, where forms of existence produce themselves as atmosphere, is interrupted by the consumption of carbon to produce and expand one form of life: late liberalism."[52]

Thus interrupted, breath registers its extimate relations with non-life in political statements and aesthetic forms. Deleuze for one captures the sense of aesthetic interruption, which he too defines as a shortage of breath, in his analysis of the literary writings of the Marquis de Sade and Leopold von Sacher-Masoch. For Deleuze, the impersonal quality of a philosophy without breath asserts itself in the personal, merely descriptive language of Sade and Masoch's libertines. "In Sade," Deleuze writes, "we discover a surprising affinity with Spinoza—a naturalistic and mechanistic approach imbued with the mathematical spirit. . . . In the work of Masoch there is a similar transcendence of the imperative and the descriptive toward a higher function."[53] Deleuze's anoxic formula (breathlessness, death = transcendence, politics) finds its cinematic expression in *Cinema 2*, where the habitual intervals between images create a life too "intolerable" to be borne.[54] Confronted with the intolerability of the image, Deleuze's cinematic martyrs are sacrificed by a cruel film cut that trades aesthetic coherence for the impossibility of queer form. In this way, Deleuze's cinema of cruelty furthers Bersani's claim, in *The Freudian Body*, that the aesthetic is, even in its reparative modes, a tautology for masochism.[55]

First Reformed enmeshes Toller's symptomatology with the planet's, where air pollution, deforestation, species extinction, soil degradation, and overpopulation are enterically enfolded. Like the deadly incorporation of the other's voice, this emplotment of toxicity proves destructive not only to Toller's health but to the film's framing dispositif: abundant life. According to Balq Industries and the Abundant Life church that is its mouthpiece, Christ died so that human life could have its encore.

Toller's "encore" is more Lacanian in inflection.[56] He stages a martyr's death so that life, and the fantasy life that is compact with environmental destruction (the lasting imprint of heteronormativity's green thumb), can live on by other means: by refusing viability and the social imperative to live at any cost. Toller's illness isn't explicitly stated as part of his planned suicide's political message. Yet, to us, his symptoms further blur the line between an intentional and an inevitable early death amidst environmental collapse.

However apropos the film's treatment of queer and environmental negativities may be, something about *First Reformed* is eerily out of time and out of place. Megachurches like Abundant Life are staples of metropolises as well as large suburbs in the southern United States. They virtually do not exist in upstate New York, where the film is set.[57] The film's only major Black character is Abundant Life's resident pastor, Joel Jeffers (Cedric Kyles). Jeffers is a figure of corporatism. Michael, via Mary, and Toller criticize him for running his church as one would a corporation and for reducing First Reformed to a museum or souvenir shop. Jeffers also stands as a figure of bribery, prioritizing Balq's bottom line over Michael's last wishes and Toller's moral objections. Through Jeffers, *First Reformed* conflates Black religious life with carbon capitalism.

This conflation appears especially misguided in light of toxicity's disproportionate impact on the African American population. Dorceta E. Taylor explains that much of the environmental justice movement's rhetoric has relied on the assertion that hazardous facilities such as Hanstown, the toxic waste dump where Michael's ashes are scattered, are concentrated in minority and low-income communities.[58] In a study of toxic inequality in Chicago's neighborhoods at the turn of the twentieth and twenty-first centuries, Robert J. Sampson and Alix S. Winter report that the city's Black and Hispanic neighborhoods bear a great deal of the city's lead toxicity.[59] As the authors note, the debilitation through lead poisoning of a majority African American population in the Flint water crisis, begun in 2014 and still unresolved as of 2024, is not an aberration, but an exemplar of contemporary segregation as toxic management. As Mel Y. Chen observes, lead exposure tends to reach the status of social and political problem when it affects a white subject whose suffering can be sentimentalized.[60] Likewise, *First Reformed* positions a white character as the paradigmatic victim, actual or potential, of a toxicity it attributes to the joint actions of a white oil magnate and a Black megachurch pastor.

First Reformed covers up toxic inequality by having Toller internalize it. His martyred internalization of planetary destruction indeed entails the internalization of racist geographies of toxic exposure. Insofar as Toller's planned suicide is meant to spectacularize extinction, it encompasses all deaths by environmental causes, including the deaths of people of color, who are here made invisible despite their statistically higher exposure to toxicity. Toller is the world; the world is (in) Toller. Toller and the film itself thus absorb toxicity while disavowing its operation as an agent of whiteness's reproduction. This iteration of the inward turn, more sadistic than sweet, corresponds to the white subject's racial melancholy as Anne Anlin Cheng defines it: "white American identity and its authority [are] secured through the melancholic introjection of racial others that [this identity] can neither fully relinquish nor accommodate and whose ghostly presence nonetheless guarantees its centrality."[61] By containing and neutralizing racial others who are disproportionally vulnerable to toxicity, Toller can imagine that *his* explosion will be universalizable, that it will mean something on a planetary scale. One type of megalomaniac destruction, Balq's, gives way to another, Toller's. The ventriloquizing of Black suffering isn't confined to toxic matters; before a group of children, Toller describes and performs with theatrical intensity the experience of enslaved people who sought refuge in the church's hidden basement, one safe house on the Underground Railroad.

Toller's incorporation of Blackness testifies not just to an erasure that finer data about health disparities or a fuller historical archive could correct but to an expression of the inadmissibility of Blackness to being. Frantz Fanon positions Blackness outside—and, for that reason, as constitutive of—white colonial ontology. As Fanon puts it, "not only must the black man be black; he must be black in relation to the white man." And yet: "The black man has no ontological resistance in the eyes of the white man."[62] Fanon writes that "the real world"—a lower-case real, in contrast to Jacques Lacan's Real, for which Blackness might be made to stand in[63]—"robbed us of our share. In the white world, the man of color encounters difficulties in elaborating his body schema. The image of one's body is solely negating. It's an image in the third person."[64] What white liberal humanism sees as a contest of competing interests, Fanon and Afropessimism after him see as a structural antagonism; Blackness, whose ~~being~~ signifies the world's limit, figures the absence or negativity of white ontology, and so undoes the world.[65] Calvin Warren names "ontological terror" the affect "of inhabiting existence outside the precincts of humanity and its humanism."[66] "Black freedom," Warren continues, "would constitute a form of *world destruction*," for "black being incarnates metaphysical nothing, the terror of metaphysics, in an antiblack world."[67] Edelman, citing Frank B. Wilderson III's antihumanism, posits that Black identity is catachrestic: it is made to substantiate that which negates being.[68] We might say that *First Reformed* occasions a glitch in this substantiation. The film indeed parodies humanism by collapsing recognition (the insistence that experiences of toxic exposure count) and appropriation (the personification of such experiences by a subject who, structurally, benefits from them).

STYLES OF TRANSCENDENCE

First Reformed styles environmental collapse as a break in rhythm, a fluttering of breath, and a disaster in form. Although the film begins in a clinical mode, surveying the signs of a dying planet, it ends in a critical mode. Its question is not the everyday question posed on American bumper stickers, *What would Jesus do?* but rather the philosophical one, *What would Tarkovsky do?* If the name Andrei Tarkovsky has become emblematic, thanks in part to Deleuze, of a certain post-Kantian mode of thinking about time and difference in twentieth-century avant-garde cinema, it did so, according to director Paul Schrader, at the expense of narrative cohesion. A cinema released from narrative gave way to an image of time without movement—what Schrader, in deference to the films of Ingmar Bergman, Robert Bresson, Carl Theodor Dreyer, and Yasujirō Ozu, calls "transcendental cinema."

In 1971, then a film student, Schrader wrote a book entitled *Transcendental Style in Film*. The book was republished in 2018, with a new introduction by the author, titled "Rethinking Transcendental Style." Schrader's object of analysis, as he clarifies in this new piece, is not any religious content per se but rather religious style, more precisely a filmic style of thought about the Holy. "Church people had been using movies since they first moved to illustrate religious belief," Schrader writes, "but this was something different. The convergence of spirituality and cinema would occur in style, not content."[69] Schrader goes on:

> Transcendental style can be seen . . . as part of a larger movement, the movement away from narrative. . . . By delaying edits, not moving the camera, forswearing music cues, not employing coverage, and heightening the mundane, transcendental style creates a sense of unease the viewer must resolve. The film maker assists the viewer's impulse for resolution by the use of a Decisive Moment, an unexpected image or act, which then results in a stasis, an acceptance of parallel reality—transcendence. . . . World War II dates the rough demarcation of a shift, more in Europe than America, from movement-image to time-image. Screen movement still occurred, of course, but it was increasingly "subordinated to time."[70]

By distancing itself from narrative technique, transcendental style affirms what can only be asserted by negation: it is a spiritual style for a dead God, "an acceptance of parallel reality—transcendence."[71] This parallel reality exists because it is denied; it appears only through the medium of the editorial cut, or the film's wandering caesura, its bated breath. Although Schrader never says so, transcendental style is melodramatic—not to mention queer—in that it wrests the image from any given so as to give witness to a reality in excess of the world thus composed. Schrader goes on to clarify his point regarding film's subordination to time and the "non-rational cuts" it engenders:

> Man exits one room, enters another—that's movement-image editing. Man exits one room, shot of trees in the wind, shot of train passing—that's time-image editing. . . . Deleuze called this the "non-rational cut." The non-rational cut breaks from sensorimotor logic. . . . Movement-image is informed by Aristotelian logic: "A" can never equal "not A." Time-image rejects the Aristotelian principle of non-contradiction, posits a world where something and its opposite can coexist: "A" can be "not A."[72]

Transcendental style rejects organic wholeness. Instead of creating a larger whole (life, the heterosexual unit), it produces explosive differences: of time, materiality, thought, and sex. This is a cinema in which parts without predetermined wholes combine to further their radical disjunctions: "A" can be "not A."

We recognize the wandering temporality of the cut, which *First Reformed* makes coextensive with the planetary carbon cycle's interruptive and spasmodic temporal reorganization of life and nonlife, in the film's penultimate scene of transcendental collapse. Toller appears at his desk, his diary open, soaking his insides with alcohol (80-proof and above will burn). Mary knocks unannounced. Grief-stricken over the loss of her husband, she turns to Toller for guidance. The room is austere and dimly lit. The camera frame is static, matched to the architecture of the room. Mary and Toller come together at a distance at first. The restrictive 4:3 aspect ratio, consistent throughout the film, gives the viewer less while filling the frame with more: more of the human face, and more emotion. Deleuze and Félix Guattari write of the face in close-up that it is not a part of the diegetic whole but a part unto itself.[73] As in our previous discussion of the voice-object, the face, once partialized, stands outside narrative sequence and intensifies the viewer's relationship to time, charging it with affect. As we linger over Mary's face, we hear her explain to Toller the "thing" she used to do with Michael. She states, "We used to do this thing called the Magical Mystery Tour. It sounds silly. But . . .

we would . . . share a joint and lay on top of each other fully clothed. We would try to get as much body-to-body contact as possible. We'd have our hands out and we would look straight into each other's eyes and move them in unison like right, left, right, left. And then we would breathe in rhythm." "You want me to do this?" Toller offers. Mary hesitates: "No. I didn't mean that." Moments later, she accepts Toller's overture. They walk to the middle of the hardwood floor. The camera maintains its distance as Toller asks for instruction: "Do we need music?" he asks. "No," says Mary, "we just listen to the breaths." They stretch out on the floor, their bodies horizontal. Toller lies supine, Mary prostrate and directly above. They are stacked one on top of the other, Mary's palms resting on Toller's like two fallen leaves. They look into each other's eyes as if across a chasm, but it is only a matter of inches. Their faces fill the screen like two splayed cross-sections or silhouettes. No words are exchanged, only audible breath. Their noses touch. Their mouths inhale and exhale one into the other. Mary's hair, a perfect bell shape, falls in vertical strands over their adjoined faces like a curtain, veiling their tête-à-tête from the viewer (figure 49). The final unbroken shot lasts for approximately forty-five seconds, long enough for us to feel time dilate and grow heavy, as though Mary and Toller were no longer two living, breathing persons but rather sedimentary layers, compressed by eons, their bodies one great tuning fork echoing the primordial sound of the universe: *Om*, the inexhaustible breath.

49

And then it happens. As the curtains fall on this reality, we are transported to another. The Magical Mystery Tour has begun. Mary and Toller begin to levitate in a nod to Tarkovsky's *Mirror* (1975, figure 50).[74] Mary and Toller's surroundings fade to black as we, along with them, float through outer space. It is, if not the beginning of time, the beginning of life on Earth as starry space turns to snow-capped mountains, followed by images of green hills, a pristine shore, blue sea, and vast forest. All of this appears sped up in time-lapse. It is paradise at the speed of a screensaver or a nature documentary—hence, for us, a paradise lost. In *The World Viewed: Reflections on the Ontology of Film*, Stanley Cavell writes that film "overcame subjectivity" and the problem of skepticism "in a way undreamed of by painting."[75] This is because "photography maintains the presentness of the world by accepting our absence from it." Cavell further claims that "the reality in a photograph is present to me while I am not present to it; and a world I know, and see, but to which I am nevertheless not present (through no fault of my subjectivity), is a world past."[76] Film stages the problem of skepticism—of the human subject's access to the world outside of thought—by envisioning a world in which skepticism, taken to its logical extreme, has eliminated the human subject entirely. The "automatism" of film presents the world as it is "in itself," but it is a world from which we are absent. Moreover, as Cavell points out, a world without the viewer is "a world past"; film, as a medium, is deeply melancholic. *First Reformed* reminds the viewer of this melancholy condition, and savagely so. As the Magical Mystery Tour continues, Toller peers outside the curtain of Mary's fallen hair. His face begins to darken as the forest canopy below turns to congested highways followed by landfill, industrial smokestacks, clear-cutting, plastic waste, a landscape devastated by fire, and finally, a polluted and derelict shipping yard (figure 51). By the end of the ritual, Mary and Toller have exited the frame completely. Their disappearance not only presages a world in which intentional and inevitable destruction have collapsed, but also hastens the void left by Toller's willed subtraction.

50

51

This is transcendental style for the climate change era. It moves outside the immanence of our relations to approach the unthinkable: deep time colliding with the present, and human breath fueling a planetary conflagration. The decision of "an unexpected image or act"—Schrader calls this the "Decisive Moment"—is not to be confused with the choice of an alternate reality, as in the film *Another Earth* (2011), where a duplicate planet Earth is found, promising individuals the chance of a better life elsewhere.[77] Nor is it the quantum reality imagined by the patriarchal parable *Interstellar* (2014), in which a father communicates with his daughter across infinite time and space to stave off human extinction.[78] In *First Reformed*, there is only this world. Such is the film's cruelty: it makes us powerless before the image of the Earth's, and our, annihilation. Yet this powerlessness to think other worlds does not prevent the film from envisioning the world as an open whole. On the contrary, it is because *First Reformed* is freed from having to think a truer world that it can release the image to novel variations. The critique of "bad transcendence" by anti-foundationalist thinkers such as Morton and Butler had the unintended consequence of reinstalling immanence as a transcendental ground. By contrast, *First Reformed* aligns transcendence with the foreclosure of queerness to think time and transcendence—they mean the same thing, according to Schrader—without the human eye as anchor. Transcendence, here, comes not from above (the Archimedean point of view) but rather vertiginously from within. It is a baseless spiral.

In the film's final scene, spiral is what we get. Toller has been performing his last rites before the start of the First Reformed reconsecration ceremony: visiting the scenes of Balq Industries' toxic runoff, stalking the streets, and staring introspectively in the mirror (a callback to Schrader's screenplay for *Taxi Driver* [1976], featuring one Travis Bickle, a former U.S. Marine turned suicidal saint).[79] On the day of the reconsecration, we see Toller buttoning his suicide vest and gazing at it in the mirror. Among the wires and explosives, a patch with the names and faces of two murdered ecological activists appears stitched to the upper-left corner of the vest. Happy with the fit, Toller conceals the suicide vest with his vestments. While sitting at his desk, he pens the final words of his diary. Before taking the podium, he decamps to the window for a final look outside. He fills the frame of the window like a coffin. That's when he sees Mary enter the First Reformed church. Distraught, he ambles back and forth, pausing only to let out a strangulated scream. He is forced to improvise. He emerges from a dark pantry, barbed wire and Drano bottle in hand. The barbed wire was salvaged from the church garden; when we last saw it, a dead animal hung from its edges. Cut scene.

When we return to Toller, it's now his flesh that the barbed wire pierces; he wears it wrapped around his naked chest like a crown of thorns fashioned into bondage gear (figure 52). "Leaning on the Everlasting Arms," a song of refuge, plays in the background. When we next see him, Toller is wearing a white robe. The blood from his mutilated flesh blossoms rose petals on the white of his linen. He fills a glass with Drano. "FULL CLOG DESTROYER," the product's epithet, appears vertically in the left-hand side of the screen as sodium hydroxide the color of honey runs down the middle of the frame. Toller's shoulders and head are curiously lopped from the frame—a visual reminder of Michael Mensana's blown-off head. The parishioners are waiting. We are waiting. Time is charged to the bursting point. Toller takes the cup in hand. Then . . . Mary. She calls him: "Ernst." The glass hits the floor, spilling its contents, and Toller walks steadfast to Mary. The camera, static throughout the film, begins to rotate. It spins around Mary and Toller as they kiss and embrace (figure 53). The barbed wire, seemingly not an impediment, can only sink deeper as they coil arms and edges around each other. The camera too rings around them, until it stops. After two slow rotations, the screens cuts to black.

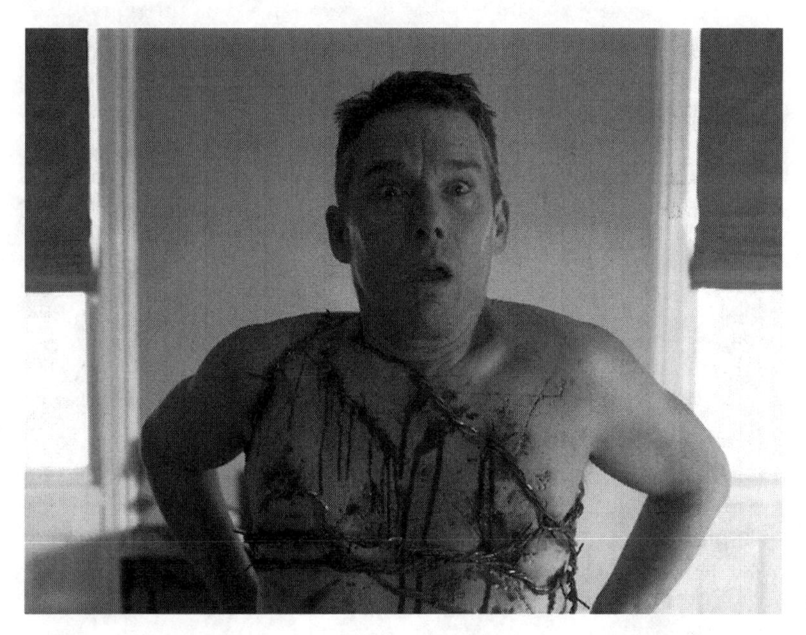

52

53

The ending is quickly followed by filmic collapse. Put differently, *First Reformed* ends twice. Schrader first gives us a false happy ending of the kind often found in Sirk's melodramas. In such a happy ending, characters move beyond the impasse—or delude themselves into thinking they can do so—by disavowing a loss hidden in plain sight. Toller and Mary's embrace affirms life *qua* heterosexual romance and reproductive futurism (Mary being, of course, an archetype for motherhood) while disavowing its enmeshment with morbid queerness—an enmeshment that, Goldberg indicates, is the metaphysical location of the impossible situation. But in mere seconds, this false happy ending is brought past its point of ignition. The film spirals, inasmuch as suicide and preservation lose their ontological grounding against the backdrop of environmental catastrophe. The camera spins around the duo until narrative shatters and the film cuts to black. The instantaneous cut is the film's second ending. Transcendental style appears in the void of unthinkability left by irresolvable contradictions.

The film's conclusion confirms that Mary was never an agentive character, but instead a biblical emblem of feminine plenitude threatened by queer forces: first Michael, then Toller. Reductively, instrumentally, Mary *is* childbearing, and later child-rearing. The meaning of her ultimate absorption into the void of negativity, illegible in terms of personal motivations or intentions, is symbolic rather than biographical.[80]

Mary—or what she represents—is siphoned. This isn't a *folie à deux*. The *folie* is queer, and the queerness is Toller's.

First Reformed only dampens the violence of Toller's suicidal rampage by baking it into the formal detonation of an impossible situation. The formalization, as void, of the unbearable confluence of individual and species destructions brings us, the spectators, much relief. Buckel's suicide and Dickey's wildfire, by contrast, didn't cut to black. In the wake of these events, we remain in melodramatic and ethical suspension, where the queer dictum "More life!" sounds increasingly perverse. In lieu of that dictum, let us be haunted by Roland Barthes's questions: "Someone tells me: this kind of love is not viable. But how can you *evaluate* viability? Why is the viable a Good Thing? Why is it better to *last* than to *burn*?"[81] We are still inhabiting an impossible situation—for now.

Acknowledgments

We thank Brian Price for believing in this book and welcoming it into *Superimpositions: Philosophy and the Moving Image.*

Faith Wilson Stein is an ideal editor: incisive, knowledgeable, and forward-thinking. We thank her for her expert guidance and incomparable good humor.

We are grateful to our anonymous readers for their thought-provoking reports.

Thanks to our copyeditor and first reader, Daniella Sanader, for combing through this book with a keen eye for detail. We also thank Matthew John Phillips, with whom it is always a pleasure to work, for crafting an index both accessible and creative.

Of the interlocutors who inspired this book, we give special thanks to Lynne Huffer, Ashley Shelden, and Elizabeth A. Wilson for inviting us into their reading group and giving us a much-needed intellectual jolt.

The American Comparative Literature Association (ACLA) and the Association for the Study of Literature and Environment provided stimulating homes for our research. Special thanks to Erin Prior and Scott Jackshaw for admitting us into their ACLA seminar, "Ruined Hope: Experiments in Negation, Nihilism, and Possibility," where we test-drove the introduction and received many helpful comments.

Our thanks to James Leo Cahill, whose Copernican cinema animates ours, for publishing our first collaborative piece. This earlier version of chapter 3 appeared as "Destructive Environmentalism: The Queer Impossibility of *First Reformed*" in *Discourse: Journal for Theoretical Studies in Media and Culture* 43, no. 1 (2021): 3–30.

Brian Teare's poem "Clear Water Ranga" is derived from *Doomstead Days*. Copyright © 2019 Nightboat Books, excerpted with the permission of Nightboat Books.

York University and Baruch College provided timely financial contributions to the production of this book. We thank them for their assistance.

Lastly, we thank three extraordinary teachers who died during the writing of this book: Lauren Berlant, Leo Bersani, and Jonathan Goldberg. We mourn their loss and celebrate their genius. This book is for them.

* * *

Steven Swarbrick thanks his colleagues at Baruch College—in particular, Timothy Aubry, Christina Christoforatou, Allison Deutermann, Claire Grandy, Laura Kolb, Jessica Lang, Mary McGlynn, Rick Rodriguez, and Evan Smith—for creating a stimulating environment in which to teach and write.

He thanks his union, the PSC-CUNY, for striving to make a more just university.

Kyle Black and Brian Whitney hosted numerous film screenings during the writing of this book. Their knowledge and friendship have been a refuge and joy.

Steven thanks his colleagues Drew Daniel, Jessie Hock, Benjamin Parris, and Christine Varnado, brilliant scholars and cherished interlocutors, for making early modern studies a place where theory can still have a home.

He thanks Frédéric Neyrat, existentialist of the stars, for disturbing his dogmatic ecological slumbers.

Rebecca van Laer's bountiful intellect and singular love make not only writing but living possible and fun. She and their cats, Milton and Gus, are a constant inspiration.

Finally, he owes his greatest debt to Jean-Thomas Tremblay, whose contributions to this book are immense. Jean-Thomas proves that not all our entanglements are bad after all. They can be exceptional. Thanks to Jean-Thomas for being an exceptional thinker, collaborator, and friend.

* * *

Jean-Thomas Tremblay wishes to thank colleagues at York University for energizing exchanges, especially Jody Berland, David Cecchetto, Shama Rangwala, and Joan Steigerwald. Thanks to Ravi de Costa for championing research. Thanks, also, to YUFA comrades for modeling solidarity.

Jean-Thomas is grateful to Jules Gill-Peterson and Dan Guadagnolo: dazzling thinkers and fierce friends.

Thanks to Sam Creely for thinking through it all, together.

The symmetry is hardly surprising, given our alignment throughout this project: final thanks are owed to Steven Swarbrick, exemplary coauthor and interlocutor, generous beyond belief, a mind so fructuous, it makes you believe again in all that this book distrusts (pedagogy, connection, abundance). Here's to hoping we're just getting started.

Notes

PREFACE

1. Donna J. Haraway, *Staying with the Trouble: Making Kin in the Chthulucene* (Durham, NC: Duke University Press, 2016), 55.
2. Haraway, *Staying with the Trouble*, 1, 2, 101, emphasis added.
3. Haraway, *Staying with the Trouble*, 101.
4. Haraway, *Staying with the Trouble*, 100.
5. Brian Teare, *Doomstead Days* (New York: Nightboat Books, 2019), 13. Another title in the aforementioned genealogy would be Sarah Dowling, *Entering Sappho* (Toronto: Coach House Books, 2020).
6. Brian Gyamfi, "The Ecological Part of Gender: An Interview with Brian Teare," *Michigan Quarterly Review*, November 2021, https://sites.lsa.umich.edu/mqr/2021/11/the-ecological-part-of-gender-an-interview-with-brian-teare/.
7. Jean-Thomas Tremblay, *Breathing Aesthetics* (Durham, NC: Duke University Press, 2022), 151.
8. Louis-Georges Schwartz, "Cinema and the ~~Meaning~~ of 'Life,'" *Discourse* 28, nos. 2–3 (2006): 7–27.
9. André Bazin, *What Is Cinema? Volume 1*, ed. and trans. Hugh Gray (Berkeley: University of California Press, 1967), 155.
10. Kara Keeling, *The Witch's Flight: The Cinematic, the Black Femme, and the Image of Common Sense* (Durham, NC: Duke University Press, 2007), esp. 3–5.
11. Jennifer Fay, *Inhospitable Worlds: Cinema in the Time of the Anthropocene* (New York: Oxford University Press, 2018), 3. See also Jennifer Fay's "Do I Know the Anthropocene When I See It?" *Representations* 157, no. 1 (2022): 41–67.
12. Derek Woods, "Terraforming Earth: Climate and Recursivity," *Diacritics* 47, no. 3 (2019): 8, 7.
13. On the "thoughtlessness" that "eludes representation and belief" on film, see Jennifer Fay, "Thinking on Film with Arendt and Cavell," *Critical Inquiry* 49, no. 2 (2023): 250.

14. Lauren Berlant and Lee Edelman, *Sex, or the Unbearable* (Durham, NC: Duke University Press, 2013), 88.
15. Berlant and Edelman, *Sex, or the Unbearable*, 93–94.
16. On the universality of non-belonging, see Todd McGowan, *Enjoyment Right and Left* (Portland, OR: Sublation, 2022): "The emancipatory position, the stance of a leftist enjoyment, is to occupy the contradiction. Leftism discovers universality in the social contradiction where there is no recognition or authorization. This contradictory position is universal because it is available to everyone regardless of social status or political power" (11).
17. Jacques Lacan makes separation the cornerstone of psychoanalytic treatment in *The Seminar of Jacques Lacan, Book XI: The Four Fundamental Concepts of Psychoanalysis*, ed. Jacques-Alain Miller, trans. Alan Sheridan (New York: Norton, 1998), 214, 218–19. Subjects, through analysis, separate and thus gain theoretical distance from the fantasy structure that has organized their psychic life. By separating from their fundamental fantasy, subjects gain a foothold on the lack that is their true source of freedom. For a related theory of separation, tuned to the pitch of ecology and its stifling entanglements, see Frédéric Neyrat, *The Unconstructable Earth: An Ecology of Separation*, trans. Drew S. Burk (New York: Fordham University Press, 2019), 150–54.
18. Alain Badiou, *Being and Event*, trans. Oliver Feltham (London: Continuum, 2005), 105. For Badiou, a "situation" refers to a structured multiple: any act of ordering or sense-making that privileges countable, recognizable units or sets to the exclusion of the null set, which he sees as universal and emancipatory. The situation, for Badiou, orders vision, while the null set haunts vision as a remainder or gap. See, on this point, Jean-Paul Sartre's *Being and Nothingness*, trans. Hazel E. Barnes (London: Routledge, 2003), which underwrites Badiou's text by likewise treating nothingness as the ground of vision and every situation.

INTRODUCTION

1. Jacques Lacan, *The Seminar of Jacques Lacan, Book VII: The Ethics of Psychoanalysis, 1959–1960*, ed. Jacques-Alain Miller, trans. Dennis Porter (New York: Norton, 1992), 88.
2. Our use of the term "ecocriticism" encompasses the practices of scholars within what are increasingly called the "environmental humanities"—practices that may be water-, air-, or land-based and may focus on plants or animals. Ecocriticism includes, in addition to ecological literary and film criticism, a range of fields and subfields that exist in the vicinity of the "theory" rubric and cultivate an aesthetic attention to the world.
3. A survey of the wonder-filled ecocritical literature on nature-as-pedagogue, one to which we will add titles throughout *Negative Life*, begins with Ruth DeFries, *What Would Nature Do? A Guide for Our Uncertain Times* (New York: Columbia University Press, 2021); Aimee Nezhukumatathil, *World of Wonders: In Praise of Fireflies, Whale Sharks, and Other Astonishments* (Minneapolis, MN: Milkweed, 2020); and Hugh Raffles, *Insectopedia* (New York: Vintage, 2010).

4. We notice this logic in environmental humanities job postings that expect candidates to demonstrate the ways their research and teaching perform the exo-disciplinary task of directly meeting the challenges brought about by the climate emergency.
5. Patrick Whitmarsh, *Writing Our Extinction: Anthropocene Fiction and Vertical Science* (Stanford, CA: Stanford University Press, 2023), 12.
6. *Die Wand* (*The Wall*), dir. Julian Pölsler (2012; Vienna and Munich: Coop99 Filmproduktion and Starhaus Filmproduktion, 2013).
7. The wall in *The Wall* impossibly occurs, blocking aesthetic recuperation and provoking a thinking that, according to Tom Cohen and Claire Colebrook, suspends phenomenalization. Such thinking resists the resistance to theory that Paul de Man maintained is at the heart of aesthetic ideology, including the new aesthetic ideologies of ecocriticism. Against the rampant calls to connect with animals and plants and repair one's milieu, "theory," Colebrook argues, following de Man, "steps back from, or disengages from, relations, and does not (yet) have a world in all its richness of affect and meaning. Theory would be, as [Paul] de Man suggested, an attention to *reading* rather than assuming that the matters of a text simply offered themselves as meaningful" (92). De Man's sublime materialism registers in a purely negative, purely formal manner as anti-matter—a hole in reference: it "is," de Man writes, "an absolute, radical formalism that entertains no notion of reference or semiosis . . . [that is] entirely a-referential, a-phenomenal, a-pathetic" (128). Such is the wall that we encounter in *The Wall* and frame as negative life. In Colebrook's view, "such a sublime would be aesthetic in de Man's sense *not* because it has to do with art and composition, but because it would propose a mode of seeing *without sense or teleology*" (120). Tom Cohen, Claire Colebrook, and J. Hillis Miller, *Twilight of the Anthropocene Idols* (London: Open Humanities, 2016); Paul de Man, *Aesthetic Ideology*, ed. Andrzej Warminski (Minneapolis: University of Minnesota Press, 1996).
8. *Persona*, dir. Ingmar Bergman (1966; Stockholm: AB Svensk Filmindustri, 2004).
9. Martin Heidegger, in *Being and Time*, trans. John Macquarrie and Edward Robinson (New York: Harper and Row, 1962), privileges the hand as the organ suitable to Dasein's way of being-in-the-world as "present-to-hand" (*vorhandenheit*) and "ready-to-hand" (*zuhandenheit*). From *Being and Time* onward, Heidegger views handiwork (*Handwerk*) and the hand itself as a manner of thinking distinct from conceptual or technological grasping. For Heidegger, the hand monstrates; it signs. We think through the hand and not just with it. Jacques Derrida observes that the monstration of the hand also borders on monstrosity. Heidegger's hand enmeshes Dasein in a lifeworld as a being whose essence is being-*in*-the-world. At the same time, this handiwork makes the human being into a monster—a thing apart. "Thus man's hand would be a thing apart, not as separable organ," Derrida writes, "but because it is different, dissimilar (*verschieden*) from all prehensile organs (paws, claws, talons); it is infinitely (*unendlich*) removed from these through the abyss of its being." Jacques Derrida, "Heidegger's Hand (*Geschlecht* II)," trans. John P. Leavey Jr. and Elizabeth Rottenberg, in *Psyche: Inventions of the Other, Volume II*, ed. Peggy Kamuf and Elizabeth Rottenberg (Stanford, CA: Stanford University Press, 2008), 41. For Derrida, unsurprisingly, the philosopher's hand is also the hand of writing, and that writing is always already divided, in touch with something other, in this

case, the animal. (In Bergman's *Persona*, the hand touches sexual difference—the subject of Derrida's other essay, "*Geschlecht* I: Sexual Difference, Ontological Difference," *Research in Phenomenology* 13 [1983]: 65–83.) The hand of thought becomes abyssal in Derrida's reading. Nonetheless, it is this abyss of thought that Heidegger makes central to Dasein's being all along and which, in the case of *The Wall*, separates the woman from the pastoral setting. In Heidegger's words, we are creatures "*held* out into the nothing"—a monstrous condition. Martin Heidegger, "What Is Metaphysics?" in *Basic Writings*, ed. and trans. David Farrell Krell (1977; New York: HarperCollins, 1993), 103, emphasis added.

10. *Bhopal Express*, dir. Mahesh Mathai (1999; Mumbai: Highlight Films, 2004); *First Reformed*, dir. Paul Schrader (2017; New York, London, Los Angeles, and Beverly Hills: Killer Films, Omeira Studio Partners, Fibonacci Films, Arclight Films, and Big Indie Productions, 2017); *First Cow*, dir. Kelly Reichardt (2019; Webster, TX, and New York: FilmScience and IAC Films, 2019); *Minari*, dir. Lee Isaac Chung (2020; Los Angeles: Plan B Entertainment, 2020); *Antichrist*, dir. Lars von Trier (2009; Copenhagen, Paris, Trollhättan, Stockholm, and Mainz: Zentropa Entertainments, arte France Cinéma, Canal+, Danmarks Radio, Film i Väst, Svenska Filminstitutet, Sveriges Television, and ZDF, 2009); *Annihilation*, dir. Alex Garland (2018; Santa Monica, London, New York, and Beijing: Skydance, DNA Films, Scott Rudin Productions, and Huahua Media, 2018); *In the Earth*, dir. Ben Wheatley (2021; Bridport, UK, and London: Rook Films and Protagonist Pictures, 2021); *Dýrið* (*Lamb*), dir. Valdimar Jóhannsson (2021; Paris, Stockholm, Warsaw, Trollhättan, and Malmö: Go to Sheep, Boom Films, Black Spark Productions, Madants/NEM Corp, Film i Väst, Chimney Sweden, Chimney Poland, and Rabbit Hole Productions, 2021); *X*, dir. Ti West (2022; Los Angeles: Little Lamb and Mad Solar Productions, 2022).

11. Eugenie Brinkema, *Life-Destroying Diagrams* (Durham, NC: Duke University Press, 2022), 27–29.

12. We shall address, in *Negative Life*'s first interlude, our formalism's imperfect alignment with Brinkema's with regard to spectatorship.

13. Of particular relevance to the genesis of our project are Leo Bersani, *The Freudian Body: Psychoanalysis and Art* (New York: Columbia University Press, 1986); Leo Bersani, *Homos* (Cambridge, MA: Harvard University Press, 1995); Leo Bersani, *Is the Rectum a Grave? And Other Essays* (Chicago: University of Chicago Press, 2010); Leo Bersani and Adam Phillips, *Intimacies* (Chicago: University of Chicago Press, 2008); Lee Edelman, *Bad Education: Why Queer Theory Teaches Us Nothing* (Durham, NC: Duke University Press, 2023); Lee Edelman, *No Future: Queer Theory and the Death Drive* (Durham, NC: Duke University Press, 2004); Jonathan Goldberg, *Melodrama: An Aesthetics of Impossibility* (Durham, NC: Duke University Press, 2016); Jonathan Goldberg, *Sodometries: Renaissance Texts, Modern Sexualities* (New York: Fordham University Press, 2010); and Elizabeth A. Wilson, "Acts against Nature," *Angelaki: Journal of the Theoretical Humanities* 23, no. 1 (2018): 19–31.

14. Berlant and Edelman, *Sex, or the Unbearable*, vii–viii.

15. See, for example, Bersani, *Is the Rectum a Grave?* 172–76.

16. Mari Ruti, *The Ethics of Opting Out: Queer Theory's Defiant Subjects* (New York: Columbia University Press, 2017), 131.

17. Nadia Bozak, *The Cinematic Footprint: Lights, Camera, Natural Resources* (New Brunswick, NJ: Rutgers University Press, 2012), 9; James Leo Cahill, *Zoological Surrealism: The Nonhuman Cinema of Jean Painlevé* (Minneapolis: University of Minnesota Press, 2019); Fay, *Inhospitable World.* See also Anat Pick and Guinevere Narraway, "Intersecting Ecology and Film," in *Screening Nature: Cinema beyond the Human*, ed. Anat Pick and Guinevere Narraway (New York: Berghahn Books, 2013), 1–18. Bozak's, Cahill's, Fay's, and our own treatment of the cinema as an ecological medium deviates from Adam O'Brien's survey, in *Film and the Natural Environment: Elements and Atmospheres* (London: Wallflower, 2018), of titles that merely "engage the natural environment with deliberate care and considerable imagination" (96). O'Brien contends that "films are never categorically 'environmental' any more than we are, but they can—like us—develop a rich and multifaceted relationship with their environment, not least by reminding us that such relationships are a matter of both perception and physical circumstance" (96). We hold greater faith in the cinema's ability not just to provide a snapshot of ecological relations but to expose and explode ecological contradictions.

18. The phrasing, "in a bad situation," is derived from the source material. Marlen Haushofer, *The Wall*, trans. Shaun Whiteside (1968; Berkeley, CA: Cleis, 2012), 11.

19. Lacan: "the most general formula that I can give you of sublimation is the following: it raises an object . . . to the dignity of the Thing"—the "Thing" being, in Lacan's idiom, the incognizable Real of the Other's desire, *das Ding*. Lacan, *The Ethics of Psychoanalysis, 1959–1960*, 112.

20. "I stretched out my hand," remembers the woman in Haushofer's novel, "and touched something smooth and cool: a smooth, cool resistance where there should be nothing but air" (*The Wall*, 8). Lacan writes: "The lamella is something extra-flat, which moves like the amoeba. . . . This lamella, this organ, whose characteristic is not to exist, but which is nevertheless an organ . . . is the libido. It is the libido, *qua* pure life instinct, that is to say, immortal life, or irrepressible life, life that has need of no organ, simplified, indestructible life." Lacan, *Four Fundamental Concepts*, 197–98.

21. Alexandre Kojève, *Introduction to the Reading of Hegel: Lectures on the "Phenomenology of Spirit,"* assembled by Raymond Queneau, ed. Allan Bloom, trans. James H. Nichols, Jr. (Ithaca, NY: Cornell University Press, 1969), 4, 5.

22. Haushofer's novel provides a different, and no less interesting, account of the human estrangement from animality. The narrator claims, "In my dreams I bring children into the world, and they aren't only human children; there are cats among them, dogs, calves, bears and quite peculiar furry creatures. But they emerge from me, and there is nothing about them that could frighten or repel me. It only looks off-putting when I write it down, in human writing and human words" (*The Wall*, 207). Here, it is the subsumption of entanglement into language that imposes a human–nonhuman dualism. Still, the novel does not locate a pastoral of entanglement in a pre- or post-linguistic moment; no such moment exists. The woman is bound to language. She is compelled to write, and thereby reestablish the impossible grounds—"human writing and human words"—of her multispecies reverie.

23. Levi Bryant, Nick Srnicek, and Graham Harman, "Towards a Speculative Philosophy," in *The Speculative Turn: Continental Materialism and Realism*, ed. Levi Bryant, Nick Srnicek, and Graham Harman (Melbourne, AU: re.press, 2011), 3, 13; Quentin Meillassoux, *After Finitude: An Essay on the Necessity of Contingency*, trans. Ray Brassier (London: Continuum, 2010), 5; Ian Bogost, *Alien Phenomenology, or What It's Like to Be a Thing* (Minneapolis: University of Minnesota Press, 2012), 10.
24. Timothy Morton, *The Ecological Thought* (Cambridge, MA: Harvard University Press, 2010), 47; see also 28, 29; Timothy Morton, *Hyperobjects: Philosophy and Ecology after the End of the World* (Minneapolis: University of Minnesota Press, 2013), 83, 118.
25. Karen Barad, *Meeting the Universe Halfway: Quantum Physics and the Entanglement of Matter and Meaning* (Durham, NC: Duke University Press, 2007), 175, 33.
26. David Hollingshead, "Neko Case and the Molecular Turn," *GLQ: A Journal of Lesbian and Gay Studies* 25, no. 4 (2019): 618.
27. Melody Jue and Rafico Ruiz, "Thinking with Saturation beyond Water: Thresholds, Phase Change, and the Precipitate," in *Saturation: An Elemental Politics*, ed. Melody Jue and Rafico Ruiz (Durham, NC: Duke University Press, 2021), 19.
28. Steven Swarbrick, "Nature's Queer Negativity: Between Barad and Deleuze," *Postmodern Culture* 29, no. 2 (2019): doi: 10.1353/pmc.2019.0003.
29. Karen Barad, "On Touching—The Inhuman That Therefore I Am," *differences* 23, no. 5 (2012): 214; Jane Bennett, *Vibrant Matter: A Political Ecology of Things* (Durham, NC: Duke University Press, 2010), 112, 14; Thom van Dooren, *Flight Ways: Life and Loss at the Edge of Extinction* (New York: Columbia University Press, 2014), 4–5, 92; Eben Kirksey, Craig Schuetze, and Stefan Helmreich, "Introduction," in *The Multispecies Salon*, ed. Eben Kirksey (Durham, NC: Duke University Press, 2014), 1; Karin Bolender, "R. A. W. Assmilk Soap," in Kirksey, *The Multispecies Salon*, 77.
30. Richard Powers, *The Overstory* (New York: W.W. Norton, 2018).
31. See William Cronon's ever-insightful "The Trouble with Wilderness; or, Getting Back to the Wrong Nature," *Environmental History* 1, no. 1 (1996): 7–28.
32. Tremblay, *Breathing Aesthetics*.
33. Tremblay, *Breathing Aesthetics*, 1–2, 5, 22–23, 33–36, 93.
34. Tremblay, *Breathing Aesthetics*, 94–138. These divergent models of respiratory ethics appear in a pair of chapters that achieve contrasting conclusions from the premise that we are all breathers, but none of the same kind.
35. Eva Haifa Giraud, *What Comes after Entanglement? Activism, Anthropocentrism, and an Ethics of Exclusion* (Durham, NC: Duke University Press, 2019), 2.
36. Giraud, *What Comes after Entanglement?* 2.
37. Giraud, *What Comes after Entanglement?* 69.
38. Ryan Hediger, *Homesickness: Of Trauma and the Longing for Place in a Change Environment* (Minneapolis: University of Minnesota Press, 2019); Bruno Latour, "An Attempt at a 'Compositionist Manifesto,'" *New Literary History* 41, no. 3 (2010): 471–90; Haraway, *Staying with the Trouble*; Anna Lowenhaupt Tsing, *The Mushroom at the End of the World: On the Possibility of Life in Capitalist Ruins* (Princeton, NJ: Princeton University Press, 2015); María Puig de la Bellacasa, *Matters of Care: Speculative Ethics in More Than Human Worlds* (Minneapolis: University of Minnesota Press, 2017); Jeffrey Jerome Cohen and Lowell Duckert, eds., *Elemental Ecocriticism:*

Thinking with Earth, Air, Water, and Fire (Minneapolis: University of Minnesota Press, 2015); Donna J. Haraway, *When Species Meet* (Minneapolis: University of Minnesota Press, 2008); Deborah Bird Rose, *Wild Dog Dreaming: Love and Extinction* (Charlottesville: University of Virginia Press, 2011); Thom van Dooren and Matthew Chrulew, eds., *Kin: Thinking with Deborah Bird Rose* (Durham, NC: Duke University Press, 2022).

39. Elizabeth DeLoughrey, "Submarine Futures of the Anthropocene," *Comparative Literature* 69, no. 1 (2017): 33; Elspeth Probyn, *Eating the Ocean* (Durham, NC: Duke University Press, 2016); Melody Jue, *Wild Blue Media: Thinking through Seawater* (Durham, NC: Duke University Press, 2020), 3.

40. Stacy Alaimo, *Exposed: Environmental Politics and Pleasures in Posthuman Times* (Minneapolis: University of Minnesota Press, 2016), 8.

41. Alaimo, *Exposed*, 8.

42. Alaimo, *Exposed*, 8.

43. Sigmund Freud, *Civilization and Its Discontents* (1930), in *The Standard Edition of the Complete Psychological Works of Sigmund Freud*, vol. 21, ed. and trans. James Strachey (London: Hogarth Press and the Institute of Psychoanalysis, 1953–74), 65.

44. See Frank B. Wilderson III, interview by Jared Ball et al., "'We're Trying to Destroy the World': Anti-Blackness and Police Violence after Ferguson," Ill Will, November 2014, https://illwill.com/print/were-trying-to-destroy-the-world; and Frank B. Wilderson III, *Afropessimism* (New York: Liveright, 2020). Wilderson's polemic, "We're Trying to Destroy the World," bares a structural insight. If some privileged parts of humanity and post-humanity experience the end of the world as an open invitation to re-create the world in the image of a better, truer "us," they miss Wilderson's point: that Humanity as such defines itself as anti-Black. Anti-Blackness is, according to Wilderson, a matter of health not only for the human community but for every political project that stakes its claim to recognition in the slogan: we are human, too. Indeed, for Afropessimism, what underwrites the claim to being recognized within the human community is "the aggressivity towards Blackness not as a form of discrimination, but as being a form of psychic health and well-being for the rest of the community" ("We're Trying to Destroy the World," 7). On Afropessimism and Black nihilism, see Saidiya Hartman, *Scenes of Subjection: Terror, Slavery, and Self-Making in Nineteenth-Century America* (Oxford: Oxford University Press, 1997); Jared Sexton, "Afro-Pessimism: The Unclear Word," *Rhizomes* 29 (2016): doi.org/10.20415/rhiz/029.e02; Calvin L. Warren, *Ontological Terror: Blackness, Nihilism, and Emancipation* (Durham, NC: Duke University Press, 2018); and Frank B. Wilderson III, *Red, White & Black: Cinema and the Structure of U.S. Antagonisms* (Durham, NC: Duke University Press, 2010). On Blackness as a problem for coalitional and identity-based politics, including ecological politics, see Zakiyyah Iman Jackson, *Becoming Human: Matter and Meaning in an Antiblack World* (New York: New York University Press, 2020); and David Marriott, *Whither Fanon? Studies in the Blackness of Being* (Stanford, CA: Stanford University Press, 2018). For a study of recent titles in Black ecology, see Jean-Thomas Tremblay, "Black Ecologies (Humanity, Animality, Property)," *GLQ: A Journal of Lesbian and Gay Studies* 29, no. 1 (2023): 129–39. The anti-sentimentalism that typifies many of the above titles complicates the incorporation of Blackness into a regime of attention that would hold out "the promise of multispecies justice"; see Eben Kirksey and Sophie Chao, "Introduction: Who Benefits from Multispecies Justice?" in *The Promise of Multispecies Justice*, ed. Sophie Chao, Karen Bolender, and Eben Kirksey (Durham, NC: Duke University Press, 2022), 1–21.

45. Wilderson, *Afropessimism*, 229. On the declaration "Black Lives Matter" and its ontological limits, see Warren, *Ontological Terror*, 1–2.

46. Alexis Shotwell, *Against Purity: Living Ethically in Compromised Times* (Minneapolis: University of Minnesota Press, 2016), 5, 15, 25–35.

47. Gayatri Chakravorty Spivak, *A Critique of Postcolonial Reason: Toward a History of the Vanishing Present* (Cambridge, MA: Harvard University Press, 1999), 9–13.

48. See Claire Colebrook, "End-Times for Humanity," Aeon, June 1, 2017, https://aeon.co/essays/the-human-world-is-not-more-fragile-now-it-always-has-been. Recall too that in the debate waged over Descartes's alleged expulsion and capture of madness by reason, it was Michel Foucault who, according to Derrida, tried to free madness (to let it speak) by enlisting the aquatic, the murmur of water, as the anti-logos and antithesis of Western reason: "madness is the manifestation in man of an obscure, aquatic element, a dark, disordered, shifting chaos, the germ and death of all things as opposed to the luminous, adult stability of the mind. So the ship of fools resonates in the Western imagination." Michel Foucault, *History of Madness*, trans. Jonathan Murphy and Jean Khalfa (1964; New York: Routledge, 2006), 12. And so it does. Derrida's point, however, is that even this anti-logos (the aquatic element as antithesis to reason) serves the operation of eco-logistics: that is, it stabilizes the logic of opposition by setting a determined solid ("adult stability of mind") against a determined liquid (madness, vitality). Rather than setting madness free, in other words, Foucault's early and unintended plunge into the blue humanities recaptures madness, the water element, under the horizon of indubitability. Jacques Derrida, "Cogito and the History of Madness," in *Writing and Difference*, trans. Alan Bass (Chicago: University of Chicago Press, 1978), 56.

49. Heidegger defines "being-toward-death" as Dasein's ownmost existential possibility, unique from other possibilities in that it cannot be apprehended: "Death is the possibility of the absolute impossibility of Dasein. Thus death reveals itself as that *possibility which is one's ownmost, which is non-relational, and which is not to be outstripped* [*unüberholbare*]. As such, death is something *distinctively* impending" (*Being and Time*, 294). For Dasein, death is an absolute limit. Comporting oneself to that limit is, for Heidegger, essential to living an authentic life. For Freud and Lacan, by contrast, the death drive allows no such authentic temporal existence, for two reasons: first, the death drive is repetitive and thus atemporal; it is, in Lacan's words, the "immortal life" of the human animal (*Four Fundamental Concepts*, 198). Second, the death drive feeds on self-sabotage. Consequently, it forbids authenticity in any straightforward sense.

50. Elizabeth A. Grosz, *Time Travels: Feminism, Nature, Power* (Durham, NC: Duke University Press, 2005), 4–5, 177–80; Jed Samer, *Lesbian Potentiality and Feminist Media in the 1970s* (Durham, NC: Duke University Press, 2022), 17, 34–37; Catherine Malabou, *The Ontology of the Accident: An Essay on Destructive Plasticity*, trans. Carolyn Shread (Cambridge: Polity, 2012); Alison Kafer, *Feminist, Queer, Crip* (Bloomington: Indiana University Press, 2013), 26; Gayle Salamon, *Assuming* *a Body: Transgender and Rhetorics of Materiality* (New York: Columbia University Press, 2010), 21; Elizabeth Freeman, *Time Binds: Queer Temporalities, Queer Histories* (Durham, NC: Duke University Press, 2010), 1, 142, 148; José Esteban Muñoz, *Cruising Utopia: The Then and There of Queer Futurity* (New York: New York University Press, 2009), 29, 32.

51. Haushofer, *The Wall*, 209.

52. The term "ab-sense" derives from Lacan's text "L'Étourdit," which is the focus of two essays, one by Alain Badiou and the other by Barbara Cassin, that appeared together under the title *There's No Such Thing as a Sexual Relationship*, trans. Susan Spitzer and Kenneth Reinhard (New York: Columbia University Press, 2017). Kenneth Reinhard distinguishes ab-sense from nonsense in the book's introduction: "Aristotle and much of the philosophic tradition thereafter assume that a key function of noncontradiction is the separation of meaning from nonsense (or in Lacan's terms, *sens* from *non-sens*)" (xviii). According to Reinhard, "Lacan introduces a third category in 'L'Étourdit,' in excess of the sense/nonsense opposition: *ab-sense*" (xviii). Badiou links ab-sense to the Lacanian Real and stresses that what "needs to be understood concerning the complex decision Lacan is making here is that ab-sense must be absolutely distinguished from non-sense. . . . It is not an assertion of the non-sense of the real. Rather, it is an assertion that an access to the real can be opened only if it is assumed that the real is like an absence in sense, an ab-sense, or a subtraction of, or from, sense. Everything hinges on the distinction between ab-sense and non-sense" (49–50). In the introduction to *Bad Education*, Edelman furthers Badiou's claim that "the impossible, hence the real, is . . . linked to ab-sense and, in particular, to the absence of any relationship, which means the absence of any sexual meaning" (Badiou, *There's No Such Thing*, 50). According to Edelman, this absence of any sexual meaning entails that "what we 'know' as sex forecloses sex as senseless negativity, as the unknowable cut or division that precedes the (id)entities that cut makes possible" (*Bad Education*, 8–9). For our part, we locate the senseless cut of negativity in the cinema of extinction's assertion of (id)entities that fail the test of interconnectedness. These films witness a lack of ecological relationship, and thus a lack of ecological meaning. They are riddled with ab-sense.

53. Edelman, *Bad Education*, 47.

54. Edelman, *Bad Education*, 47.

55. Edelman, *Bad Education*, 52, 48.

56. Barad, "On Touching," 209, 213; Sam See, *Queer Natures, Queer Mythologies*, ed. Christopher Looby and Michael North (New York: Fordham University Press, 2020), 25.

57. Edelman, *Bad Education*, xiv; see also 200; Marriott, *Whither Fanon?*; James Bliss, "Hope Against Hope: Queer Negativity, Black Feminist Theorizing, and Reproduction without Futurity," *Mosaic* 48, no. 1 (2015): 83–98.

58. Edelman, *Bad Education*, xiv.

59. Angela Hume and Samia Rahimtoola, "Introduction: Queering Ecopoetics," *ISLE: Interdisciplinary Studies in Literature and Environment* 25, no. 1 (2018): 136.

60. Hume and Rahimtoola, "Introduction," 136. The latest (as of our writing this) entry in the literature on this debate is Lee Edelman's own "On Solidarity," *Representations* 158, no. 1 (2022): 93–105.

61. Samia Rahimtoola, "The Poetics of Drift: Coloniality, Place, and Environmental Racialization," in *Avant-Gardes in Crisis: Art and Politics in the Long 1970s*, ed. Jean-Thomas Tremblay and Andrew Strombeck (Albany: State University of New York Press, 2021), 39–60.
62. Mark Bould, *The Anthropocene Unconscious: Climate Catastrophe Culture* (New York: Verso, 2021), 15–16.
63. Steven Swarbrick, *The Environmental Unconscious: Ecological Poetics from Spenser to Milton* (Minneapolis: University of Minnesota Press, 2023), 27. Swarbrick's definition of the "environmental unconscious" quarrels with Lawrence Buell's—"the impossibility of individual or collective perception coming to full consciousness at whatever level"—in the latter's *Writing for an Endangered World: Literature, Culture, and Environment in the U.S. and Beyond* (Cambridge, MA: Belknap Press of Harvard University Press, 2001), 22. "What is above all striking in Buell's definition," writes Swarbrick, "is the extent to which it foreshortens the insights of psychoanalysis. The Freudian theory of sexuality is not on Buell's list of explanatory causes of environmental destruction: 'scientific ignorance, inattention,' and so on" (*The Environmental Unconscious*, 14).
64. Swarbrick, *The Environmental Unconscious*, 14.
65. Jean Laplanche, *New Foundations for Psychoanalysis*, trans. David Macey (Cambridge, MA: Basil Blackwell, 1989), 125–30.
66. On Freud's "going astray" and Laplanche's general theory of seduction, see Jean Laplanche, *Life and Death in Psychoanalysis*, trans. Jeffrey Mehlman (Baltimore, MD: Johns Hopkins University Press, 1976); Jean Laplanche, "The Unfinished Copernican Revolution," trans. Luke Thurston, in *Essays on Otherness*, ed. John Fletcher (New York: Routledge, 1999), 52–83; and Jean Laplanche, *The Temptation of Biology: Freud's Theories of Sexuality*, trans. Donald Nicholson-Smith (New York: The Unconscious in Translation, 2015). For a queer-theoretical investigation of Laplanche's theory of sexuality, see Gila Ashtor, *Homo Psyche: On Queer Theory and Erotophobia* (New York: Fordham University Press, 2021).
67. Laplanche: "[Sándor] Ferenczi stops short of the further consideration that what he calls the 'language of passion' (adult language) is traumatic only in so far as it conveys an unknown meaning, or only in so far as it manifests the presence of the parental unconscious. . . . I am, then, using the term primal seduction to describe a fundamental situation in which an adult proffers to a child verbal, non-verbal and even behavioral signifiers which are pregnant with unconscious sexual significations" (*New Foundations for Psychoanalysis*, 125–26).
68. See Emmanuel Levinas, *Entre Nous: Thinking-of-the-Other*, trans. Michael B. Smith and Barbara Harshav (New York: Columbia University Press, 1998); Emmanuel Levinas, *Otherwise Than Being, or Beyond Essence*, trans. Alphonso Lingis (Pittsburgh, PA: Duquesne University Press, 1998); Judith Butler, *Giving an Account of Oneself* (New York: Fordham University Press, 2005); and Judith Butler, *Precarious Life: The Powers of Mourning and Violence* (New York: Verso, 2004). On the Levinasian influence on thinkers concerned with Anthropocene ethics, see Seán Hand, "Being for Every Other: Levinas in the Anthropocene," *Frontiers of Narrative Studies* 7, no. 2 (2021): 156–75. For evidence of this influence, see, for example, Haraway, *When Species Meet*; Puig de la Bellacasa, *Matters of Care*; and Michael Marder,

Plant-Thinking: A Philosophy of Vegetal Life (New York: Columbia University Press, 2013). Environmental justice, too, predicates itself, more often than not, on an ethics of recognition. See, for example, Brendan Coolsaet and Pierre-Yves Néron, "Recognition and Environmental Justice," in *Environmental Justice: Key Issues*, ed. Brendan Coolsaet (London: Routledge, 2020): 52–63; Adrian Martin et al., "Justice and Conservation: The Need to Incorporate Recognition," *Biological Conservation* 197 (2016): 254–61; and Kyle Whyte, "The Recognition Paradigm of Environmental Injustice," in *The Routledge Handbook of Environmental Justice*, ed. Ryan Holifield, Jayajit Chakraborty, and Gordon Walker (New York: Routledge, 2017), 113–23.

69. Laplanche, *New Foundations for Psychoanalysis*, 126–27.

70. Conventional periodization places the Lacan of the symbolic in the early seminars before *Seminar VII* and the emergence of *das Ding*. See Laplanche, *New Foundations for Psychoanalysis*, 125–30.

71. Jacques Lacan, "The Mirror Stage as Formative of the *I* Function as Revealed in Psychoanalytic Experience," in *Écrits: The First Complete Edition in English*, trans. Bruce Fink (New York: Norton, 2006), 75–81.

72. Edelman, *Bad Education*, 48.

73. Edelman, *Bad Education*, 46.

74. Lacan, *The Ethics of Psychoanalysis*, 90.

75. Although, as Cahill notes, the human self-estrangement triggered by the Copernican revolution may be a bid to regain humanity: "A profound ambivalence subtends Copernican thought and its instrumentation. Together they produce a cosmic 'humiliation' of being displaced from the center of the universe and being confronted with one's own 'parochial' perception. But they also supported a humanist triumph of *reason* and *technique*, capable of loosening human imagination from the perceptual limitations of its situated embodiment through prostheses 'overcoming' perceived defects and extending perceptual and cognitive capacities. Copernican thought sustains a dialectical interplay between anti-anthropocentric displacement and a recentering humanist affirmation of human ingenuity" (*Zoological Surrealism*, 17–18). We land on an alternative version of recalcitrant humanity in the next section.

76. Grosz, *Time Travels*, 3, 19, 37, 41, 47.

77. See, *Queer Natures, Queer Mythologies*, 14. On See's equation between nature, queerness, art, and modernism; on the clash between Grosz's and See's Darwinisms around the question of sexual difference; and on both theorists' ultimately counter-Darwinian, pastoral recuperation of the accidentality of nature and sex, see Jean-Thomas Tremblay and Jules Gill-Peterson, "Sex in Nature: Darwin, Depastoralized," *Regeneration: Environment, Art, Culture* 1, no. 1 (2024), forthcoming.

78. See, for example, Sam See, "Bersani in Love," *Henry James Review* 32, no. 3 (2011): 195–203.

79. Grosz, *Time Travels*, 18, 22; Elizabeth Grosz, "The Nature of Sexual Difference: Irigaray and Darwin," *Angelaki* 17, no. 2 (2012): 90.

80. Grosz, *Time Travels*, 41.

81. We detect a similar problem in the ecophilosophy of Rosi Braidotti's *Nomadic Subjects: Embodiment and Sexual Difference in Contemporary Feminist Theory*, 2nd ed. (New York: Columbia University Press, 2011). Like Grosz, Braidotti frames sexual difference not as an anchoring point for essentialism but as a multiplier of differences and becomings that are queer and posthuman. "The subject is both sexed and split," Braidotti writes, "both resting on one of the poles of the sexual dichotomy and unfastened to it, constantly off-center and in motion between structures and social indicators. The theoretical core of the feminism of sexual difference is the assertion of the not-One-ness at the origin of the subject and hence also within each subject" (98). We notice, however, that the lack of One-ness in Braidotti's posthumanism decamps from the One only to reassert it on a higher level where all things, human and nonhuman, interconnect. In a reading of Clarice Lispector's novel *The Passion According to G.H.*, Braidotti highlights G.H.'s encounter with an insect to posit a nature that is "uncoded" and "open," where "social identity" is unfixed and becoming-animal equates to a "becoming one with all that lives outside the human": "In the uncoded space that opens up, G.H. shreds all the forms of belonging that had framed her social identity until then and is open to becoming one with all that lives outside the human; animal, divine, and even cosmic diversions beacon out of her" (117). The anti-naturalism that Braidotti critiques finds its complement in a theory of life that is connected rather than fractured, positive rather than negative, and posthuman rather than human.

82. Laplanche: "the primacy of sexuality opens directly onto the question of the other, and in the case of the child, onto the adult other in his or her alien-ness" ("The Unfinished Copernican Revolution," 64). Jacques Lacan formulates this question as the *Chè vuoi?* (What do you want?) in "The Subversion of the Subject and the Dialectic of Desire," in *Écrits*, 690. For an analysis of the *Chè vuoi?* in relation to the Lacanian big Other, see Slavoj Žižek, "From *Che Vuoi?* to Fantasy: Lacan with *Eyes Wide Shut*," in *How to Read Lacan* (New York: Norton, 2006), 40–60.

83. Fascinatingly, Haushofer's novel does not espouse the format of a diary. It reads, quite simply, as a novel, one with paragraph breaks but no chapter divisions. This implies a supplementary mediation: either the woman novelized her own report after writing it, or a third party did. In either case, the distance established by generic and formal remediation further estranges us, as readers, from the woman's lonely existence.

84. See, for example, Ursula K. Heise, *Imagining Extinction: The Cultural Meanings of Endangered Species* (Chicago: University of Chicago Press, 2016), 5, 244; and van Dooren, *Flight Ways*.

85. Lydia Pyne, *Endlings: Fables for the Anthropocene* (Minneapolis: University of Minnesota Press, 2022), 1.

86. Pyne, *Endlings*, 73–74.

87. Pyne, *Endlings*, 79.

88. See Wojciech Małecki et al., "About Empirical Ecocriticism," Empirical Ecocriticism, n.d., https://empiricalecocriticism.com/about-empirical-ecocriticism/.

89. Wojciech Małecki et al., "Can Fiction Make Us Kinder to Other Species? The Impact of Fiction on Pro-Animal Attitudes and Behavior," *Poetics* 66 (February 2018): doi.org/10.1016/j.poetic.2018.02.004; W. P. Małecki et al., "Extinction Stories Matter: The Impact of Narrative Representations of Endangered Species across Media," *ISLE: Interdisciplinary Studies in Literature and Environment* (2021): doi.org/10.1093/isle/isab094.

90. *The Cabin in the Woods*, dir. Drew Goddard (2011; Los Angeles: Mutant Enemy Productions, 2012).
91. Brinkema, *Life-Destroying Diagrams*, 150.
92. Brinkema, *Life-Destroying Diagrams*, 150. All words proximate to "failure" are printed in gray ink, rather than black ink, in the chapter "Grid, Table, Failure, Line." We have omitted the stylization for legibility.
93. Brinkema, *Life-Destroying Diagrams*, 152.
94. Brinkema, *Life-Destroying Diagrams*, 161n.xi.
95. Brinkema, *Life-Destroying Diagrams*, 151n.vii.
96. "Nothing is underneath the grid," writes Brinkema; "it does not loan or transfer its sense to anything else; the grid is only its formal extension and optimal saturation" (*Life-Destroying Diagrams*, 180n.xxiv).

CHAPTER ONE

1. Sigmund Freud, "Negation" (1925), in *The Standard Edition of the Complete Psychological Works of Sigmund Freud*, vol. 19, ed. and trans. James Strachey (London: Hogarth Press and the Institute of Psychoanalysis, 1953–74), 233–40.
2. Lucretius, *On the Nature of Things*, trans. W. H. D. Rouse, revised by Martin Ferguson Smith, Loeb Classical Library (Cambridge, MA: Harvard University Press, 1982), 15.
3. William Shakespeare, *The Tragedy of King Lear* (Folio version), in *The Norton Shakespeare*, 3rd ed., ed. Stephen Greenblatt et al. (New York: Norton, 2016), 2331–493.
4. Badiou, *Being and Event*, 24–25.
5. From *apo-*, "off," and *kalýptein*, "to cover." "Apocalypse," *Merriam-Webster.com Dictionary*, Merriam-Webster, https://www.merriam-webster.com/dictionary/apocalypse.
6. Freud, "Negation," 235. We catch sight of negation's operation in Freud's very analogy. "It is as though the patient had said" something, Freud begins, implying that the patient has not, in fact, said it—not in those terms, anyway.
7. Freud, "Negation," 235.
8. Freud, "Negation," 236, emphasis added.
9. For Badiou, too, being as number begins at nothing, which he denotes as the empty set {∅}. In Badiou's mathematical ontology, the void {∅} extrudes being: "The unpresentable is that to which nothing, no multiple, belongs; consequently, it cannot present itself in its difference. . . . This singular axiom . . . is *the axiom of the void-set*. . . . In its metaontological formulation the axiom says: the unpresentable is present, as a subtractive term" (*Being and Event*, 67).
10. Freud, "Negation," 235.
11. Freud, "Negation," 236.
12. Freud, "Negation," 237–38.
13. For Zupančič, the "missing signifier" refers to "a constitutive lack in the Other." She explains: "In this precise sense the signifying order could be said to begin, not with One (nor with multiplicity), but with a 'minus one.' . . . It is *in the place of this gap* or negativity that *appears the surplus-enjoyment* which stains the signifying

structure: the heterogeneous element pertaining to the signifying structure, yet irreducible to it." Alenka Zupančič, *What IS Sex?* (Cambridge, MA: MIT Press, 2017), 42.
14. *Old Joy*, dir. Kelly Reichardt (2006; Webster, TX, and New York: Film Science, Van Hoy/Knudsen Productions, and Washington Square Films, 2007); *Wendy and Lucy*, dir. Kelly Reichardt (2008; Webster, TX, and New York: Field Guide Films, Film Science, Glass Eye Pix, and Washington Square Films, 2009); *Meek's Cutoff*, dir. Kelly Reichardt (2010; Webster, TX, and New York: Evenstar Films, Film Science, Harmony Productions, and Primitive Nerd, 2011); *Night Moves*, dir. Kelly Reichardt (2013; Santa Monica, Webster, TX, and São Paulo: Maybach Film Productions, Film Science, Tipping Point Productions, and RT Features, 2014).
15. Rob Nixon, *Slow Violence and the Environmentalism of the Poor* (Cambridge, MA: Harvard University Press, 2011).
16. Katherine Fusco and Nicole Seymour, *Kelly Reichardt* (Champaign: University of Illinois Press, 2017), 3.
17. Georg Wilhelm Friedrich Hegel, *Phenomenology of Spirit*, trans. A. V. Miller (Oxford: Oxford University Press, 1977), 6.
18. Jacques Lacan, *The Seminar of Jacques Lacan, Book II: The Ego in Freud's Theory and in the Technique of Psychoanalysis, 1954–1955*, ed. Jacques-Alain Miller, trans. Sylvana Tomaselli (New York: Norton, 1991), 201.
19. Rancière's political philosophy rests on the distinction between what something is and where it is in space. He calls "policing" the distribution of bodies in space—a distribution that governs ways of appearing or not: "The police is thus first an order of bodies that defines the allocation of ways of doing, ways of being, and ways of saying, and sees that those bodies are assigned by name to a particular place and task; is an order of the visible and the sayable that sees that a particular activity is visible and another is not, that this speech is understood as discourse and another as noise." Jacques Rancière, *Disagreement: Politics and Philosophy*, trans. Julie Rose (Minneapolis: University of Minnesota Press, 1999), 29.
20. Jacques Lacan, *The Seminar of Jacques Lacan, Book XX: On Feminine Sexuality, the Limits of Love and Knowledge, 1972–1973 (Encore)*, ed. Jacques-Alain Miller, trans. Bruce Fink (New York: Norton, 1998), 22, 77, 121. Lacan's translator, Bruce Fink, notes that "Lacan uses it [ex-sistence] to talk about an existence that stands apart, which insists as it were from the outside, something not included on the inside. Rather than being intimate, it is 'extimate'" (22n.24).
21. Lacan's full reasoning reads: "Nothing in the way of intersubjectivity is decisive here, because once the measures of the real are made tight, once a perimeter, a volume, is defined once and for all, there is nothing to lead one to suspect that when all is said and done even a letter might escape. If nonetheless the fact that they can't find it is convincing, it is because the domain of significations continues to exist, even in the mind of people assumed to be as stupid as policemen. . . . In the same way, one thinks that when one has reached a certain point of comprehension in psychoanalysis, one can grab it and say—Here it is, we've got it. On the contrary, signification as such is never where one thinks it must be." Lacan, *The Ego in Freud's Theory and in the Technique of Psychoanalysis*, 187.

22. See, for example, Haraway, *Staying with the Trouble*, 99–103; Linsey E. Haram et al., "A Plasticene Lexicon," *Marine Pollution Bulletin* 150 (2020): doi.org/10.1016/j.marpolbul.2019.110714.

23. On ecocriticism and anamorphism, see Tremblay, *Breathing Aesthetics*, 42–43; and Swarbrick, *The Environmental Unconscious*, 242. We are inspired by Todd McGowan's Lacanian reformulation of the cinematic gaze as "the site of a traumatic encounter with the [anamorphic] Real, with the utter failure of the spectator's seemingly safe distance and assumed mastery," in "Looking for the Gaze: Lacanian Film Theory and Its Vicissitudes," *Cinema Journal* 42, no. 3 (2003): 29.

24. Michel Foucault, *The History of Sexuality: Volume 1: An Introduction*, trans. Robert Hurley (New York: Pantheon, 1978), 10–13.

25. *Fantastic Fungi*, dir. Louie Schwartzberg (2019; Los Angeles: Moving Art, 2019); Merlin Sheldrake, *Entangled Life: How Fungi Make Our Worlds, Change Our Minds & Shape Our Futures* (New York: Random House, 2020).

26. Tsing, *The Mushroom at the End of the World*, vii.

27. Tsing, *The Mushroom at the End of the World*, vii.

28. Tsing, *The Mushroom at the End of the World*, vii.

29. Tsing, *The Mushroom at the End of the World*, viii.

30. Tsing, *The Mushroom at the End of the World*, 22, 24, 61, 20, viii, 4.

31. Tsing, *The Mushroom at the End of the World*, 22–23, 218.

32. Tsing, *The Mushroom at the End of the World*, 23.

33. Tsing, *The Mushroom at the End of the World*, 98.

34. Natalia Cecire and Samuel Solomon, "Mycoaesthetics; or, Why Mushrooms Can Never Run Out of Steam," *Critical Inquiry* 50, no. 4 (2024), forthcoming.

35. Cecire and Solomon, "Mycoaesthetics."

36. Cecire and Solomon, "Mycoaesthetics."

37. See, for example, Jacques Derrida's "Signature Event Context" on the indeterminate nature of the signifier in *Margins of Philosophy*, trans. Alan Bass (Chicago: University of Chicago Press, 1982), 307–30.

38. "In a language," Saussure asserts, "there are only differences, *and no positive terms*." Ferdinand de Saussure, *Course in General Linguistics*, ed. Charles Bally et al., trans. Roy Harris (Chicago: Open Court, 1983), 118.

39. Joan Copjec, *Read My Desire: Lacan against the Historicists* (1994; New York: Verso, 2015), 201–36.

40. Copjec: "Emphasizing the 'synchronic perspective' of the linguist and his community, Saussure eventually decided to give priority to the contemporaneous system of signifiers operating at some (hypothetical) frozen moment: the present" (*Read My Desire*, 206).

41. Copjec, *Read My Desire*, 206.

42. Lacan, *On Feminine Sexuality*, 57, 7.

43. See Anna Lowenhaupt Tsing et al., "Introduction: Haunted Landscapes of the Anthropocene," in *Arts of Living on a Damaged Planet: Ghosts and Monsters of the Anthropocene*, ed. Anna Lowenhaupt Tsing, Heather Anne Swanson, Elaine Gan, and Nils Bubandt (Minneapolis: University of Minnesota Press, 2017), G1–G14.

44. On the empirical versus transcendental distinction in Lacan's thought, see Todd McGowan, *Enjoying What We Don't Have: The Political Project of Psychoanalysis* (Lincoln: University of Nebraska Press, 2013). Whereas "the hermeneutic thinker renders the missing signifier both transcendent and empirical," McGowan notes, "it is neither one nor the other. The status of the missing signifier is transcendental. Its absence serves only to curve the signifying structure" (274).

45. *Sans toit ni loi* (*Vagabond*), dir. Agnès Varda (1985; New York and Paris: Janus Films and Ciné-Tamaris, 2007).

46. Todd McGowan links Varda's *Vagabond* to the structure of signification and the drifter to the missing signifier in "Signification and Subjectivity," July 17, 2021, video, 26:00, https://youtu.be/AF7QBX9t28c?si=l929tFDgApLyKHYl.

47. *Twin Peaks*, created by Mark Frost and David Lynch (1990–91; Los Angeles: Lynch/Frost Productions, Propaganda Films, Spelling Television, and Twin Peaks Productions, 1990–91); *Twin Peaks: The Return*, created by Mark Frost and David Lynch (2017; Los Angeles and New York: Lynch/Frost Productions, Propaganda Films, Spelling Television, Twin Peaks Productions, CBS Television, and Showtime, 2017).

48. T. J. Clark, *The Sight of Death: An Experiment in Art Writing* (New Haven, CT: Yale University Press, 2006), 174; *Blue Velvet*, dir. David Lynch (1986; Wilmington, NC: De Laurentiis Entertainment Group, 2001).

49. *Fire of Love*, dir. Sara Dosa (2022; New York, Montreal, and Los Angeles: Sandbox Films, Intuitive Pictures, Cottage M, 2022).

50. Jean Laplanche, "Note on Afterwardsness," in *Essays on Otherness*, ed. John Fletcher (New York: Routledge, 1999), 260–65.

51. Jean Laplanche, "Time and the Other," trans. Luke Thurston, in *Essays on Otherness*, ed. John Fletcher (New York: Routledge, 1999), 234.

52. Laplanche, "The Unfinished Copernican Revolution," 82–83.

53. Laplanche, "Time and the Other," 235.

54. Laplanche, "The Unfinished Copernican Revolution," 73, 78–79.

55. Laplanche, "Time and the Other," 255.

56. The formulation appears in an excerpt that reads, in full: "The 'other thing' is quite simply the unconscious. There is no reason to deny this 'other thing' the characteristics of timelessness and above all the absence of negation. The absence of negation, the absence of discursivity from the diachronic point of view, and the absence of 'value' (in the Saussurean sense of structural opposition) from the synchronic. . . . The unconscious cannot in any way be considered the kernel of our being. . . . Far from being my kernel, it is the other implanted in me, the metabolized product of the other in me: forever an 'internal foreign body.'" Laplanche, "Time and the Other," 256.

57. Laplanche, "Time and the Other," 259.

58. *Tampopo*, dir. Juzo Itami (1985; New York: Itami Productions and New Century Producers, 1998).

59. Todd McGowan, *Only a Joke Can Save Us: A Theory of Comedy* (Evanston, IL: Northwestern University Press, 2017), esp. 19–48.

60. Mark Rifkin, *Settler Time: Temporal Sovereignty and Indigenous Self-Determination* (Durham, NC: Duke University Press, 2017), x.

61. Laplanche, "Time and the Other," 258.
62. Sigmund Freud, *Project for a Scientific Psychology* (1950 [1895]), in *The Standard Edition of the Complete Psychological Works of Sigmund Freud*, vol. 1, ed. and trans. James Strachey (London: Hogarth Press and the Institute of Psychoanalysis, 1953–74), 327–28.
63. Todd McGowan explains in "The Satisfaction of an Ending," in *Cinematic Cuts: Theorizing Film Endings*, ed. Sheila Kunkle (Albany: State University of New York Press, 2016), that "desire's relation to the object is metonymic. This is because whatever the subject's desire finds never provides the satisfaction it expects. Desire moves from object to object in search of a satisfaction that no object is able to provide but that the next object always promises" (136).
64. Philippe van Haute, *Against Adaptation: Lacan's "Subversion of the Subject,"* trans. Paul Crowe and Miranda Vankerk (New York: Other Press, 2002), 144.
65. Van Haute, *Against Adaptation*, 287–88.
66. Barbara J. Fields and Karen E. Fields. *Racecraft: The Soul of Inequality in American Life* (New York: Verso, 2022), 18.
67. Fields and Fields, *Racecraft*, 18.
68. Fields and Fields, *Racecraft*, 20.
69. Fields and Fields, *Racecraft*, 21–22.
70. Copjec, *Read My Desire*, 209.
71. Fred Moten, *Stolen Life* (Durham, NC: Duke University Press, 2018).
72. Hortense Spillers, "Mama's Baby, Papa's Maybe: An American Grammar Book," *Diacritics* 17, no. 2 (1987): 67, emphasis removed.
73. James Baldwin, "My Dungeon Shook: Letter to My Nephew on the One Hundredth Anniversary of the Emancipation," in *James Baldwin: Collected Essays*, ed. Toni Morrison (New York: Library of America, 1998), 295.
74. Cari M. Carpenter, *Seeing Red: Anger, Sentimentality, and American Indians* (Columbus: Ohio State University Press, 2008), 11.
75. Carpenter, *Seeing Red*, 3, 11.
76. Carpenter, *Seeing Red*, 134.
77. Xine Yao, *Disaffected: The Cultural Politics of Unfeeling in Nineteenth-Century America* (Durham, NC: Duke University Press, 2021), 7, 5, 12.
78. Nicole Seymour, *Bad Environmentalism: Irony and Irrelevance in the Ecological Age* (Minneapolis: University of Minnesota Press, 2018), 26.
79. Elisabeth R. Anker, *Ugly Freedoms* (Durham, NC: Duke University Press, 2022), 6, 163.
80. Anker, *Ugly Freedoms*, 5.

INTERLUDE. THE HORROR OF ENTANGLEMENT I: *IN THE EARTH*, *ANNIHILATION*

1. Stephen Sondheim and James Lapine's 1987 stage musical *Into the Woods*: another excursus toward negativity.
2. *In the Earth* shares with the utopian mycoaesthetes some interpretations of mushroom life but prompts us as well to dwell on the threat that such interpretations

might pose to human sensation, perception, or health. Cecire and Solomon inventory these interpretations in "Mycoaesthetics": "'Mushrooms thrive in depleted environments' is high on the list of frequently repeated points, along with 'mushrooms let trees communicate,' 'mushrooms have x genders' (for some large number x), 'some mushrooms cannot be cultivated and are thus "nonscalable,"' and 'mushrooms are more closely related to animals than to plants.'"

3. Didier Anzieu, *The Skin-Ego*, trans. Naomi Segal (New York: Routledge, 2018), esp. 103–14.

4. In Jeff VanderMeer's 2014 novel *Annihilation*, the film's source material, the expedition comprises four women: an anthropologist, a surveyor, a psychologist, and a biologist (the narrator). We will not belabor the differences between the two versions, of which there are many. The film's five-person count doesn't strike us as thematically significant, only dramaturgically so. Other deviations on Garland's part appear motivated by the cinematic imperative to represent what otherwise resists visualization—for instance, a "tower . . . [that] plunges into the earth" or "words . . . made of fungi." Jeff VanderMeer, *Area X: The Southern Reach Trilogy* (New York: Farrar, Straus and Giroux, 2014), 3, 17.

5. Christy Tidwell, "Monstrous Natures Within: Posthuman and New Materialist Ecohorror in Mira Grant's *Parasite*," *ISLE: Interdisciplinary Studies in Literature and Environment* 21, no. 3 (2014): 538–39.

6. Tidwell, "Monstrous Natures Within," 539.

7. Tidwell, "Monstrous Natures Within," 541, 543.

8. Tidwell, "Monstrous Natures Within," 543.

9. Tidwell, "Monstrous Natures Within," 547, 548.

10. Sarah Dillon, "The Horror of the Anthropocene," *C21 Literature: Journal of 21st-Century Writing* 6, no. 1 (2018): 20. Dillon is here citing John Clute, "The Darkening Garden: A Short Lexicon of Horror," in *Stay* (Harold Wood, UK: Beccon, 2014), 269–343. To be clear: Dillon bemoans vastation, ultimately tasking literature with "conceiv[ing] of *story moves other than horror* that will transit all us critters into a future present in which the dust does not lie thickly over the planet" (22). New objects, same desire.

11. Christy Tidwell and Carter Soles, "Introduction: Ecohorror in the Anthropocene," in *Fear and Nature: Ecohorror Studies in the Anthropocene*, ed. Christy Tidwell and Carter Soles (University Park, PA: Penn State University Press, 2021), 1–20. See also Dawn Keetley and Matthew Sivils, eds., *Ecogothic in Nineteenth-Century American Literature* (New York: Routledge, 2018); Bernice M. Murphy, *The Rural Gothic in American Popular Culture: Backwoods Horror and Terror in the Wilderness* (New York: Palgrave Macmillan, 2013); and Alison Sperling, "Queer Ingestions: Weird and Vegetative Bodies in Jeff VanderMeer's Fiction," in *Plants in Science Fiction: Speculative Vegetation*, ed. Katherine E. Bishop, David Higgins, and Jerry Määtä (Cardiff: University of Wales Press, 2020), 194–213.

12. Tidwell and Soles, "Introduction," 5. On the self-conscious Anthropocene, or the epoch wherein human beings are aware of their status as geological agents, see Lynn Keller, *Recomposing Ecopoetics: North American Poetry of the Self-Conscious Anthropocene* (Charlottesville: University of Virginia Press, 2017), esp. 1–30.

13. Linda Williams, "Film Bodies: Gender, Genre, and Excess," *Film Quarterly* 44, no. 4 (1991): 2–3.
14. Williams, "Film Bodies," esp. 4, 7, 9.
15. Brinkema, *Life-Destroying Diagrams*, 193, 22, 279.
16. Brinkema, *Life-Destroying Diagrams*, 1.
17. Brinkema, *Life-Destroying Diagrams*, 4.
18. Tremblay, *Breathing Aesthetics*, 33–64; Jean-Thomas Tremblay, "Diagnostic Spectatorship: Modern Physical Culture and White Masculinity," *Modernism/modernity Print Plus* 6, no. 2 (2021): doi.org/10.26597/mod.0206; Steven Swarbrick, "The Violence of the Frame: Image, Animal, Interval in Lars von Trier's *Nymphomaniac*," *Cultural Critique* 113 (2021): 135–37.
19. Jamieson Webster, *Conversion Disorder: Listening to the Body in Psychoanalysis* (New York: Columbia University Press, 2019), 44.
20. Webster, *Conversion Disorder*, 44.
21. Melody Jue and Rafico Ruiz, *Saturation: An Elemental Politics* (Durham, NC: Duke University Press, 2021).
22. Brinkema, *Life-Destroying Diagrams*, 21, 298–99. Brinkema is here at her most deconstructive. Here is Drucilla Cornell on deconstruction, from *The Philosophy of the Limit* (New York: Routledge, 1992): "The philosophy of the limit does not leave us to wander in circles before the limit we have reached at the 'end of metaphysics.' The limit challenges us to reopen the question—to think again" (71). And here is Brinkema on formalism, decision, and speculation: "Radical formalism is, once more, an act of decision, which at the root is a term best thought as a formal problem the *de-/caedere* that is a cutting in two, which is to say a division that is a multiplication of an aspect of something's form"; "The point of radical formalism is not merely to displace contextualist readings, but to activate and launch the speculative potential of texts, one only available through readings that proceed without guarantee" (*Life-Destroying Diagrams*, 281, 259–60).
23. Frédéric Neyrat, *Atopias: Manifesto for a Radical Environmentalism*, trans. Walt Hunter and Lindsay Turner (New York: Fordham University Press, 2018), 5, 127. In orienting ourselves toward the edge, we pursue what Eugene Thacker calls "*the horror of philosophy*: the isolation of those moments in which philosophy reveals its own limitations and constraints, moments in which thinking enigmatically confronts the horizon of its possibility—the thought of the unthinkable that philosophy cannot pronounce but via a non-philosophical language" (*In the Dust of This Planet: Horror of Philosophy, Vol. 1* [Winchester, UK: Zero Books, 2011], 2). Thacker continues: "The genre of supernatural horror is a privileged site in which this paradoxical thought of the un-thinkable takes place. What an earlier era would have described through the language of darkness mysticism or negative theology, our contemporary era thinks of in terms of supernatural horror" (2). "This also means," Thacker later sums up, "that horror is not simply about fear, but instead about the enigmatic thought of the unknown" (8–9).
24. Gilbert Simondon, *Individuation in Light of Notions of Form and Information*, trans. Taylor Adkins (Minneapolis: University of Minnesota Press, 2020), 179.
25. Simondon, *Individuation in Light of Notions of Form and Information*, 179.
26. Simondon, *Individuation in Light of Notions of Form and Information*, 179.

27. See Ashley Dawson, *Mongrel Nation: Diasporic Culture and the Making of Postcolonial Britain* (Ann Arbor: University of Michigan Press, 2007).

28. Immanuel Kant, *Critique of Judgment*, trans. Werner S. Pluhar (Indianapolis, IN: Hackett, 1987), 122–23.

29. Monique Allewaert, *Ariel's Ecology: Plantations, Personhood, and Colonialism in the American Tropics* (Minneapolis: University of Minnesota Press, 2013), 29–50.

30. Rebecca Duncan, "Anthropocene Gothic, Capitalocene Gothic: The Politics of Ecohorror," in *The Edinburgh Companion to Globalgothic*, ed. Rebecca Duncan (Edinburgh: University of Edinburgh Press, 2023), 118; Anna Krauthamer, "Would That the Earth Could Stop Us," Public Books, June 2, 2022, https://www.publicbooks.org/ecohorror-gaia-in-the-earth/. Duncan's observation pertains to South African dramatist and filmmaker Jaco Bouwer's *Gaia* (2021; Los Angeles and Cape Town: XYZ Films, Film Initiative Africa, and kykNET Films, 2021), which, like *In the Earth*, follows a pair of characters on a mission amid ancient woodland; Krauthamer's point pertains to both *In the Earth* and *Gaia*.

31. These projects include the albums *Biophilia* (2011), *Utopia* (2017), and *Fossora* (2022), as well as the concert tour Cornucopia (2019–23), all of which constitute inquiries, often with live and virtual-reality components, into the interplay between organic and aesthetic forms. Of her latest album as of this writing, *Fossora*, Björk says, "I sometimes use visual shortcuts when I'm explaining an album to my engineer. I'll go, 'Oh, this is my mushroom album.' . . . Mushrooms, they're fun, right? They're psychedelic and they're bubbly. They pop up everywhere. They're mostly traveling through the whole forest." "Björk on Mushrooms and the Meaning behind Her New Album *Fossora*," Pitchfork, YouTube, September 20, 2022, https://www.youtube.com/watch?v=1poSSch7pSo.

32. See, *Queer Natures, Queer Mythologies*, 27.

33. See, *Queer Natures, Queer Mythologies*, 14–15, 20–21, 28–36.

34. Jacques Rancière, *The Politics of Aesthetics: The Distribution of the Sensible*, ed. and trans. Gabriel Rockhill (New York: Bloomsbury, 2004), 7–14.

35. Berlant and Edelman, *Sex, or the Unbearable*, 98–99.

36. "I am not returning home," concludes VanderMeer's novel (*Area X*, 128).

37. "*Mushroom*: A Film by Danilo Parra," Ford Canada, YouTube, October 12, 2022, https://www.youtube.com/watch?v=Gkyq71JYz-8.

CHAPTER TWO

1. Edward Broughton, "The Bhopal Disaster and Its Aftermath: A Review," *Environmental Health* 4, no. 6 (2005): doi:10.1186/1476-069X-4-6; Pramod N. Nayar, *Bhopal's Ecological Gothic: Disaster, Precarity, and the Biopolitical Uncanny* (Lanham, MD: Lexington Books, 2017), xiii.

2. Jessica Hurley, *Infrastructures of Apocalypse: American Literature and the Nuclear Complex* (Minneapolis: University of Minnesota Press, 2020), 26.

3. Dipesh Chakrabarty, *The Climate of History in a Planetary Age* (Chicago: University of Chicago Press, 2021), 26, 4.

4. Tobias Menely's "stratigraphic criticism," for example, sees "any poem" as "a symbolic mediation of the work that made it," which is to say that it "can be understood, in its world making and time shaping, to offer a mediation on the enigmatic yet omnipresent nature of energy, in its planetary and social manifestations." Tobias Menely, *Climate and the Making of Worlds: Toward a Geohistorical Poetics* (Chicago: University of Chicago Press, 2021), 18, 14; see also 212.
5. Cahill, *Zoological Surrealism*, 22; see also 214.
6. Elizabeth A. Povinelli concludes *Geontologies: A Requiem to Late Liberalism* (Durham, NC: Duke University Press, 2016) by making the eroded distinction between Life and Nonlife a locus of radical thought. If geontopower, or the aggregation of discourses, affects, and tactics that ontologize Life and Nonlife, is wielded in the late-liberal governance of difference and markets, then to demagnetize the poles that are Life and Nonlife would sink the grounds on which extinction actually means anything. "So extinction," Povinelli sums up, "may well be a concept dependent on other concepts whose discursive and affective impact depend on other concepts that produce other concepts—biology and geology, for instance—and that produce modes and tactics of power, that produce social figures, that produce other concepts and without these concepts, without species, without population, without Life and Nonlife, there is no extinction, no mass death" (175). See also Elizabeth A. Povinelli, *Between Gaia and Ground: Four Axioms of Existence and the Ancestral Catastrophe of Late Liberalism* (Durham, NC: Duke University Press, 2021), esp. 63–130.
7. Quoting the filmmaker Douglas Sirk, Jonathan Goldberg, in *Melodrama*, identifies the compositional indistinction between "'a dead thing and a live thing'" as a defining trait of the melodramatic impossible situation, a situation out of which there is no way without loss (25). Goldberg adds: "The point about this point about objects, persons, and the camera's correlation of them is that it posits a relationship between the absolute opposition of life and death; this is the metaphysical location of the impossible situation" (25). We consider the implications for ecological thought of this melodramatic undead, as it were, in chapter 3.
8. Sigmund Freud, *The Uncanny*, trans. David McLintock (London: Penguin Books, 2003), 124.
9. Barry J. Barnett, "The U.S. Farm Financial Crisis of the 1980s," *Agricultural History* 74, no. 2 (2010): 366–80; Neil E. Harl, *The Farm Debt Crisis of the 1980s* (Ames: Iowa State University Press, 1990).
10. Jenna Ryu, "Here's Why *Minari* Is Truly an American Story, Even If the Golden Globes Disagree," *USA Today*, February 11, 2021, https://www.usatoday.com/story/entertainment/movies/2021/02/11/minari-american-film-even-if-golden-globes-disagree/4340916001/. See also Jen Yamato, "*Minari* Wins Best Foreign Language Film at Golden Globes. Yes, It's American," *Los Angeles Times*, February 28, 2021, https://www.latimes.com/entertainment-arts/movies/story/2021-02-28/minari-golden-globes-2021-foreign-language. Chung was born in Denver and grew up on an Arkansas farm.
11. Lulu Wang (@thumbelulu), Twitter post, December 20, 2020, https://twitter.com/thumbelulu/status/1341606647572045824?s=20.

12. Coleen Lyle, *America's Asia: Racial Form and American Literature, 1893–1945* (Princeton, NJ: Princeton University Press, 2015), 9.
13. Wayne Patterson, *The Korean Frontiers in America: Immigration to Hawaii, 1896–1910* (Honolulu: University of Hawaii Press, 1988), 50.
14. In 1990, only 1,037 Korean Americans were reported to live in Arkansas, compared to 345,882 in California. "Korean American Population Data," National Association of Korean Americans, 2021, http://www.naka.org/resources/.
15. Lyle sums up, in *America's Asia*: "The American identification of the Asiatic as a sign of globalization was not arbitrary; it was rooted in the material history of U.S. relations with East Asia" (9–10). On Asiatic figures as "global generic subject[s]," see Jane Hu, "Ang Lee's Tears: Digital Global Melodrama in *The Wedding Banquet*, *Hulk*, and *Gemini Man*," *Verge: Studies in Global Asias* 7, no. 2 (2021): 152.
16. Chloe Ahmann and Alison Kenner, "Breathing Late Industrialism," *Engaging Science, Technology, and Society* 6 (2020): 422.
17. Kim Fortun, "From Latour to Late Industrialism," *HAU: A Journal of Ethnographic Theory* 4, no. 1 (2014): 310.
18. Fortun, "From Latour to Late Industrialism," 312.
19. Fortun, "From Latour to Late Industrialism," 312.
20. Jacques Lacan, *The Seminar of Jacques Lacan, Book III: The Psychoses, 1955–1956*, ed. Jacques-Alain Miller, trans. Russell Grigg (New York: Norton, 1993), 268.
21. Lacan, *The Psychoses*, 268.
22. Lacan, *The Psychoses*, 268, 266.
23. This is how Todd McGowan, in "The Satisfaction of an Ending," in *Cinematic Cuts: Theorizing Film Endings*, ed. Sheila Kunkle (Albany: State University of New York Press, 2016), describes the romantic union, that "most common ideological film ending": "The romantic union functions ideologically because it provides spectators with the fantasy of overcoming the most intractable antagonism through romance. Films begin by showing the antagonism that keeps the couple apart, and then they conclude with a fantasy of them coming together in spite of this antagonism. The idea behind the concluding romantic union is that antagonism is not intractable, that through compromise or sacrifice or work we can overcome antagonism and achieve social harmony" (139). *Minari*'s and *Bhopal Express*'s endings ask the romantic union to perform an impossible ideological smoothing out; such a union both does and does not, can and cannot, resolve antagonism. What results from the clash between a "pure" form of life like the marital or familial unit and an "impure" living condition like precarity or toxicity is a denaturalization of environmental histories of toxification *and* purification, one that recalls the denaturalization of sexual histories of repression *and* expression in Todd Haynes's anachronistic cinema. See Jean-Thomas Tremblay, "The Haynes Code," *Los Angeles Review of Books*, April 8, 2022, https://lareviewofbooks.org/article/the-haynes-code/.
24. This absent cause is, in Lacanian parlance, the *objet a* (impossible object of desire), which neither history nor narrative, including evolutionary narratives, can account for. The non sequitur produces the *objet a* as a break in narrative sequence. This break remains even when the family unit reasserts itself, forestalling narrative closure.

25. Frank Kermode, *The Sense of an Ending: Studies in the Theory of Fiction* (1966; Oxford: Oxford University Press, 2000), 46.
26. Edelman, *No Future*, 44.
27. Hugh S. Manon, "Resolution, Truncation, Glitch," in *Cinematic Cuts: Theorizing Film Endings*, ed. Sheila Kunkle (Albany: State University of New York Press, 2016), 25.
28. See, for example, Amitav Ghosh, *The Great Derangement: Climate Change and the Unthinkable* (Chicago: University of Chicago Press, 2016), 15–24, 28–33; Ursula K. Heise, *Imagining Extinction: The Cultural Meanings of Endangered Species* (Chicago: University of Chicago Press, 2016), 5, 44; Heather Houser, *Ecosickness in Contemporary U.S. Fiction: Environment and Affect* (New York: Columbia University Press, 2014); Min Hyoung Song, *Climate Lyricism* (Durham, NC: Duke University Press, 2022); van Dooren, *Flight Ways*; and Jennifer Wenzel, *The Disposition of Nature: Environmental Crisis and World Literature* (New York: Fordham University Press, 2019).
29. Alain Badiou defines the "immanent exception" as "an exception to the world in which it takes place, even though it is made with materials and things from this very world," in *Badiou by Badiou*, trans. Bruno Bosteels (Stanford, CA: Stanford University Press, 2022), 13.
30. One such fellow Lacanian being, of course, Edelman. The queer, he posits, embodies the social "order's traumatic encounter with its own inescapable failure, its encounter with the illusion of the future as suture to bind the constitutive wound of the subject's subjection to the signifier, which divides it, paradoxically, both from and into itself" (*No Future*, 26). Edelman anticipates Lauren Berlant's critique of the drama of trauma in *Sex, or the Unbearable*: "Lauren would see the word 'traumatic' as an instance of my making grandiose what she invites us to dedramatize, while I would worry that dramatization is the emptying out, the attempt to neutralize the force of that encounter itself. Not always—and not in Lauren's work—but maybe in our normative relations to ourselves as continuous or viable subjects" (9). Berlant would go on to develop a heuristics of the not-quite-traumatic in *On the Inconvenience of Other People* (Durham, NC: Duke University Press, 2022): "The minima of inconvenience can go under the radar, or not, but it does not register at first as a traumatic or transformative event. At minimum intensity, though, the affective sense of inconvenience is harder, less easy to shake off or step around" (4). To live with inconvenience, or "to loosen up at the moment when everything in me would prefer not to," according to Berlant, necessitates a "transformational infrastructure" (150). We are interested precisely in the horror of continuity and viability, one that can make itself felt when the dramatic intensity reached through a properly traumatic event persists even after a resolution has been achieved by way of the normative.
31. Mari Ruti, *Distillations: Theory, Ethics, Affect* (New York: Bloomsbury, 2018), 165.
32. Ruti, *Distillations*, 165.
33. See Rebekah Sheldon, *The Child to Come: Life after Human Catastrophe* (Minneapolis: University of Minnesota Press, 2016), esp. 40–42.
34. All quoted dialogue from *Minari* and *Bhopal Express* relays the English translation provided by subtitles.

35. *Beoning*, dir. Lee Chang-dong (2018; Seoul and Tokyo: Pinehouse Film, Now Film, and NHK, 2018).
36. Edelman, *No Future*, 44; Swarbrick, "Nature's Queer Negativity."
37. Edelman, *No Future*, 33.
38. The story's beats are as follows: a narrator's friend takes an impulsive trip to Africa and returns accompanied. Her companion, unnamed like the other two characters, admits to burning barns, not greenhouses, on occasion. The narrator is cataloging nearby barns, expecting one to be set on fire, when the woman vanishes.
39. Haruki Murakami, "Barn Burning," trans Alfred Birnbaum, in *The Elephant Vanishes: Stories* (New York: Vintage, 1993), 147–48.
40. On the intertextual flows between Faulkner, Murakami, and Lee, see Björn Boman, "The Multifold Intertextuality in Lee Chang Dong's *Burning*," *Social Sciences & Humanities Open* 3, no. 1 (2021): doi:10.1016/j.ssaho.2021.100119.
41. William Faulkner, "Barn Burner," in *Selected Stories of William Faulkner* (New York: Modern Library, 2012), 3–26.
42. John Locke, *Two Treatises of Government*, ed. Peter Laslett (Cambridge: Cambridge University Press, 1988), 35, 37.
43. Angela Mitropoulos, *Contract and Contagion: From Biopolitics to Oikonomia* (Brooklyn, NY: Autonomedia, 2012), 12, 11.
44. Mitropoulos, *Contract and Contagion*, 11–12.
45. Joshua Schuster and Derek Woods, *Calamity Theory: Three Critiques of Existential Risk* (Minneapolis: University of Minnesota Press, 2021), esp. 2, 5–9.
46. Mitropoulos, *Contract and Contagion*, 12, 15, 18, 85–86.
47. Albert Camus, *The Myth of Sisyphus and Other Essays*, trans. Justin O'Brien (New York: Vintage, 1991), 28.
48. Camus, *The Myth of Sisyphus*, 31.
49. Camus, *The Myth of Sisyphus*, 3, 54.
50. Camus, *The Myth of Sisyphus*, 55.
51. Camus, *The Myth of Sisyphus*, 120.
52. Camus, *The Myth of Sisyphus*, 120–21.
53. Camus, *The Myth of Sisyphus*, 120–21.
54. Camus, *The Myth of Sisyphus*, 120–21.
55. Camus, *The Myth of Sisyphus*, 55.
56. Rose, *Wild Dog Dreaming*, 42.
57. Rose, *Wild Dog Dreaming*, 43–44.
58. Rose, *Wild Dog Dreaming*, 44. The introduction to a volume dedicated to Rose's scholarship finds in her emphasis on plenitude a "commit[ment] to life: to exploring the living world in its beauty and its challenges [and] to making a stand for flourishing, for inclusive possibilities." Thom van Dooren and Matthew Chrulew, "World of Kin: An Introduction," in *Kin: Thinking with Deborah Bird Rose*, ed. Thom van Dooren and Matthew Chrulew (Durham, NC: Duke University Press, 2022), 10. The reduction of nature to its "inclusive possibilities" constitutes yet another iteration of the exclusionary gesture (flourishing, not wilting; inclusion, not exclusion) that *Negative Life* associates with contemporary ecocriticism.
59. Schuster and Woods, *Calamity Theory*, 89. See also Puig de la Bellacasa, *Matters of Care*, esp. 1–12.

60. Rose, *Wild Dog Dreaming*, 44.
61. Camus, *The Myth of Sisyphus*, 9.
62. Neyrat, *Atopias*.
63. Neyrat, *Atopias*, 5.
64. Neyrat, *Atopias*, 6.
65. Neyrat, *Atopias*, 7.
66. Neyrat, *Atopias*, 28.
67. Neyrat, *Atopias*, 30, 29.
68. Neyrat, *Atopias*, 81.
69. See Todd McGowan's lecture on the Lacanian quilting point in "Signification and Subjectivity," July 17, 2021, video, 12:40, https://youtu.be/AF7QBX9t28c.
70. Kermode, *The Sense of an Ending*, 44.
71. Kermode, *The Sense of an Ending*, 44–45. Kermode adds: "We can perceive a duration only when it is organized. It can be shown by experiment that subjects who listen to rhythmic structures such as *tick-tock*, repeated identically, 'can reproduce the intervals within the structure accurately, but they cannot grasp spontaneously the interval between the rhythmic groups,' that is, between *tock* and *tick*, even when this remains constant. The first interval is organized and limited, the second not" (45).
72. Kermode, *The Sense of an Ending*, 45.
73. Kermode, *The Sense of an Ending*, 46, 47.
74. In *Reading for the Plot: Design and Intention in Narrative* (Cambridge, MA: Harvard University Press, 1984), Peter Brooks writes: "Narratives both tell of desire—typically present some story of desire—and arouse and make use of desire as dynamic of signification. Desire is in this view like Freud's notion of Eros, a force including sexual desire but larger and more polymorphous. . . . Desire as Eros, desire in its plastic and totalizing function, appears to me central to our experience of reading narrative" (37). He adds: "Desire is the wish for the end, for fulfillment" (111). Brooks conflates desire with Eros, the totalizing function of narrative. His thesis is contradicted by the fact that Freud defines desire *not* as the desire for fulfillment but as the desire for *repetition*, that is, false endings. The absence of death drive in Brooks's argument ruins its progressive thesis.
75. Nayar, *Bhopal's Ecological Gothic*, xvi.
76. Nayar, *Bhopal's Ecological Gothic*, xvi.
77. Nayar, *Bhopal's Ecological Gothic*, xvii.
78. Gilles Deleuze, *Cinema 2: The Time-Image*, trans. Hugh Tomlinson and Robert Galeta (Minneapolis: University of Minnesota Press, 1989), 20, 21. "Now this is what a cliché is. A cliché is a sensory-motor image of the thing. As Bergson says, we do not perceive the thing or the image in its entirety, we always perceive less of it. . . . We therefore normally perceive only clichés" (20). Although Deleuze would likely perceive the happy ending of *Bhopal Express* as a reterritorialization of time by the cliché, we maintain that the film's retroactivity, precisely its *atemporal* dimension, makes the clichéd ending something other than a mere cliché. Joan Copjec, writing in *Read My Desire* on Deleuze's philosophical influence, Henri Bergson, highlights the problem with Deleuzian-Bergsonian theories of time: they remain progressivist, clichéd theories. "There is simply no way to understand *organic elasticity* and *inertia* as synonymous," Copjec asserts, "so long as we hold to the Bergsonian model"

(45–46). One would have to think instead with the Freud of *Beyond the Pleasure Principle* to grasp the possibility that the "aim of life is not evolution but regression, or, in its most seemingly contradictory form, the aim of life is death" (46).

79. Mari Ruti, *The Singularity of Being: Lacan and the Immortal Within* (New York: Fordham University Press, 2012), 14–16.

80. Ruti, *The Singularity of Being*, 14–15.

81. Anil Narine, for instance, idealizes traumas as their very own treatment by arguing that "eco-trauma cinema" equips audiences with the means to overcome their own saturation or paralysis: "This is the challenge of our age: to overcome our disavowal, to reflect on the unsavory forces reshaping our earth and to acknowledge our role in the production of the very mechanisms responsible for the induced eco-traumas such as e-waste and carbon emissions. . . . If documented, filmed realities, as well as dramatized and digitally rendered worlds, can serve as our cognitive maps, aiding us in our quest to make sense of our age of anxiety, we may very well *avoid* this stasis, situate ourselves as political beings and embrace our responsibilities as the earth's most powerful habitants" ("Introduction: Eco-Trauma Cinema," in *Eco-Trauma Cinema*, ed. Anil Narine [New York: Routledge, 2015], 22).

82. *Terminator II: Judgment Day*, dir. James Cameron (1991; Los Angeles, Santa Monica, and Paris: Carolco Pictures, Pacific Western Productions, Lightstorm Entertainment, and Le Studio Canal+, 2000); *12 Monkeys*, dir. Terry Gilliam (1995; Los Angeles: Atlas Entertainment Classico, 2005); *Tenet*, dir. Christopher Nolan (2020; Los Angeles: Syncopy, 2020).

83. Sigmund Freud, "Analysis Terminable and Interminable" (1937), in *The Standard Edition of the Complete Psychological Works of Sigmund Freud*, vol. 23, ed. and trans. James Strachey (London: Hogarth Press and the Institute of Psychoanalysis, 1953–74), 209–54.

84. McGowan, *Enjoying What We Don't Have*, 16–22.

85. Ghosh, *The Great Derangement*, 16–17, 24–25, 30–31.

86. Ray Brassier, *Nihil Unbound: Enlightenment and Extinction* (New York: Palgrave Macmillan, 2007), 238.

87. Brassier, *Nihil Unbound*, 238.

88. Brassier, *Nihil Unbound*, 238–39.

89. Sigmund Freud, *Studies on Hysteria* (1895), in *The Standard Edition of the Complete Psychological Works of Sigmund Freud*, vol. 2, ed. and trans. James Strachey (London: Hogarth Press and the Institute of Psychoanalysis, 1953–74), 305.

90. Brassier, *Nihil Unbound*, 239.

91. Hurley, *Infrastructures of Apocalypse*, 3–4, 7, 204–5, 222.

92. Hurley, *Infrastructures of Apocalypse*, 2.

93. See Catherine Malabou, *Ontology of the Accident: An Essay on Destructive Plasticity*, trans. Carolyn Shread (Cambridge: Polity, 2012).

94. Ruti, *The Singularity of Being*, 40–41, 162. Ruti links "surplus vitality" to the undeadness of the drives, "a paradoxical kind of immortality or incapacity to die . . . that infuses the subject with an uncontrollable vitality" (22).

95. Lacan's lamella is the clearest example of the "indestructible life" of the drive. The lamella "survives any division," is "irrepressible," and "immortal" (Lacan, *Four Fundamental Concepts*, 197, 198).

96. We remain faithful to the two trains of desire, one leading, in Edelman's queer, drive-oriented sense, to negativity, the other leading to Verma and all spectators chasing after a narrative end. As Edelman notes, these two tracks are impossible to disentangle: "However attenuated, qualified, ironized, interrupted, or deconstructed it may be, a story implies a direction; it signals, as story, a movement that leads toward some payoff or profit, some comprehension or closure, however open-ended. . . . Absent that framework of expectation, it isn't a story at all, just metonymic associations attached to a given nucleus" (Berlant and Edelman, *Sex, or the Unbearable*, 3). Edelman seems to check the impulse of *No Future* to sever the negativity of the drive from the fantasy structure of desire that he attaches to heteronormative futurism.

INTERLUDE. THE HORROR OF ENTANGLEMENT II: *ANTICHRIST*, *LAMB*, *X*

1. Stanley Cavell, *A Pitch of Philosophy: Autobiographical Exercises* (Cambridge, MA: Harvard University Press, 1994), 140.
2. Cavell, *A Pitch of Philosophy*, 144.
3. "The loss of the world—of say being—is philosophy's cause," Cavell writes in *Emerson's Transcendental Etudes* (Stanford, CA: Stanford University Press, 2003), "which it tries to overcome even as it causes" (132). Cavell extends this cause to cinema.
4. Cavell, *A Pitch of Philosophy*, 140.
5. Stanley Cavell, *The World Viewed: Reflections on the Ontology of Film* (Cambridge, MA: Harvard University Press, 1979), 18.
6. Jacques Derrida, *Rogues: Two Essays on Reason*, trans. Pascale-Anne Brault and Michael Naas (Stanford, CA: Stanford University Press, 2005), xii.
7. Derrida, *Rogues*, xii, 4.
8. Stanley Cavell, *Contesting Tears: The Hollywood Melodrama of the Unknown Woman* (Chicago: University of Chicago Press, 1996), 42; Adriana Cavarero, *For More Than One Voice: Toward a Philosophy of Vocal Expression*, trans. Paul A. Kottman (Stanford, CA: Stanford University Press, 2005), 167. Cavarero specifies: "Unlike the Muses or the Homeric Sirens, however, Echo's voice is not a singing or narrating voice, but rather a voice that results, like a mere residual material, from its subtraction from the semantic register of logos. Rather than repeating the words, Echo repeats their sounds" (166). Cavarero explains de-semanticization by incorporating it into a broadly psychoanalytic model of regression: "As in the case of the infant who repeats the mother's words, stripping them of their meaning, Echo is an acoustic repetition, not intentioned toward meaning. Just as the myth recounts, her story alludes to a sort of regression to the mimetic vocalizations of infancy, to the so-called la-la language" (168). For a related account of sound and voice in Cavell's work, see Cary Wolfe, *What Is Posthumanism?* (Minneapolis: University of Minnesota Press, 2010), 169–202. Wolfe draws on Kaja Silverman's influential study, *The Acoustic Mirror: The Female Voice in Psychoanalysis and Cinema* (Bloomington: Indiana University Press, 1998), to posit "a crucial and altogether symptomatic aporia . . .

at the heart of his [Cavell's] understanding of voice in relation to sound," that is, "how the interiority of voice as expression can be quarantined from the *exteriority* that is its material medium and condition of possibility in sound" (179). With Silverman and following Lacan's interweaving of Symbolic and Real, Wolfe insists that "meaning and materiality, subject and object, are always complicated and interwoven in a symbolic and psychic economy of *imbalance*," rather than opposed, as in Cavell's philosophy—an opposition that Wolfe notes feeds into "a nuclear heteronormativity that (at the least) lurks in the background of Cavell's speculations on (re)marriage" (180, 174).

9. Cavell, *A Pitch of Philosophy*, 132, 140.

10. Cavell, *The World Viewed*, 18.

11. Cavell, *Contesting Tears*, 4.

12. Cavell derives this idiosyncratic definition of marriage from none other than the poet John Milton: "Pervading each moment of the texture and mood of remarriage comedy is the mode of *conversation* that binds or sweeps together the principal pair. . . . Conversation is given a beautiful theory in John Milton's revolutionary tract to justify divorce, making the willingness for conversation (for "a meet and happy conversation") the basis of marriage, even making conversation what I might call the *fact* of marriage" (*Contesting Tears*, 5).

13. Cavell, *Contesting Tears*, 43.

14. Eduardo Kohn, *How Forests Think: Toward an Anthropology beyond the Human* (Berkeley: University of California Press, 2013).

15. Morton, *Hyperobjects*, 9.

16. Morton, *Hyperobjects*, 11; Graham Harman, *Tool-Being: Heidegger and the Metaphysics of Objects* (Chicago: Open Court, 2002). For Harman, objects are "forever withdrawing from view into a distant background" (24). There is an unknown, melodramatic dimension to objects, which we only catch sight of partially. This is true, Harman contends, not only for humans but for all objects. Objects, including humans, interact in a vacuum: "if my perception of a bridge reduces its bridge-being to a mere caricature, the same is equally true," Harman argues, "for the pigeon that lands on it, the hailstones that strike it, and the military satellites that spy on it" (127). Crucial to object-oriented ontology is that it is a *substantialist* ontology. Harman stakes his claim to the withdrawn nature of objects in Aristotle's theory of substance, which holds that a being simply is itself. A is A, without division. Harman: "The tool-being of a thing is what that thing simply *is*, quite aside from any of the faces that it manifests to view" (269–70). Our theory of negative life could not be more different. While we attend to the withdrawn nature of things, we maintain that a thing is never identical to itself. The chasm that Harman locates between objects and their appearances we locate *within* objects. A is and is not A. This point is made salient by Lacan's theory of the *objet a*, an insubstantial scrap that inheres in objects, making all objects, nonobjects, desirable for that reason.

17. Morton, *Hyperobjects*, 18.

18. Lacan, *Le Séminaire XXI: Les Non-dupes errent*, 1973–74, manuscript, session of April 23, 1974, Todd McGowan's translation. McGowan writes in *Enjoying What We Don't Have*: "For psychoanalysis, the link between knowledge and progress dooms the possibility of progress. Rather than desiring to know, the subject desires not to know and organizes its existence around the avoidance of knowledge" (17).

19. Wilson, "Acts against Nature," 19–31. On queer theories of sodomy, specifically within the cultures of sex without condoms, see Tim Dean, *Unlimited Intimacy: Reflections on the Subculture of Barebacking* (Chicago: University of Chicago Press, 2009); and Ricky Varghese, ed., *Raw: PrEP, Pedagogy, and the Politics of Barebacking* (Regina, SK: University of Regina Press, 2019).

20. Karen Barad, "Nature's Queer Performativity (The Authorized Version)," *Women, Gender, and Research (Kvinder, Køn oh Korkning)* 1–2 (2012): 47. Qtd. in Wilson, "Acts against Nature," 22.

21. Wilson, "Acts against Nature," 20.

22. Wilson, "Acts against Nature," 26.

23. Christopher Chitty, *Sexual Hegemony: Statecraft, Sodomy, and Capital in the Rise of the World System*, ed. Max Fox (Durham, NC: Duke University Press, 2020), 37, 119.

24. Andil Gosine, *Nature's Wild: Love, Sex, and Law in the Caribbean* (Durham, NC: Duke University Press, 2021), 19–21, 27.

25. *The Texas Chainsaw Massacre*, dir. Tobe Hooper (1974; Vortex, 2004).

26. We align *X*'s denaturing of pastoral with Leo Bersani's critique of a "pastoral impulse" that he counters with his own demand that sex be seen as "anticommunal, antiegalitarian, antinurturing, antiloving." Bersani, *Is the Rectum a Grave?* 22.

27. Ruti, *The Singularity of Being*, 92. Joan Copjec echoes this deathless account of the drive in *Imagine There's No Woman: Ethics and Sublimation* (Cambridge, MA: MIT Press, 2002): "Directed not outward toward the constituted world, but away from it, the death drive aims at the past, at a time *before* the subject found itself where it is now, imbedded in time and moving toward death" (33). Badiou, likewise, sutures subjects to "eternal truths," through which "we," Badiou contends, "raise or resurrect ourselves as Immortals," in *Logics of Worlds*, 513.

28. Andrea Dworkin, *Pornography: Men Possessing Women* (1979; New York: Plume, 1989), 137–38.

29. Lacan, *The Ethics of Psychoanalysis*, 243–90.

30. Alain Badiou, *Saint Paul: The Foundations of Universalism*, trans. Ray Brassier (Stanford, CA: Stanford University Press, 2003), 4, 107.

31. Mladen Dolar theorizes the voice-object "as a blind spot in the call and as a disturbance of aesthetic appreciation" in *A Voice and Nothing More* (Cambridge, MA: MIT Press, 2006), 4.

32. Foucault, *The History of Sexuality*, 48.

33. Lacan, *On Feminine Sexuality*, 44, 101.

34. "As a substitute for what cannot be seen, the money shot can be viewed as yet another form of cinematic perversion." Linda Williams, *Hard Core: Power, Pleasure, and the "Frenzy of the Visible"* (Berkeley: University of California Press, 1989), 95.

35. Kant gives grist to the object-oriented ontologist mill when he writes that "appearances are not things in themselves, but," and this point is decisive for modern thought, "only representations, which in turn have their object, which therefore cannot be further intuited by us, and that may therefore be called the non-empirical, i.e., transcendental "object = *X*." Immanuel Kant, *Critique of Pure Reason*, ed. and trans. Paul Guyer and Allen Wood (Cambridge: Cambridge University Press, 1998), 233.

36. McGowan, *Enjoying What We Don't Have*, 26–27.
37. Lacan's $<>*a* delineates four procedures: <, >, ∧, ∨. As Bruce Fink interprets it, "This diamond or lozenge (poinçon) designates the following relations: 'envelopment-development-conjunction-disjunction,' alienation (∨) and separation (∧), greater than (>), less than (<), and so on. It is most simply read, 'in relation to,' or 'desire for,' as in $<>*a*, the subject in relation to the object, or the subject's desire for the object." Bruce Fink, *The Lacanian Subject: Between Language and Jouissance* (Princeton, NJ: Princeton University Press, 1995), 174.
38. Eugene Thacker proffers this view of the "world-without-us," where death registers as total human annihilation, in *In the Dust of This Planet*, 5–6. Eugenie Brinkema likewise asserts Heidegger's notion of "being-towards-death" as the ultimate horizon of horror ("Death is the aesthetic force of possibility in horror" [73]), including ecohorror, in *Life-Destroying Diagrams*, 73–77.
39. Joan Copjec identifies "being-towards-sex" as the Lacanian rejoinder to Heideggerian phenomenology. For Freud and Lacan, repetition, not temporality (enjoyment, not death), is the true traumatic kernel of subjectivity. Here is Copjec: "Lacan once proffered the term 'being-towards-sex,' clearly referencing Heidegger's term 'being-towards-death,' in order presumably to displace the latter. The coinage of the new term goes beyond a simple terminological substitution by seeming to call for a rethinking of the arguments that led up to the original term. Where Heidegger links anxiety to the encounter with death, for example, Lacan insists that we see anxiety as, instead, an encounter with jouissance." Joan Copjec, "Sexual Difference," Political Concepts: A Critical Lexicon, November 3, 2014, https://www.politicalconcepts.org/sexual-difference-joan-copjec/8/.
40. Badiou's four truth procedures are science, politics, art, and love. Notably, Badiou views love as the "sublimation of sexuality, not in the sense of its negation—even though this is a tendency in philosophy—but on the contrary in the sense of its exaltation, its affirmation" (*Badiou by Badiou*, 9). Relatedly, he sees his philosophy as a philosophy of life, not death. Alain Badiou, *Logics of Worlds: Being and Event II*, trans. Alberto Toscano (2009; London: Bloomsbury, 2013), 508–9. He also, as Claire Colebrook argues in "Cinemas and Worlds," *Diacritics* 45, no. 1 (2017): 25–48, diminishes the truth value of cinema relative to the other arts, including poetry. Badiou theorizes the subject's fidelity to truth in *Saint Paul*, 5, 7, 11, 14–15, 107–11.

CHAPTER THREE

1. Jesse Barron, "David Buckel, a Lifetime of Service Ended in Self-Immolation," *New York Times*, December 27, 2018, https://www.nytimes.com/interactive/2018/12/27/magazine/lives-they-lived-david-buckel.html.
2. Jeffery C. Mays, "Prominent Lawyer in Fight for Gay Rights Dies after Setting Himself on Fire in Prospect Park," *New York Times*, April 14, 2018, https://www.nytimes.com/2018/04/14/nyregion/david-buckel-dead-fire.html.
3. Barron, "David Buckel, a Lifetime of Service Ended in Self-Immolation."

4. Amir Vera, "Border Patrol Agent's Gender Reveal Party Ignited a 47,000-Acre Wildfire," CNN, October 2, 2018, https://www.cnn.com/2018/10/02/us/az-off-duty-border-patrol-agent-wildfire/index.html.
5. Barron, "David Buckel, a Lifetime of Service Ended in Self-Immolation."
6. Jason Silverstein, "Why the Ashes of People with AIDS on the White House Lawn Matter," Vice, August 29, 2016, https://www.vice.com/en_us/article/vdqv34/why-the-ashes-of-aids-victims-on-the-white-house-lawn-matter.
7. Edelman, *No Future*.
8. Wilson, "Acts against Nature," 22.
9. Edelman, *No Future*, 25; Bersani, *Homos*, 113.
10. Edelman, *No Future*, 29.
11. Neel Ahuja, "Intimate Atmospheres: Queer Theory in a Time of Extinctions," *GLQ: A Journal of Lesbian and Gay Studies* 21, nos. 2–3 (2015): 365.
12. Ahuja, "Intimate Atmospheres," 372.
13. Goldberg, *Melodrama*, ix.
14. Deleuze, *Cinema 2*, 169, 2.
15. Gilles Deleuze, *Cinema 1: The Movement-Image*, trans. Hugh Tomlinson and Barbara Habberjam (Minneapolis: University of Minnesota Press, 1986), xiv.
16. Bersani, *Homos*, 7.
17. Edelman, *No Future*.
18. Nicole Seymour, *Strange Natures: Futurity, Empathy, and the Queer Ecological Imagination* (Urbana: University of Illinois Press, 2003), 6.
19. Seymour, *Strange Natures*, 6.
20. Goldberg, *Melodrama*, 3.
21. Goldberg, *Melodrama*, 25, 79.
22. Catriona Sandilands, "Melancholy Natures, Queer Ecologies," in *Queer Ecologies: Sex, Nature, Politics, Desire*, ed. Catriona Sandilands and Bruce Erickson (Bloomington: Indiana University Press, 2010), 331–58.
23. Sigmund Freud, "Mourning and Melancholia" (1917), in *The Standard Edition of the Complete Psychological Works of Sigmund Freud*, vol. 14, ed. and trans. James Strachey (London: Hogarth Press and the Institute of Psychoanalysis, 1953–74), 257.
24. Sandilands, "Melancholy Natures, Queer Ecologies," 342.
25. David Eng, *Racial Castration: Managing Masculinity in Asian America* (Durham, NC: Duke University Press, 2001); José Esteban Muñoz, *Disidentifications: Queers of Color and the Performance of Politics* (Minneapolis: University of Minnesota Press, 1999).
26. Judith Butler, *The Psychic Life of Power: Theories in Subjection* (Stanford, CA: Stanford University Press, 1997), 147.
27. Timothy Morton, *Ecology without Nature: Rethinking Environmental Aesthetics* (Cambridge, MA: Harvard University Press, 2007), 181; Timothy Morton, "Queer Ecology," *PMLA* 125, no. 2 (2010): 274.
28. Morton, *Ecology without Nature*, 186.
29. Morton, *Ecology without Nature*, 186.
30. Morton, *Ecology without Nature*, 187.
31. Morton, *Ecology without Nature*, 187.

32. See Stacy Alaimo, *Bodily Natures: Science, Environment, and the Material Self* (Bloomington: Indiana University Press, 2010); Barad, "Nature's Queer Performativity," 25–53.
33. Morton, *Ecology without Nature*, 197.
34. Neyrat, *Atopias*, 4.
35. Goldberg, *Melodrama*. See Deleuze, *Cinema 2*; and Berlant and Edelman, *Sex, or the Unbearable*.
36. Elizabeth A. Wilson, *Gut Feminism* (Durham, NC: Duke University Press, 2015), 74.
37. Wilson, *Gut Feminism*, 85, 88.
38. See also, more recently, Patricia Stuelke, *The Ruse of Repair: US Neoliberal Empire and the Turn from Critique* (Durham, NC: Duke University Press, 2021), esp. 5–17, 30.
39. As Nicole Seymour demonstrates, environmentalism frequently conjures up the figure of the innocent child as the imaginary victim of environmental collapse and the benefactor of environmental activism. Similarly, Rebekah Sheldon argues that, amidst crisis, the child is invested with "the emergent energies of posthumanity." Seymour, *Bad Environmentalism*; Sheldon, *The Child to Come*, 21.
40. Amplifying resonances between queer theory and environmental studies, Sarah Ensor posits that cruising, a scene dear to many male-identifying queer theorists, "might inspire an ecological ethic more deeply attuned to our impersonal intimacies with the human, nonhuman, and elemental strangers that constitute both our environment and ourselves." According to Ensor's utopian account, in cruising, "anonymity and impersonality can be the ground of intimacy rather than barriers to it." The suicidal ideation and performance of self-annihilation in *First Reformed* reject the idea that, at this stage of planetary destruction, an ethics may be rooted in cross-species intimacies, however thrillingly impersonal. Michael, like Davis S. Buckel, sees his own survival as an obstacle to other organic beings. Sarah Ensor, "Queer Fallout: Samuel R. Delany and the Ecology of Cruising," *Environmental Humanities* 9, no. 1 (2017): 150, 155.
41. Freud: "What consciousness is aware of in the work of melancholia is thus not the essential part of it, nor is it even the part which we may credit with an influence in bringing the ailment to an end. We see that the ego debases itself and rages against itself, and we understand as little as the patient what this can lead to and how it can change" ("Mourning and Melancholia," 257).
42. Slavoj Žižek, *Looking Awry: An Introduction to Jacques Lacan through Popular Culture* (Cambridge, MA: MIT Press, 1991), 126.
43. Richard Powers, *Gain* (New York: Farrar, Straus and Giroux, 1998).
44. Michelle Murphy, *Sick Building Syndrome and the Problem of Uncertainty: Environmental Politics, Technoscience, and Women Workers* (Durham, NC: Duke University Press, 2006).
45. Povinelli, *Geontologies*.
46. Povinelli, *Geontologies*, 5.
47. Bennett, *Vibrant Matter*.
48. Bennett, *Vibrant Matter*, 112.
49. Edelman, *No Future*; Bersani, *Is the Rectum a Grave?*
50. Bersani, *Is the Rectum a Grave?* 70.
51. Povinelli, *Geontologies*, 42.

52. Povinelli, *Geontologies*, 46.
53. Gilles Deleuze, *Masochism: Coldness and Cruelty*, trans. Jean McNeil (New York: Zone Books, 1991), 20.
54. Deleuze, *Cinema 2*, 169.
55. Bersani, *The Freudian Body*.
56. Lacan, *On Feminine Sexuality*.
57. According to data compiled by the Hartford Institute for Religious Research, the largest church in the state of New York outside of the New York City boroughs boasts an average attendance of 3,500 parishioners. Hartford Institute for Religious Research, "Database of Megachurches in the U.S.," 2015, http://hirr.hartsem.edu/megachurch/database.html.
58. Dorceta E. Taylor, *Toxic Communities: Environmental Racism, Industrial Pollution, and Residential Mobility* (New York: New York University Press, 2014).
59. Robert J. Sampson and Alix S. Winter, "The Racial Ecology of Lead Poisoning: Toxic Inequality in Chicago Neighborhoods, 1995–2013," *Du Bois Review: Social Science Research on Race* 13, no. 2 (2016): 261–83.
60. Mel Y. Chen, *Animacies: Biopolitics, Racial Mattering, and Queer Affect* (Durham, NC: Duke University Press, 2012).
61. Anne Anlin Cheng, *The Melancholy of Race: Psychoanalysis, Assimilation, and Hidden Grief* (Oxford: Oxford University Press), xi.
62. Frantz Fanon, *Black Skin, White Masks*, trans. Richard Philcox (New York: Grove, 2008), 90.
63. See Wilderson, *Red, White & Black*, 75; and Edelman, *Bad Education*, 17.
64. Fanon, *Black Skin, White Masks*, 90.
65. See Marriott, *Whither Fanon?* esp. 6, 201, 314–63.
66. Warren, *Ontological Terror*, 4.
67. Warren, *Ontological Terror*, 6, 5. On this point, Warren diverges from Zakiyyah Iman Jackson, who argues, in *Becoming Human*, that "blackness, and the abject fleshly figures that bear the weight of *the* world, is a being (something rather than nothing, perhaps even everything)" (85).
68. Edelman, *Bad Education*, xiii; Wilderson, *Afropessimism*, 14.
69. Paul Schrader, *Transcendental Style in Film: Ozu, Bresson, Dreyer* (Oakland: University of California Press, 2018), 2.
70. Schrader, *Transcendental Style in Film*, 3.
71. Schrader, *Transcendental Style in Film*, 3.
72. Schrader, *Transcendental Style in Film*, 4.
73. Gilles Deleuze and Félix Guattari, *A Thousand Plateaus: Capitalism and Schizophrenia* (Minneapolis: University of Minnesota Press, 1987).
74. *Mirror*, dir. Andrei Tarkovsky (1975; Moscow: Mosfilm, 2007).
75. Cavell, *The World Viewed*, 23.
76. Cavell, *The World Viewed*, 23.
77. Schrader, *Transcendental Style in Film*, 3; *Another Earth*, dir. Mike Cahill (2011; New York: Artists Public Domain, 2011).
78. *Interstellar*, dir. Christopher Nolan (2014; Burbank, Los Angeles, and Culver City: Legendary Pictures, Syncopy, and Lunda Obst Productions, 2014).

79. *Taxi Driver*, dir. Martin Scorsese (1976; New York: Bill/Phillips Productions and Italo/Judeo Productions, 2007).

80. Schrader describes Mary as though she were a symbol, rather than a character, in an interview whose publication coincided with the film's theatrical release: "On one level, Grace descends and he's saved from his suicidal ways. On the other hand, there he is in Gethsemane with the cup in his hand and he's saying, 'Lord, please let this cup pass from me.' But he doesn't, and he drinks it, and now he's on all fours, purging out his stomach. And God, who hasn't talked to him for the whole film, now comes over to him and says, 'Rev. Toller, would you like to see what heaven looks like?' . . . It looks like one long kiss." Eric Cortellessa, "Paul Schrader on *First Reformed*'s Provocative Ending and Its Many Influences," *Slate*, June 13, 2018, https://slate.com/culture/2018/06/first-reformeds-ending-paul-schrader-explains-why-its-designed-to-be-ambiguous.html.

81. Roland Barthes, *A Lover's Discourse: Fragments*, trans. Richard Howard (New York: Farrar, Straus and Giroux, 1978), 23.

Filmography

Bergman, Ingmar, dir. *Persona*. 1966; Stockholm: AB Svensk Filmindustri, 2004.

Bouwer, Jaco, dir. *Gaia*. 2021; Los Angeles and Cape Town: XYZ Films, Film Initiative Africa, and kykNET Films, 2021.

Cahill, Mike, dir. *Another Earth*. 2011; New York: Artists Public Domain, 2011.

Cameron, James, dir. *Terminator II: Judgment Day*. 1991; Los Angeles, Santa Monica, and Paris: Carolco Pictures, Pacific Western Productions, Lightstorm Entertainment, and Le Studio Canal+, 2000.

Chang-dong, Lee, dir. *Beoning* (*Burning*). 2018; Seoul and Tokyo: Pinehouse Film, Now Film and NHK, 2018.

Chung, Lee Isaac, dir. *Minari*. 2020; Los Angeles: Plan B Entertainment, 2020.

Dosa, Sara, dir. *Fire of Love*, 2022; New York, Montreal, and Los Angeles: Sandbox Films, Intuitive Pictures, and Cottage M, 2022.

Frost, Mark, and David Lynch, creators. *Twin Peaks*. 1990–91; Los Angeles: Lynch/Frost Productions, Propaganda Films, Spelling Television, Twin Peaks Productions, and ABC Network.

Frost, Mark, and David Lynch, creators. *Twin Peaks: The Return*. 2017; Los Angeles and New York: Lynch/Frost Productions, Propaganda Films, Spelling Television, Twin Peaks Productions, CBS Television, and Showtime.

Garland, Alex, dir. *Annihilation*. 2018; Santa Monica, London, New York, and Beijing: Skydance, DNA Films, Scott Rudin Productions, and Huahua Media, 2018.

Gilliam, Terry, dir. *12 Monkeys*. 1995; Los Angeles: Atlas Entertainment Classico, 2005.

Goddard, Drew, dir. *The Cabin in the Woods*. 2011; Los Angeles: Mutant Enemy Productions, 2012.

Hooper, Tobe, dir. *The Texas Chainsaw Massacre*. 1974; Vortex, 2004.

Itami, Juzo, dir. *Tampopo*. 1985; New York: Fox Lorber Home Video, Itami Productions, and New Century Producers, 1998.

Jóhannsson, Valdimar, dir. *Dýrið* (*Lamb*). 2021; Paris, Stockholm, Warsaw, Trollhättan, and Malmö: Go to Sheep, Boom Films, Black Spark Productions, Madants/NEM Corp, Film i Väst, Chimney Sweden, Chimney Poland, and Rabbit Hole Productions, 2021.

Lynch, David, dir. *Blue Velvet*. 1986; Wilmington, NC: De Laurentiis Entertainment Group, 2001.

Mathai, Mahesh, dir. *Bhopal Express*. 1999; Mumbai: Highlight Films, 2004.

Nolan, Christopher, dir. *Interstellar*. 2014; Burbank, Los Angeles, and Culver City: Legendary Pictures, Syncopy, and Lunda Obst Productions, 2014.

Nolan, Christopher, dir. *Tenet*. 2020; Los Angeles: Syncopy, 2020.

Parra, Danilo, dir. "*Mushroom*: A Film by Danilo Parra." Ford Canada, YouTube. October 12, 2022. https://www.youtube.com/watch?v=Gkyq71JYz-8.

Pölsler, Julian, dir. *Die Wand* (*The Wall*). 2012; Vienna and Munich: Coop99 Filmproduktion and Starhaus Filmproduktion, 2013.

Reichardt, Kelly, dir. *First Cow*. 2019; Webster, TX and New York: Film Science and IAC Films, 2019.

Reichardt, Kelly, dir. *Meek's Cutoff*. 2010; New York and Webster, TX: Evenstar Films, Film Science, Harmony Productions, and Primitive Nerd, 2011.

Reichardt, Kelly, dir. *Night Moves*. 2013. Santa Monica, Webster, TX, and São Paulo: Maybach Film Productions, Film Science, Tipping Point Productions, and RT Features, 2014.

Reichardt, Kelly, dir. *Old Joy*. 2006; Webster, TX, and New York: Film Science, Van Hoy/Knudsen Productions, and Washington Square Films, 2007.

Reichardt, Kelly, dir. *Wendy and Lucy*. 2008; Webster, TX, and New York: Field Guide Films, Film Science, Glass Eye Pix, and Washington Square Films, 2009.

Schrader, Paul, dir. *First Reformed*. 2017; New York, London, Los Angeles, and Beverly Hills: Killer Films, Omeira Studio Partners, Fibonacci Films, Arclight Films, and Big Indie Productions, 2017.

Schwartzberg, Louie, dir. *Fantastic Fungi*. 2019; Los Angeles: Moving Art, 2019.

Scorsese, Martin, dir. *Taxi Driver*. 1976; New York: Bill/Phillips Productions and Italo/Judeo Productions, 2007.

Tarkovsky, Andrei, dir. *Mirror*. 1975; Moscow: Mosfilm, 2007.

Varda, Agnès, dir. *Sans toit ni loi* (*Vagabond*). 1985; New York and Paris: Janus Films and Ciné-Tamaris, 2007.

Von Trier, Lars, dir. *Antichrist*. 2009; Copenhagen, Paris, Trollhättan, Stockholm, and Mainz: Zentropa Entertainments, arte France Cinéma, Canal+, Danmarks Radio, Film i Väst, Svenska Filminstitutet, Sveriges Television, and ZDF, 2009.

West, Ti, dir. *X*. 2022; Los Angeles: Little Lamb and Mad Solar Productions, 2022.

Wheatley, Ben, dir. *In the Earth*. 2021; Bridport, UK, and London: Rook Films and Protagonist Pictures, 2021.

Bibliography

Ahmann, Chloe, and Alison Kenner. "Breathing Late Industrialism." *Engaging Science, Technology, and Society* 6 (2020): doi.org/10.17351/ests2020.673.

Ahuja, Neel. "Intimate Atmospheres: Queer Theory in a Time of Extinctions." *GLQ: A Journal of Lesbian and Gay Studies* 21, nos. 2–3 (2015): 365–85.

Alaimo, Stacy. *Bodily Natures: Science, Environment, and the Material Self.* Bloomington: Indiana University Press, 2010.

———. *Exposed: Environmental Politics and Pleasures in Posthuman Times.* Minneapolis: University of Minnesota Press, 2016.

Allewaert, Monique. *Ariel's Ecology: Plantations, Personhood, and Colonialism in the American Tropics.* Minneapolis: University of Minnesota Press, 2013.

Anker, Elisabeth R. *Ugly Freedoms.* Durham, NC: Duke University Press, 2022.

Anzieu, Didier. *The Skin-Ego.* Translated by Naomi Segal. New York: Routledge, 2018.

Ashtor, Gila. *Homo Psyche: On Queer Theory and Erotophobia.* New York: Fordham University Press, 2021.

Badiou, Alain. *Badiou by Badiou.* Translated by Bruno Bosteels. Stanford, CA: Stanford University Press, 2022.

———. *Being and Event.* Translated by Oliver Feltham. London: Continuum, 2005.

———. *Logics of Worlds: Being and Event II.* Translated by Alberto Toscano. 2009; London: Bloomsbury, 2013.

———. *Saint Paul: The Foundations of Universalism.* Translated by Ray Brassier. Stanford, CA: Stanford University Press, 2003.

Badiou, Alain, and Barbara Cassin. *There's No Such Thing as a Sexual Relationship.* Translated by Susan Spitzer and Kenneth Reinhard. New York: Columbia University Press, 2017.

Baldwin, James. "My Dungeon Shook: Letter to My Nephew on the One Hundredth Anniversary of the Emancipation." In *James Baldwin: Collected Essays*, edited by Toni Morrison, 291–95. New York: Library of America, 1998.

Barad, Karen. *Meeting the Universe Halfway: Quantum Physics and the Entanglement of Matter and Meaning.* Durham, NC: Duke University Press, 2007.

———. "Nature's Queer Performativity." *Qui Parle* 19, no. 2 (2011): 121–58.

——. "Nature's Queer Performativity (The Authorized Version)." *Women, Gender, and Research (Kvinder, Køn oh Korkning)* 1–2 (2012): 25–53.
——. "On Touching—The Inhuman That Therefore I Am." *differences* 23, no. 5 (2012): 206–23.
Barnett, Barry J. "The U.S. Farm Financial Crisis of the 1980s." *Agricultural History* 74, no. 2 (2010): 366–80.
Barthes, Roland. *A Lover's Discourse: Fragments*. Translated by Richard Howard. New York: Farrar, Straus and Giroux, 1978.
Bazin, André. *What Is Cinema? Volume 1*. Edited and translated by Hugh Gray. Berkeley: University of California Press, 1967.
Bennett, Jane. *Vibrant Matter: A Political Ecology of Things*. Durham, NC: Duke University Press, 2010.
Berlant, Lauren. *On the Inconvenience of Other People*. Durham, NC: Duke University Press, 2022.
Berlant, Lauren, and Lee Edelman. *Sex, or the Unbearable*. Durham, NC: Duke University Press, 2013.
Bersani, Leo. *The Freudian Body: Psychoanalysis and Art*. New York: Columbia University Press, 1986.
——. *Homos*. Cambridge, MA: Harvard University Press, 1995.
——. *Is the Rectum a Grave? And Other Essays*. Chicago: University of Chicago Press, 2010.
Bersani, Leo, and Adam Phillips. *Intimacies*. Chicago: University of Chicago Press, 2008.
Bliss, James. "Hope Against Hope: Queer Negativity, Black Feminist Theorizing, and Reproduction without Futurity." *Mosaic* 48, no. 1 (2015): 83–98.
Bogost, Ian. *Alien Phenomenology, or What It's Like to Be a Thing*. Minneapolis: University of Minnesota Press, 2012.
Bolender, Karin. "R. A. W. Assmilk Soap." In *The Multispecies Salon*, edited by Eben Kirksey, 64-86. Durham, NC: Duke University Press, 2014.
Boman, Björn. "The Multifold Intertextuality in Lee Chang Dong's *Burning*." *Social Sciences & Humanities Open* 3, no. 1 (2021): doi:10.1016/j.ssaho.2021.100119.
Bould, Mark. *The Anthropocene Unconscious: Climate Catastrophe Culture*. New York: Verso, 2021.
Bozak, Nadia. *The Cinematic Footprint: Lights, Camera, Natural Resources*. New Brunswick, NJ: Rutgers University Press, 2012.
Braidotti, Rosi. *Nomadic Subjects: Embodiment and Sexual Difference in Contemporary Feminist Theory*, 2nd edition. New York: Columbia University Press, 2011.
Brassier, Ray. *Nihil Unbound: Enlightenment and Extinction*. New York: Palgrave Macmillan, 2007.
Brinkema, Eugenie. *Life-Destroying Diagrams*. Durham, NC: Duke University Press, 2022.
Brooks, Peter. *Reading for the Plot: Design and Intention in Narrative*. Cambridge, MA: Harvard University Press, 1984.
Broughton, Edward. "The Bhopal Disaster and Its Aftermath: A Review." *Environmental Health* 4, no. 6 (2005): doi:10.1186/1476-069X-4-6.
Bryant, Levi, Nick Srnicek, and Graham Harman. "Towards a Speculative Philosophy." In *The Speculative Turn: Continental Materialism and Realism*, edited by Levi Bryant, Nick Srnicek, and Graham Harman, 1–18. Melbourne, AU: re.press, 2011.

Buell, Lawrence. *Writing for an Endangered World: Literature, Culture, and Environment in the U.S. and Beyond*. Cambridge, MA: Belknap Press of Harvard University Press, 2001.

Butler, Judith. *Giving an Account of Oneself*. New York: Fordham University Press, 2005.

———. *Precarious Life: The Powers of Mourning and Violence*. New York: Verso, 2004.

———. *The Psychic Life of Power: Theories in Subjection*. Stanford, CA: Stanford University Press, 1997.

Cahill, James Leo. *Zoological Surrealism: The Nonhuman Cinema of Jean Painlevé*. Minneapolis: University of Minnesota Press, 2019.

Camus, Albert. *The Myth of Sisyphus and Other Essays*. Translated by Justin O'Brien. New York: Vintage, 1991.

Carpenter, Cari M. *Seeing Red: Anger, Sentimentality, and American Indians*. Columbus: Ohio State University Press, 2008.

Cavarero, Adriana. *For More Than One Voice: Toward a Philosophy of Vocal Expression*. Translated by Paul A. Kottman. Stanford, CA: Stanford University Press, 2005.

Cavell, Stanley. *Contesting Tears: The Hollywood Melodrama of the Unknown Woman*. Chicago: University of Chicago Press, 1996.

———. *Emerson's Transcendental Etudes*. Stanford, CA: Stanford University Press, 2003.

———. *A Pitch of Philosophy: Autobiographical Exercises*. Cambridge, MA: Harvard University Press, 1994.

———. *The World Viewed: Reflections on the Ontology of Film*. Cambridge, MA: Harvard University Press, 1979.

Cecire, Natalia, and Samuel Solomon. "Mycoaesthetics; or, Why Mushrooms Can Never Run Out of Steam." *Critical Inquiry* 50, no. 4 (2024), forthcoming.

Chakrabarty, Dipesh. *The Climate of History in a Planetary Age*. Chicago: University of Chicago Press, 2021.

Chen, Mel Y. *Animacies: Biopolitics, Racial Mattering, and Queer Affect*. Durham, NC: Duke University Press, 2012.

Cheng, Anne Anlin. *The Melancholy of Race: Psychoanalysis, Assimilation, and Hidden Grief*. Oxford: Oxford University Press.

Chitty, Christopher. *Sexual Hegemony: Statecraft, Sodomy, and Capital in the Rise of the World System*. Edited by Max Fox. Durham, NC: Duke University Press, 2020.

Clark, T. J. *The Sight of Death: An Experiment in Art Writing*. New Haven, CT: Yale University Press, 2006.

Clute, John. "The Darkening Garden: A Short Lexicon of Horror." In *Stay*, 269–343. Harold Wood, UK: Beccon, 2014.

Cohen, Jeffrey Jerome, and Lowell Duckert, editors. *Elemental Ecocriticism: Thinking with Earth, Air, Water, and Fire*. Minneapolis: University of Minnesota Press, 2015.

Cohen, Tom, Claire Colebrook, and J. Hillis Miller. *Twilight of the Anthropocene Idols*. London: Open Humanities, 2016.

Colebrook, Claire. "Cinemas and Worlds." *Diacritics* 45, no. 1 (2017): 25–48.

———. "End-Times for Humanity." Aeon. June 1, 2017. https://aeon.co/essays/the-human-world-is-not-more-fragile-now-it-always-has-been.

Coolsaet, Brendan, and Pierre-Yves Néron. "Recognition and Environmental Justice." In *Environmental Justice: Key Issues*, edited by Brendan Coolsaet, 52–63. London: Routledge, 2020.

Copjec, Joan. *Imagine There's No Woman: Ethics and Sublimation*. Cambridge, MA: MIT Press, 2002.

———. *Read My Desire: Lacan against the Historicists*. 1994; New York: Verso, 2015.

———. "Sexual Difference." Political Concepts: A Critical Lexicon. November 3, 2014. https://www.politicalconcepts.org/sexual-difference-joan-copjec/8/.

Cornell, Drucilla. *The Philosophy of the Limit*. New York: Routledge, 1992.

Cronon, William. "The Trouble with Wilderness; or, Getting Back to the Wrong Nature." *Environmental History* 1, no. 1 (1996): 7–28.

Dawson, Ashley. *Mongrel Nation: Diasporic Culture and the Making of Postcolonial Britain*. Ann Arbor: University of Michigan Press, 2007.

De Man, Paul. *Aesthetic Ideology*. Edited by Andrzej Warminski. Minneapolis: University of Minnesota Press, 1996.

De Saussure, Ferdinand. *Course in General Linguistics*. Edited by Charles Bally et al., translated by Roy Harris. Chicago: Open Court, 1983.

Dean, Tim. *Unlimited Intimacy: Reflections on the Subculture of Barebacking*. Chicago: University of Chicago Press, 2009.

DeFries, Ruth. *What Would Nature Do? A Guide for Our Uncertain Times*. New York: Columbia University Press, 2021.

Deleuze, Gilles. *Cinema 1: The Movement-Image*. Translated by Hugh Tomlinson and Barbara Habberjam. Minneapolis: University of Minnesota Press, 1986.

———. *Cinema 2: The Time-Image*. Translated by Hugh Tomlinson and Robert Galeta. Minneapolis: University of Minnesota Press, 1989.

———. *Masochism: Coldness and Cruelty*. Translated by Jean McNeil. New York: Zone Books, 1991.

Deleuze, Gilles, and Félix Guattari. *A Thousand Plateaus: Capitalism and Schizophrenia*. Minneapolis: University of Minnesota Press, 1987.

DeLoughrey, Elizabeth. "Submarine Futures of the Anthropocene." *Comparative Literature* 69, no. 1 (2017): 32–44.

Derrida, Jacques. "Cogito and the History of Madness." In *Writing and Difference*, translated by Alan Bass, 31–63. Chicago: University of Chicago Press, 1978.

———. "*Geschlecht* I: Sexual Difference, Ontological Difference." *Research in Phenomenology* 13 (1983): 65–83.

———. "Heidegger's Hand (*Geschlecht* II)." Translated by John P. Leavey Jr. and Elizabeth Rottenberg. In *Psyche: Inventions of the Other, Volume II*, edited by Peggy Kamuf and Elizabeth Rottenberg, 27–61. Stanford, CA: Stanford University Press, 2008.

———. *Rogues: Two Essays on Reason*. Translated by Pascale-Anne Brault and Michael Naas. Stanford, CA: Stanford University Press, 2005.

———. "Signature Event Context." In *Margins of Philosophy*, translated by Alan Bass, 307–30. Chicago: University of Chicago Press, 1982.

Dillon, Sarah. "The Horror of the Anthropocene." *C21 Literature: Journal of 21st-Century Writing* 6, no. 1 (2018): doi.org/10.16995/c21.38.

Dolar, Mladen. *A Voice and Nothing More*. Cambridge, MA: MIT Press, 2006.

Dowling, Sarah. *Entering Sappho*. Toronto: Coach House Books, 2020.

Duncan, Rebecca. "Anthropocene Gothic, Capitalocene Gothic: The Politics of Ecohorror." In *The Edinburgh Companion to Globalgothic*, edited by Rebecca Duncan, 114–30. Edinburgh: University of Edinburgh Press, 2023.

Dworkin, Andrea. *Pornography: Men Possessing Women*. 1979. New York: Plume, 1989.

Edelman, Lee. *Bad Education: Why Queer Theory Teaches Us Nothing*. Durham, NC: Duke University Press, 2023.

———. *No Future: Queer Theory and the Death Drive*. Durham, NC: Duke University Press, 2004.

———. "On Solidarity." *Representations* 158, no. 1 (2022): 93–105.

Eng, David. *Racial Castration: Managing Masculinity in Asian America*. Durham, NC: Duke University Press, 2001.

Ensor, Sarah. "Queer Fallout: Samuel R. Delany and the Ecology of Cruising." *Environmental Humanities* 9, no. 1 (2017): 149–66.

Fanon, Frantz. *Black Skin, White Masks*. Translated by Richard Philcox. New York: Grove, 2008.

Faulkner, William. "Barn Burner." In *Selected Stories of William Faulkner*, 3–26. New York: Modern Library, 2012.

Fay, Jennifer. "Do I Know the Anthropocene When I See It?" *Representations* 157, no. 1 (2022): 41–67.

———. *Inhospitable World: Cinema in the Time of the Anthropocene*. New York: Oxford University Press, 2018.

———. "Thinking on Film with Arendt and Cavell." *Critical Inquiry* 49, no. 2 (2023): 227–50.

Fields, Barbara J., and Karen E. Fields. *Racecraft: The Soul of Inequality in American Life*. New York: Verso, 2022.

Fink, Bruce. *The Lacanian Subject: Between Language and Jouissance*. Princeton, NJ: Princeton University Press, 1995.

Fortun, Kim. "From Latour to Late Industrialism." *HAU: A Journal of Ethnographic Theory* 4, no. 1 (2014): 209–29.

Foucault, Michel. *History of Madness*. Translated by Jonathan Murphy and Jean Khalfa. 1964. New York: Routledge, 2006.

———. *The History of Sexuality, Volume 1: An Introduction*. Translated by Robert Hurley. New York: Pantheon, 1978.

Freeman, Elizabeth. *Time Binds: Queer Temporalities, Queer Histories*. Durham, NC: Duke University Press, 2010.

Freud, Sigmund. "Analysis Terminable and Interminable" (1937). In *The Standard Edition of the Complete Psychological Works of Sigmund Freud*, vol. 23, edited and translated by James Strachey, 209–54. London: Hogarth Press and the Institute of Psychoanalysis, 1953–74.

———. *Civilization and Its Discontents* (1930). In *The Standard Edition of the Complete Psychological Works of Sigmund Freud*, vol. 21, edited and translated by James Strachey, 64–148. London: Hogarth Press and the Institute of Psychoanalysis, 1953–74.

———. "Mourning and Melancholia" (1917). In *The Standard Edition of the Complete Psychological Works of Sigmund Freud*, vol. 14, edited and translated by James Strachey, 237–58. London: Hogarth Press and the Institute of Psychoanalysis, 1953–74.

——. "Negation" (1925). In *The Standard Edition of the Complete Psychological Works of Sigmund Freud*, vol. 19, edited and translated by James Strachey, 233–40. London: Hogarth Press and the Institute of Psychoanalysis, 1953–74.

——. *Project for a Scientific Psychology* (1895). In *The Standard Edition of the Complete Psychological Works of Sigmund Freud*, vol. 1, edited and translated by James Strachey, 283–98. London: Hogarth Press and the Institute of Psychoanalysis, 1953–74.

——. *Studies on Hysteria* (1895). In *The Standard Edition of the Complete Psychological Works of Sigmund Freud*, vol. 2, edited and translated by James Strachey, 1–312. London: Hogarth Press and the Institute of Psychoanalysis, 1953–74.

——. *The Uncanny*. Translated by David McLintock. London: Penguin Books, 2003.

Fusco, Katherine, and Nicole Seymour. *Kelly Reichardt*. Champaign: University of Illinois Press, 2017.

Ghosh, Amitav. *The Great Derangement: Climate Change and the Unthinkable*. Chicago: University of Chicago Press, 2016.

Giraud, Eva Haifa. *What Comes After Entanglement? Activism, Anthropocentrism, and an Ethics of Exclusion*. Durham, NC: Duke University Press, 2019.

Goldberg, Jonathan. *Melodrama: An Aesthetics of Impossibility*. Durham, NC: Duke University Press, 2016.

——. *Sodometries: Renaissance Texts, Modern Sexualities*. New York: Fordham University Press, 2010.

Gosine, Andil. *Nature's Wild: Love, Sex, and Law in the Caribbean*. Durham, NC: Duke University Press, 2021.

Grosz, Elizabeth. "The Nature of Sexual Difference: Irigaray and Darwin." *Angelaki* 17, no. 2 (2012): 69–93.

——. *Time Travels: Feminism, Nature, Power*. Durham, NC: Duke University Press, 2005.

Gyamfi, Brian. "The Ecological Part of Gender: An Interview with Brian Teare." *Michigan Quarterly Review*, November 2021. https://sites.lsa.umich.edu/mqr/2021/11/the-ecological-part-of-gender-an-interview-with-brian-teare/.

Hand, Seán. "Being for Every Other: Levinas in the Anthropocene." *Frontiers of Narrative Studies* 7, no. 2 (2021): 156–75.

Haram, Linsey E., James T. Carlton, Gregory M. Ruiz, and Nikolai A. Maximenko. "A Plasticene Lexicon." *Marine Pollution Bulletin* 150 (2020): doi.org/10.1016/j.marpolbul.2019.110714.

Haraway, Donna J. *Staying with the Trouble: Making Kin in the Chthulucene*. Durham, NC: Duke University Press, 2016.

——. *When Species Meet*. Minneapolis: University of Minnesota Press, 2008.

Harl, Neil E. *The Farm Debt Crisis of the 1980s*. Ames: Iowa State University Press, 1990.

Harman, Graham. *Tool-Being: Heidegger and the Metaphysics of Objects*. Chicago: Open Court, 2002.

Hartman, Saidiya. *Scenes of Subjection: Terror, Slavery, and Self-Making in Nineteenth-Century America*. Oxford: Oxford University Press, 1997.

Haushofer, Marlen. *The Wall*. Translated by Shaun Whiteside. 1968. Berkeley, CA: Cleis, 2012.

Hediger, Ryan. *Homesickness: Of Trauma and the Longing for Place in a Change Environment*. Minneapolis: University of Minnesota Press, 2019.

Hegel, Georg Wilhelm Friedrich. *Phenomenology of Spirit*. Translated by A. V. Miller. Oxford: Oxford University Press, 1977.

Heidegger, Martin. *Being and Time*. Translated by John Macquarrie and Edward Robinson. New York: Harper and Row, 1962.

———. "What Is Metaphysics?" In *Basic Writings*, edited and translated by David Farrell Krell, 89–110. 1977. New York: HarperCollins, 1993.

Heise, Ursula K. *Imagining Extinction: The Cultural Meanings of Endangered Species*. Chicago: University of Chicago Press, 2016.

Hollingshead, David. "Neko Case and the Molecular Turn." *GLQ: A Journal of Lesbian and Gay Studies* 25, no. 4 (2019): 617–47.

Houser, Heather. *Ecosickness in Contemporary U.S. Fiction: Environment and Affect*. New York: Columbia University Press, 2014.

Hu, Jane. "Ang Lee's Tears: Digital Global Melodrama in *The Wedding Banquet*, *Hulk*, and *Gemini Man*." *Verge: Studies in Global Asias* 7, no. 2 (2021): 151–76.

Hume, Angela, and Samia Rahimtoola. "Introduction: Queering Ecopoetics." *ISLE: Interdisciplinary Studies in Literature and Environment* 25, no. 1 (2018): 134–49.

Hurley, Jessica. *Infrastructures of Apocalypse: American Literature and the Nuclear Complex*. Minneapolis: University of Minnesota Press, 2020.

Jackson, Zakiyyah Iman. *Becoming Human: Matter and Meaning in an Antiblack World*. New York: New York University Press, 2020.

Jue, Melody. *Wild Blue Media: Thinking through Seawater*. Durham, NC: Duke University Press, 2020.

Jue, Melody, and Rafico Ruiz. "Thinking with Saturation beyond Water: Thresholds, Phase Change, and the Precipitate." In *Saturation: An Elemental Politics*, edited by Melody Jue and Rafico Ruiz, 1–28. Durham, NC: Duke University Press, 2021.

———. *Saturation: An Elemental Politics*. Durham, NC: Duke University Press, 2021.

Kafer, Alison. *Feminist, Queer, Crip*. Bloomington: Indiana University Press, 2013.

Kant, Immanuel. *Critique of Judgment*. Translated by Werner S. Pluhar. Indianapolis, IN: Hackett, 1987.

———. *Critique of Pure Reason*. Edited and translated by Paul Guyer and Allen Wood. Cambridge: Cambridge University Press, 1998.

Keeling, Kara. *The Witch's Flight: The Cinematic, the Black Femme, and the Image of Common Sense*. Durham, NC: Duke University Press, 2007.

Keetley, Dawn, and Matthew Sivils, editors. *Ecogothic in Nineteenth-Century American Literature*. New York: Routledge, 2018.

Keller, Lynn. *Recomposing Ecopoetics: North American Poetry of the Self-Conscious Anthropocene*. Charlottesville: University of Virginia Press, 2017.

Kermode, Frank. *The Sense of an Ending: Studies in the Theory of Fiction*. 1966. Oxford: Oxford University Press, 2000.

Kirksey, Eben, and Sophie Chao. "Introduction: Who Benefits from Multispecies Justice?" In *The Promise of Multispecies Justice*, edited by Sophie Chao, Karen Bolender, and Eben Kirksey, 1–21. Durham, NC: Duke University Press, 2022.

Kirksey, Eben, Craig Schuetze, and Stefan Helmreich. "Introduction." In *The Multispecies Salon*, edited by Eben Kirksey, 1–28. Durham, NC: Duke University Press, 2014.

Kohn, Eduardo. *How Forests Think: Toward an Anthropology beyond the Human.* Berkeley: University of California Press, 2013.

Kojève, Alexandre. *Introduction to the Reading of Hegel: Lectures on the "Phenomenology of Spirit."* Assembled by Raymond Queneau, edited by Allan Bloom, translated by James H. Nichols, Jr. Ithaca, NY: Cornell University Press, 1969.

"Korean American Population Data." National Association of Korean Americans. 2021. http://www.naka.org/resources/.

Krauthamer, Anna. "Would That the Earth Could Stop Us." Public Books. June 2, 2022. https://www.publicbooks.org/ecohorror-gaia-in-the-earth/.

Lacan, Jacques. "The Mirror Stage as Formative of the *I* Function as Revealed in Psychoanalytic Experience." In *Écrits: The First Complete Edition in English*, translated by Bruce Fink, 75–81. New York: Norton, 2006.

———. *The Seminar of Jacques Lacan, Book II: The Ego in Freud's Theory and in the Technique of Psychoanalysis, 1954–1955.* Edited by Jacques-Alain Miller, translated by Sylvana Tomaselli. New York: Norton, 1991.

———. *The Seminar of Jacques Lacan, Book III: The Psychoses, 1955–1956.* Edited by Jacques-Alain Miller, translated by Russell Grigg. New York: Norton, 1993.

———. *The Seminar of Jacques Lacan, Book VII: The Ethics of Psychoanalysis, 1959–1960.* Edited by Jacques-Alain Miller, translated by Dennis Porter. New York: Norton, 1992.

———. *The Seminar of Jacques Lacan, Book XI: The Four Fundamental Concepts of Psychoanalysis.* Edited by Jacques-Alain Miller, translated by Alan Sheridan. New York: Norton, 1977.

———. *The Seminar of Jacques Lacan, Book XX: On Feminine Sexuality, the Limits of Love and Knowledge, 1972–1973 (Encore).* Edited by Jacques-Alain Miller, translated by Bruce Fink. New York: Norton, 1998.

———. *Le Séminaire XXI: Les Non-dupes errent*, 1973–74. Manuscript, session of April 23, 1974. Translation by Todd McGowan. Quoted in *Enjoying What We Don't Have: The Political Project of Psychoanalysis*, by Todd McGowan, 17. Lincoln: University of Nebraska Press, 2013.

Laplanche, Jean. *Life and Death in Psychoanalysis.* Translated by Jeffrey Mehlman. Baltimore, MD: Johns Hopkins University Press, 1976.

———. *New Foundations for Psychoanalysis.* Translated by David Macey. Cambridge, MA: Basil Blackwell, 1989.

———. "Note on Afterwardsness." In *Essays on Otherness*, edited by John Fletcher, 260–65. New York: Routledge, 1999.

———. *The Temptation of Biology: Freud's Theories of Sexuality.* Translated by Donald Nicholson-Smith. New York: The Unconscious in Translation, 2015.

———. "Time and the Other." Translated by Luke Thurston. In *Essays on Otherness*, edited by John Fletcher, 238–63. New York: Routledge, 1999.

———. "The Unfinished Copernican Revolution." Translated by Luke Thurston. In *Essays on Otherness*, edited by John Fletcher, 52–85. New York: Routledge, 1999.

Latour, Bruno. "An Attempt at a 'Compositionist Manifesto.'" *New Literary History* 41, no. 3 (2010): 471–90.

Levinas, Emmanuel. *Entre Nous: Thinking-of-the-Other.* Translated by Michael B. Smith and Barbara Harshav. New York: Columbia University Press, 1998.

———. *Otherwise Than Being, or Beyond Essence.* Translated by Alphonso Lingis. Pittsburgh, PA: Duquesne University Press, 1998.

Locke, John. *Two Treatises of Government*. Edited by Peter Laslett. Cambridge: Cambridge University Press, 1988.

Lucretius. *On the Nature of Things*. Translated by W. H. D. Rouse, revised by Martin Ferguson Smith. Loeb Classical Library. Cambridge, MA: Harvard University Press, 1982.

Lyle, Coleen. *America's Asia: Racial Form and American Literature, 1893–1945*. Princeton, NJ: Princeton University Press, 2015.

Malabou, Catherine. *The Ontology of the Accident: An Essay on Destructive Plasticity*. Translated by Carolyn Shread. Cambridge: Polity, 2012.

Małecki, Wojciech, Bogusław Pawłowski, Marcin Cieński, and Piotr Sorokowski. "Can Fiction Make Us Kinder to Other Species? The Impact of Fiction on Pro-Animal Attitudes and Behavior." *Poetics* 66 (February 2018): doi.org/10.1016/j.poetic.2018.02.004.

Małecki, Wojciech, Matthew Schneider-Mayerson, Nicolai Skiveren, Alexa Weik von Mossner, and Frank Hakemulder. "About Empirical Ecocriticism." Empirical Ecocriticism. n.d. https://empiricalecocriticism.com/about-empirical-ecocriticism/.

Małecki, W. P., Alexa Weik von Mossner, Piotr Sorokowski, and Tomasz Frackowiak. "Extinction Stories Matter: The Impact of Narrative Representations of Endangered Species across Media." *ISLE: Interdisciplinary Studies in Literature and Environment* (2021): doi.org/10.1093/isle/isab094.

Manon, Hugh S. "Resolution, Truncation, Glitch." In *Cinematic Cuts: Theorizing Film Endings*, edited by Sheila Kunkle, 19–38. Albany: State University of New York Press, 2016.

Marder, Michael. *Plant-Thinking: A Philosophy of Vegetal Life*. New York: Columbia University Press, 2013.

Marriott, David. *Whither Fanon? Studies in the Blackness of Being*. Stanford, CA: Stanford University Press, 2018.

Martin, Adrian, Brendan Coolsaet, Esteve Corbera, Neil M. Dawson, James A. Fraser, Ina Lehmann, and Iokiñe Rodríguez. "Justice and Conservation: The Need to Incorporate Recognition." *Biological Conservation* 197 (2016): 254–61.

McGowan, Todd. *Enjoying What We Don't Have: The Political Project of Psychoanalysis*. Lincoln: University of Nebraska Press, 2013.

———. *Enjoyment Right and Left*. Portland, OR: Sublation, 2022.

———. "Looking for the Gaze: Lacanian Film Theory and Its Vicissitudes." *Cinema Journal* 42, no. 3 (2003): 29.

———. *Only a Joke Can Save Us: A Theory of Comedy*. Evanston, IL: Northwestern University Press, 2017.

———. "The Satisfaction of an Ending." In *Cinematic Cuts: Theorizing Film Endings*, edited by Sheila Kunkle, 135–46. Albany: State University of New York Press, 2016.

———. "Signification and Subjectivity." July 17, 2021, video, 37:00. https://youtu.be/AF7QBX9t28c.

Meillassoux, Quentin. *After Finitude: An Essay on the Necessity of Contingency*. Translated by Ray Brassier. London: Continuum, 2010.

Menely, Tobias. *Climate and the Making of Worlds: Toward a Geohistorical Poetics*. Chicago: University of Chicago Press, 2021.

Mitropoulos, Angela. *Contract and Contagion: From Biopolitics to Oikonomia*. Brooklyn, NY: Autonomedia, 2012.

Morton, Timothy. *The Ecological Thought*. Cambridge, MA: Harvard University Press, 2010.

——. *Ecology without Nature: Rethinking Environmental Aesthetics*. Cambridge, MA: Harvard University Press, 2007.

——. *Hyperobjects: Philosophy and Ecology after the End of the World*. Minneapolis: University of Minnesota Press, 2013.

——. "Queer Ecology." *PMLA* 125, no. 2 (2010): 273–82.

Moten, Fred. *Stolen Life*. Durham, NC: Duke University Press, 2018.

Muñoz, José Esteban. *Cruising Utopia: The Then and There of Queer Futurity*. New York: New York University Press, 2009.

——. *Disidentifications: Queers of Color and the Performance of Politics*. Minneapolis: University of Minnesota Press, 1999.

Murakami, Haruki. "Barn Burning." Translated by Alfred Birnbaum. In *The Elephant Vanishes: Stories*, 132–49. New York: Vintage, 1993.

Murphy, Bernice M. *The Rural Gothic in American Popular Culture: Backwoods Horror and Terror in the Wilderness*. New York: Palgrave Macmillan, 2013.

Murphy, Michelle. *Sick Building Syndrome and the Problem of Uncertainty: Environmental Politics, Technoscience, and Women Workers*. Durham, NC: Duke University Press, 2006.

Narine, Anil. "Introduction: Eco-Trauma Cinema." In *Eco-Trauma Cinema*, edited by Anil Narine, 1–24. New York: Routledge, 2015.

Nayar, Pramod N. *Bhopal's Ecological Gothic: Disaster, Precarity, and the Biopolitical Uncanny*. Lanham, MD: Lexington Books, 2017.

Neyrat, Frédéric. *Atopias: Manifesto for a Radical Environmentalism*. Translated by Walt Hunter and Lindsay Turner. New York: Fordham University Press, 2018.

——. *The Unconstructable Earth: An Ecology of Separation*. Translated by Drew S. Burk. New York: Fordham University Press, 2019.

Nezhukumatathil, Aimee. *World of Wonders: In Praise of Fireflies, Whale Sharks, and Other Astonishments*. Minneapolis, MN: Milkweed, 2020.

Nixon, Rob. *Slow Violence and the Environmentalism of the Poor*. Cambridge, MA: Harvard University Press, 2011.

O'Brien, Adam. *Film and the Natural Environment: Elements and Atmospheres*. London: Wallflower, 2018.

Patterson, Wayne. *The Korean Frontiers in America: Immigration to Hawaii, 1896–1910*. Honolulu: University of Hawaii Press, 1988.

Pick, Anat, and Guinevere Narraway. "Intersecting Ecology and Film." In *Screening Nature: Cinema beyond the Human*, edited by Anat Pick and Guinevere Narraway, 1–18. New York: Berghahn Books, 2013.

Povinelli, Elizabeth A. *Between Gaia and Ground: Four Axioms of Existence and the Ancestral Catastrophe of Late Liberalism*. Durham, NC: Duke University Press, 2021.

——. *Geontologies: A Requiem to Late Liberalism*. Durham, NC: Duke University Press, 2016.

Powers, Richard. *Gain*. New York: Farrar, Straus and Giroux, 1998.

——. *The Overstory*. New York: W.W. Norton, 2018.

Probyn, Elspeth. *Eating the Ocean*. Durham, NC: Duke University Press, 2016.

Puig de la Bellacasa, María. *Matters of Care: Speculative Ethics in More Than Human Worlds*. Minneapolis: University of Minnesota Press, 2017.

Pyne, Lydia. *Endlings: Fables for the Anthropocene*. Minneapolis: University of Minnesota Press, 2022.

Raffles, Hugh. *Insectopedia*. New York: Vintage, 2010.

Rahimtoola, Samia. "The Poetics of Drift: Coloniality, Place, and Environmental Racialization." In *Avant-Gardes in Crisis: Art and Politics in the Long 1970s*, edited by Jean-Thomas Tremblay and Andrew Strombeck, 39–60. Albany: State University of New York Press, 2021.

Rancière, Jacques. *Disagreement: Politics and Philosophy*. Translated by Julie Rose. Minneapolis: University of Minnesota Press, 1999.

———. *The Politics of Aesthetics: The Distribution of the Sensible*. Edited and translated by Gabriel Rockhill. New York: Bloomsbury, 2004.

Rifkin, Mark. *Settler Time: Temporal Sovereignty and Indigenous Self-Determination*. Durham, NC: Duke University Press, 2017.

Rose, Deborah Bird. *Wild Dog Dreaming: Love and Extinction*. Charlottesville: University of Virginia Press, 2011.

Ruti, Mari. *Distillations: Theory, Ethics, Affect*. New York: Bloomsbury, 2018.

———. *The Ethics of Opting Out: Queer Theory's Defiant Subjects*. New York: Columbia University Press, 2017.

———. *The Singularity of Being: Lacan and the Immortal Within*. New York: Fordham University Press, 2012.

Salamon, Gayle. *Assuming a Body: Transgender and Rhetorics of Materiality*. New York: Columbia University Press, 2010.

Samer, Jed. *Lesbian Potentiality and Feminist Media in the 1970s*. Durham, NC: Duke University Press, 2022.

Sampson, Robert J., and Alix S. Winter. "The Racial Ecology of Lead Poisoning: Toxic Inequality in Chicago Neighborhoods, 1995–2013." *Du Bois Review: Social Science Research on Race* 13, no. 2 (2016): 261–83.

Sandilands, Catriona. "Melancholy Natures, Queer Ecologies." In *Queer Ecologies: Sex, Nature, Politics, Desire*, edited by Catriona Sandilands and Bruce Erickson, 331–58. Bloomington: Indiana University Press, 2010.

Sartre, Jean-Paul. *Being and Nothingness*. Translated by Hazel E. Barnes. London: Routledge, 2003.

Schrader, Paul. *Transcendental Style in Film: Ozu, Bresson, Dreyer*. Oakland: University of California Press, 2018.

Schuster, Joshua, and Derek Woods. *Calamity Theory: Three Critiques of Existential Risk*. Minneapolis: University of Minnesota Press, 2021.

Schwartz, Louis-Georges. "Cinema and the ~~Meaning~~ of 'Life.'" *Discourse* 28, nos. 2–3 (2006): 7–27.

See, Sam. "Bersani in Love." *Henry James Review* 32, no. 3 (2011): 195–203.

———. *Queer Natures, Queer Mythologies*. Edited by Christopher Looby and Michael North. New York: Fordham University Press, 2020.

Sexton, Jared. "Afro-Pessimism: The Unclear Word." *Rhizomes* 29 (2016): doi.org/10.20415/rhiz/029.e02.

Seymour, Nicole. *Bad Environmentalism: Irony and Irrelevance in the Ecological Age*. Minneapolis: University of Minnesota Press, 2018.

———. *Strange Natures: Futurity, Empathy, and the Queer Ecological Imagination*. Urbana: University of Illinois Press, 2003.

Shakespeare, William. *The Tragedy of King Lear* (Folio version). In *The Norton Shakespeare*, 3rd edition, edited by Stephen Greenblatt et al., 2331–493. New York: Norton, 2016.

Sheldon, Rebekah. *The Child to Come: Life after Human Catastrophe*. Minneapolis: University of Minnesota Press, 2016.

Sheldrake, Merlin. *Entangled Life: How Fungi Make Our Worlds, Change Our Minds & Shape Our Futures*. New York: Random House, 2020.

Shotwell, Alexis. *Against Purity: Living Ethically in Compromised Times*. Minneapolis: University of Minnesota Press, 2016.

Silverman, Kaja. *The Acoustic Mirror: The Female Voice in Psychoanalysis and Cinema*. Bloomington: Indiana University Press, 1998.

Simondon, Gilbert. *Individuation in Light of Notions of Form and Information*. Translated by Taylor Adkins. Minneapolis: University of Minnesota Press, 2020.

Song, Min Hyoung. *Climate Lyricism*. Durham, NC: Duke University Press, 2022.

Sperling, Alison. "Queer Ingestions: Weird and Vegetative Bodies in Jeff VanderMeer's Fiction." In *Plants in Science Fiction: Speculative Vegetation*, edited by Katherine E. Bishop, David Higgins, and Jerry Määtä, 194–213. Cardiff: University of Wales Press, 2020.

Spillers, Hortense. "Mama's Baby, Papa's Maybe: An American Grammar Book." *Diacritics* 17, no. 2 (1987): 65–81.

Spivak, Gayatri Chakravorty. *A Critique of Postcolonial Reason: Toward a History of the Vanishing Present*. Cambridge, MA: Harvard University Press, 1999.

Stuelke, Patricia. *The Ruse of Repair: US Neoliberal Empire and the Turn from Critique*. Durham, NC: Duke University Press, 2021.

Swarbrick, Steven. *The Environmental Unconscious: Ecological Poetics from Spenser to Milton*. Minneapolis: University of Minnesota Press, 2023.

———. "Nature's Queer Negativity: Between Barad and Deleuze." *Postmodern Culture* 29, no. 2 (2019): doi: 10.1353/pmc.2019.0003.

———. "The Violence of the Frame: Image, Animal, Interval in Lars von Trier's *Nymphomaniac*." *Cultural Critique* 113 (2021): 135–64.

Taylor, Dorceta E. *Toxic Communities: Environmental Racism, Industrial Pollution, and Residential Mobility*. New York: New York University Press, 2014.

Teare, Brian. *Doomstead Days*. New York: Nightboat Books, 2019.

Thacker, Eugene. *In the Dust of This Planet: Horror of Philosophy, Vol. 1*. Winchester, UK: Zero Books, 2011.

Tidwell, Christy. "Monstrous Natures Within: Posthuman and New Materialist Ecohorror in Mira Grant's *Parasite*." *ISLE: Interdisciplinary Studies in Literature and Environment* 21, no. 3 (2014): 538–49.

Tidwell, Christy, and Carter Soles. "Introduction: Ecohorror in the Anthropocene." In *Fear and Nature: Ecohorror Studies in the Anthropocene*, edited by Christy Tidwell and Carter Soles, 1–20. University Park, PA: Penn State University Press, 2021.

Tremblay, Jean-Thomas. "Black Ecologies (Humanity, Animality, Property)." *GLQ: A Journal of Lesbian and Gay Studies* 29, no. 1 (2023): 129–39.

———. *Breathing Aesthetics*. Durham, NC: Duke University Press, 2022.

———. "Diagnostic Spectatorship: Modern Physical Culture and White Masculinity." *Modernism/modernity Print Plus* 6, no. 2 (2021): doi.org/10.26597/mod.0206.

———. "The Haynes Code." *Los Angeles Review of Books*. April 8, 2022. https://lareviewofbooks.org/article/the-haynes-code/.

Tremblay, Jean-Thomas, and Jules Gill-Peterson. "Sex in Nature: Darwin, Depastoralized." *Regeneration: Environment, Art, Culture* 1, no. 1 (2024), forthcoming.

Tsing, Anna Lowenhaupt. *The Mushroom at the End of the World: On the Possibility of Life in Capitalist Ruins*. Princeton, NJ: Princeton University Press, 2015.

Tsing, Anna Lowenhaupt, Heather Anne Swanson, Elaine Gan, and Nils Bubandt. "Introduction: Haunted Landscapes of the Anthropocene." In *Arts of Living on a Damaged Planet: Ghosts and Monsters of the Anthropocene*, edited by Anna Lowenhaupt Tsing, Heather Anne Swanson, Elaine Gan, and Nils Bubandt, G1–G14. Minneapolis: University of Minnesota Press, 2017.

Van Dooren, Thom. *Flight Ways: Life and Loss at the Edge of Extinction.* New York: Columbia University Press, 2014.

Van Dooren, Thom, and Matthew Chrulew, editors. *Kin: Thinking with Deborah Bird Rose*. Durham, NC: Duke University Press, 2022.

———. "World of Kin: An Introduction." In *Kin: Thinking with Deborah Bird Rose*, edited by Thom van Dooren and Matthew Chrulew, 1–14. Durham, NC: Duke University Press, 2022.

Van Haute, Philippe. *Against Adaptation: Lacan's "Subversion of the Subject."* Translated by Paul Crowe and Miranda Vankerk. New York: Other Press, 2002.

VanderMeer, Jeff. *Area X: The Southern Reach Trilogy*. New York: Farrar, Straus and Giroux, 2014.

Varghese, Ricky, editor. *Raw: PrEP, Pedagogy, and the Politics of Barebacking*. Regina, SK: University of Regina Press, 2019.

Warren, Calvin L. *Ontological Terror: Blackness, Nihilism, and Emancipation*. Durham, NC: Duke University Press, 2018.

Webster, Jamieson. *Conversion Disorder: Listening to the Body in Psychoanalysis*. New York: Columbia University Press, 2019.

Wenzel, Jennifer. *The Disposition of Nature: Environmental Crisis and World Literature*. New York: Fordham University Press, 2019.

Whitmarsh, Patrick. *Writing Our Extinction: Anthropocene Fiction and Vertical Science*. Stanford, CA: Stanford University Press, 2023.

Whyte, Kyle. "The Recognition Paradigm of Environmental Injustice." In *The Routledge Handbook of Environmental Justice*, edited by Ryan Holifield, Jayajit Chakraborty, and Gordon Walker, 113–23. New York: Routledge, 2017.

Wilderson III, Frank B. *Afropessimism*. New York: Liveright, 2020.

———. Interview by Jared Ball et al. "'We're Trying to Destroy the World': Anti-Blackness and Police Violence after Ferguson." Ill Will. November 2014. https://illwill.com/print/were-trying-to-destroy-the-world.

———. *Red, White & Black: Cinema and the Structure of U.S. Antagonisms*. Durham, NC: Duke University Press, 2010.

Williams, Linda. "Film Bodies: Gender, Genre, and Excess." *Film Quarterly* 44, no. 4 (1991): 2–13.

———. *Hard Core: Power, Pleasure, and the "Frenzy of the Visible."* Berkeley: University of California Press, 1989.

Wilson, Elizabeth A. "Acts against Nature." *Angelaki: Journal of the Theoretical Humanities* 23, no. 1 (2018): 19–31.

——. *Gut Feminism*. Durham, NC: Duke University Press, 2015.

Wolfe, Cary. *What Is Posthumanism?* Minneapolis: University of Minnesota Press, 2010.

Woods, Derek. "Terraforming Earth: Climate and Recursivity." *Diacritics* 47, no. 3 (2019): 6–29.

Yao, Xine. *Disaffected: The Cultural Politics of Unfeeling in Nineteenth-Century America.* Durham, NC: Duke University Press, 2021.

Žižek, Slavoj. "From *Che Vuoi?* to Fantasy: Lacan with *Eyes Wide Shut*." In *How to Read Lacan*, 40–60. New York: Norton, 2006.

——. *Looking Awry: An Introduction to Jacques Lacan through Popular Culture.* Cambridge, MA: MIT Press, 1991.

Zupančič, Alenka. *What IS Sex?* Cambridge, MA: MIT Press, 2017.

Credits

Figure 1. Still from *The Wall* (2012). Coop99 Filmproduktion and Starhaus Filmproduktion.
Figure 2. Still from *Persona* (1966). AB Svensk Filmindustri.
Figures 3–11. Stills from *The Wall* (2012). Coop99 Filmproduktion and Starhaus Filmproduktion.
Figure 12. Still from *Vagabond* (1985). Janus Films and Ciné-Tamaris.
Figures 13–14. Stills from *First Cow* (2019). FilmScience and IAC Films.
Figure 15. Nicolas Poussin, *Et in Arcadia Ego* (1638). WikiCommons.
Figure 16. Nicolas Poussin, *Landscape with a Man Killed by a Snake* (1648). WikiCommons.
Figures 17–18. Stills from *Blue Velvet* (1986). De Laurentiis Entertainment Group.
Figure 19. Still from *First Cow* (2019). FilmScience and IAC Films.
Figures 20–21. Stills from *Tampopo* (1985). Fox Lorber Home Video, Itami Productions, and New Century Producers.
Figures 22–25. Stills from *First Cow* (2019). FilmScience and IAC Films.
Figures 26–27. Stills from *Annihilation* (2018). Skydance, DNA Films, Scott Rudin Productions, and Huahua Media.
Figures 28–29. Stills from *In the Earth* (2018). Rook Films and Protagonist Pictures.
Figure 30. Still from *Annihilation* (2018). Skydance, DNA Films, Scott Rudin Productions, and Huahua Media.
Figures 31–32. Stills from *Minari* (2019). Plan B Entertainment.
Figures 33–34. Stills from *Burning.* (2018). Pinehouse Film, Now Film, and NHK.
Figure 35. Still from *Minari* (2019). Plan B Entertainment.
Figures 36–37. Stills from *Bhopal Express* (1999). Highlight Films.
Figures 38–39. Stills from *Lamb* (2021). Go to Sheep, Boom Films, Black Spark Productions, Madants/NEM Corp, Film i Väst, Chimney Sweden, Chimney Poland, and Rabbit Hole Productions.
Figure 40. Still from *Antichrist* (2009). Zentropa Entertainments, arte France Cinéma, Canal+, Danmarks Radio, Film i Väst, Svenska Filminstitutet, Sveriges Television, and ZDF.
Figures 41–47. Stills from *X* (2022). Little Lamb and Mad Solar Productions.
Figure 48–53. Stills from *First Reformed* (2017). Killer Films, Omeira Studio Partners, Fibonacci Films, Arclight Films, and Big Indie Productions.

Index